Avant Gardeners

Tim Richardson

with foreword by Martha Schwartz

Avant Gardeners

50 VISIONARIES OF THE CONTEMPORARY LANDSCAPE

Thames & Hudson

ON THE COVER *Front* Cao Perrot Studio, Cocoons
Back, *top row, left to right* Claude Cormier, Blue Sticks
(photo Jean-François Vézina); Topher Delaney, Craford
Residence; Gross.Max, Vertical Garden; Gustafson Porter,
HM Treasury Courtyards; *Middle row, left to right* Shunmyo
Masuno, Suifo-So; Ron Lutsko, Sustainability Gardens
(photo Ron Lutsko, Jr.); Claude Cormier, Esplanade (photo
Jean-François Vézina); RCH Studios, Baroda House (photo
Tom Bonner); *Bottom row, left to right* Martha Schwartz,
Mesa Arts Centre (photo Alan Ward); West 8, Fortis Bank
Headquarters; Shunmyo Masuno, Hofu City Crematorium;
West 8, Sphinx Garden

PAGE 1 Topotek 1, Castle Park
PAGE 2 Patricia Johanson, Fair Park Lagoon

First published in 2008 in hardcover in the United States
of America by Thames & Hudson Inc., 500 Fifth Avenue,
New York, New York 10110

thamesandhudsonusa.com

First paperback edition 2009

Library of Congress Catalog Card Number 2007905739

ISBN 978-0-500-28826-9

Printed and bound in Singapore by CS Graphics

Contents

8   Foreword by Martha Schwartz
9   Introduction by Tim Richardson

ESSAYS

32 Concept
The theoretical basis for – and a definition of –
landscape conceptualism.

96 History
The ways in which conceptualist designers both
deny and embrace ideas of history.

144 Nature
Conceptualists lead the charge against lazy,
politically expedient 'eco' solutions.

200 Plants and Other Materials
Colour, artificiality, surrealism and green growing things.

232 Maxims Towards a Conceptualist
Attitude to Landscape Design
More mini-festo than manifesto: notes on
conceptualist reality.

264 The Conceptualist Garden Show
The best international showcase for conceptual work?

304 Psychotopia
An anatomy of landscape atmosphere: the
importance of invisibles.

DESIGNERS

10 Atelier Big City
MONTREAL
Trio of architects who play with concepts of scale,
colour, volume, material and structure.

14 Lodewijk Baljon
AMSTERDAM
Analytical design with an emphasis on elegance and
a certain 'looseness'.

18 Thomas Balsley
NEW YORK
Modernist landscape architecture with
conceptualist tweaks.

22 Julia Barton
NORTHUMBERLAND (UK)
Conceptualist artist working on large-scale
installations using plant material.

26 BCA Landscape
LIVERPOOL (UK)
Industrial and folk memories provide source material
for inner-city conceptual practice.

42 Petra Blaisse
AMSTERDAM
Highly personalized cross-disciplinary art projects.

48 Jean-Pierre Brazs
PARIS
Site-specific land art and conceptualist sculpture.

54 Susanne Burger
MUNICH
Outdoor conceptualist installations in functional
landscape-architecture settings.

60 Cao Perrot Studio
LOS ANGELES, NEW YORK AND PARIS
Deeply personalized conceptual statements utilizing
innovative materials.

66 Paul Cooper
POWYS (UK)
Pioneering material experimentation including
use of exterior video.

70   **Claude Cormier**
MONTREAL
Exuberant, witty, no-holds-barred urban landscape
conceptualism.

78   **Topher Delaney**
SAN FRANCISCO
Complex and vividly realized garden spaces that
unite architecture and horticulture.

86   **Herbert Dreiseitl**
ÜBERLINGEN (GERMANY)
The world's leading conceptualist water designer,
a maker of liquid narratives.

90   **DS Landschapsarchitecten**
AMSTERDAM
Long-established art-based conceptualist practice
characterized by clarity of vision.

106   **Monika Gora**
MALMÖ (SWEDEN)
Strident forms and ideas which blur the boundaries
between art and design.

114   **Gross.Max**
EDINBURGH
Colourful and imaginative public-space solutions which
address the complexities of the urban environment.

122   **Gustafson Porter**
LONDON AND SEATTLE
Elegantly sculpted, coolly uncluttered public
space design.

130   **Fritz Haeg**
LOS ANGELES
Provocative horticultural installations in suburbia.

132   **Paula Hayes**
NEW YORK
A distinctive artistic vision melded with horticultural
curiosity.

138   **Tony Heywood**
LONDON
Dramatic landscape installations, massive writhing
forms and botanical minutiae.

154   **Patricia Johanson**
BUSKIRK (USA)
Ecologically inspired organo-conceptualism from
Korea to Canada.

156   **Karres en Brands**
HILVERSUM (THE NETHERLANDS)
Uncompromisingly high-concept public park design.

160   **Klahn + Singer**
KARLSRUHE (GERMANY)
Horticultural and architectural formal
experimentation go hand in hand.

166   **Land-I**
ROME
Art collective who construct highly worked-out
landscape installations.

170   **Die LandschaftsArchitekten**
WIESBADEN (GERMANY)
Structural minimalism offset by extensive plantings
and conceptual humour.

174   **Ron Lutsko**
SAN FRANCISCO
Botanically and ecologically nuanced conceptual
landscape design.

180   **Lützow 7**
BERLIN
Long-established deconstructivist practice promoting
a visionary conceptual outlook.

184   **William Martin**
NOORAT (AUSTRALIA)
Individualist garden-maker melding sculptural
artefacts and botanical know-how.

186   **Shunmyo Masuno**
YOKOHAMA (JAPAN)
Classical Japanese design meets contemporary
landscape conceptualism.

194   **Metagardens**
LONDON
Organically morphing and growing garden and
building structures.

198   **Meyer + Silberberg**
BERKELEY (USA)
Elegant, understated Modernism with unexpected
conceptual twists.

210   **Helle Nebelong**
GENTOFTE (DENMARK)
Environmentally ordered children's playground design.

216   **Nip Paysage**
MONTREAL
Delicate and cheeky park and garden design.

222   **Antonio Perazzi**
MILAN
Sensuous planting design with conceptualist
underpinnings.

224   **Plant**
TORONTO
Rehabilitation of difficult sites through
'experiential design'.

230   **Philippe Rahm**
PARIS AND LAUSANNE (SWITZERLAND)
Theoretical explorations of the conceptualist
landscape through thermal modelling.

242   **RCH Studios**
LOS ANGELES
Exploratory and interdisciplinary conceptual
landscape design.

250   **Janet Rosenberg**
TORONTO
Versatile conceptualism that works on all scales.

254   **Mario Schjetnan**
MEXICO CITY
Socially motivated Conceptual–Modernist work
informed by history.

256   **Martha Schwartz**
CAMBRIDGE (USA) AND LONDON
The pioneer of conceptualism, always moving
forward.

274   **Vladimir Sitta**
SURRY HILLS (AUSTRALIA)
Surreal and uncompromising conceptual design.

278   **SLA**
COPENHAGEN
Conceptual design which aims to capture a balance
between nature and urban experience.

284   **Ken Smith**
NEW YORK
The conceptualist who disavows concepts: startling
urban interruptions.

290   **Taylor Cullity Lethlean**
PRINCES HILL AND ADELAIDE (AUSTRALIA)
Functional, imaginative, distinctively Australian work.

298   **Topotek 1**
BERLIN
Conceptual landscape design with a light and
humorous touch.

314   **Trinidad**
VIENNA
Theoretical outfit with groundbreaking conceptualist
landscape ideas.

318   **Michael Van Valkenburgh**
NEW YORK AND CAMBRIDGE (USA)
Sensual, experiential landscapes, mediated by raw
nature.

326   **Brita von Schoenaich**
PETERSHAM (UK)
Individualistic designer creating her own tradition.

330   **WES & Partner**
HAMBURG
Flexible, functional spatial design based on
conceptual artistic principles.

336   **West 8**
ROTTERDAM
Well-established conceptualist outfit working on a
large scale.

344   **Directory**

Foreword

Martha Schwartz

I am extremely honoured to be asked to write the preface for this book, for it is the first that I have seen that elevates this topic of conceptualism to a 'genre' of, or movement within, landscape architecture. When I first reviewed *Avant Gardeners*, I was overwhelmed with the amount of work I had never seen and was surprised by how many people are and have been involved in doing this kind of work, and how rich the topic is.

I am also honoured to be thought of as a 'Mother of Invention' here, and have never contemplated a more holistic and comprehensive overview of this subject. Having my nose buried in the exigencies of trying to run a practice and make a living, I am very short of any parallax where I could view my role within the evolution of the profession of landscape architecture. In retrospect, I wish I had planned this as a strategy for changing the world, but I can assure you that had no such thoughts at the time of the Bagel Garden. It was, quite truthfully, a little joke I was playing on my then-husband, Pete Walker. I had no idea or forethought about publishing it. The only brilliant move was to invite my friend, Alan Ward, to bring his 4x5 camera and photograph the installation. Nor would it have occurred to me to send the image to be published were it not for my friend Marie Brenner, a writer for *New York Magazine*, nor could I ever have imagined that Grady Clay, the editor of *Landscape Architecture Magazine*, would make the decision to put the image on the front cover. What can I say – I was in the right place at the right time. I had little foresight as to where my little experiments would take me. I could never have imagined seeing the amount of work in this book and have it somehow connected to my early antics within this profession.

In the 1970s, I entered the University of Michigan's graduate school of landscape architecture after spending five years in the fine arts department at the same university. I was very aware of the earthworks artists of the 1960s – people such as Robert Smithson, Michael Heizer, Nancy Holt, Richard Long and Mary Miss; their pieces spoke, without words and statistics, of the frailty of our dwindling resources and the beauty of our natural landscapes. This was clearly an art form I wanted to pursue. That summer, in 1974, I met Pete Walker at the SWA Group internship program in Sausalito. Meeting Pete changed the course of my life. In our first meeting, while he was running our 'prognostication' problem, he excoriated us for marching along doing what people expected us to do and not bringing anything of interest or value into the world. 'Where is the art?' he asked. He was the first person I had heard all year speak about art and its relationship to the landscape, and I realized that landscape could be what I defined it as – and that it was a worthy effort to transform culture through the art of landscape. Although my interests have broadened and deepened over time, I still am guided by the desire to make landscapes that speak to people of the human condition. This is obviously a different and perhaps a more difficult 'sell' than naturalism or the next phase of naturalism, 'eco-revelatory', but I have never disassociated human beings from nature. Therein lies the dividing line.

Now, thirty years later, the profession is so much richer, with many more people who embrace this way of working in the landscape. As landscape is all-encompassing, we continue to work within a broadly defined profession. But this profession, with its myriad practices and voices, is on the verge of another transformation, which will be leveraged through the efforts of the landscape artists in this book. I am proud to be included in this collection of work, and know that collectively we are changing the way people see and use the landscape, and how we learn to live in balance with our natural environment. Ultimately, it has to be an environment that we humans cherish, respect and can thrive in, while wishing to have a life of purpose and meaning. Our need for meaning, truth and beauty are fundamental requirements that many of our landscapes must fulfil. The designers in this book fully understand and embrace this task.

Introduction

Tim Richardson

The subject of this book is conceptualist landscape design, a term which I began to use in the mid-1990s as a useful shorthand for grouping together individuals such as Martha Schwartz, Topher Delaney, Claude Cormier and Kathryn Gustafson. What these designers had in common was the harnessing of an idea, or a set of related ideas, as the starting point for work that was characterized by the use of colour, artificial materials and witty commentary on a site's history and culture. Often a readable narrative was revealed in the landscape or superimposed onto it (though an understanding of this underlying meaning was never deemed a necessity by the designers). Such a strongly conceptualist attitude marks a significant departure from the functionalist imperatives of Modernism, the decorative or romantic tradition of the 19th and 20th centuries, and the avowedly naturalistic stance developed in recent years (most notably by the New Perennials school of planting).

A monograph on Schwartz's work, which I produced in collaboration with the designer in 2004, was a further catalyst for thought about the possibility that a conceptualist movement in landscape was developing worldwide. Further research revealed that most designers remained unaware of the output of contemporaries working in a similar mode (with the exception of a handful of celebrated or notorious individuals, such as Schwartz). It was a gratifying surprise, therefore, to find that in 2007 some fifty landscape designers and companies are now working, at least partly, in a conceptualist vein. Of course they all have their differing emphases and idiosyncrasies: for example, many conceptualist designers celebrate the urban and the artificial, while others are interested in the role and potential of plants and trees in human lives and in the wider ecology. But on the other hand, not a single designer in this book objected to being described as 'conceptualist'.

Conceptualist landscape architecture is related to conceptualist art, but should not be viewed as a sub-section of that broad movement. Gallery-based artefact-art does not have a monopoly on notions of conceptualism, after all (as Marcel Duchamp would be the first to agree). While conceptual art went through a crisis of confidence after it was realized that the purity of 'Idea Art' is compromised by its reliance on the commercial art world, an element of functionalism is inherent in most conceptual landscape spaces. Some would argue that this proves that landscape design is not an artform – which is fine: toppling the self-serving hierarchies of the mainstream art world is not a priority for the designers in this book.

It now appears that landscape conceptualism might be emerging as the landscape correlative to the Postmodern attitude, which overtook architecture as a way of thinking in the 1980s. Leading architects such as Zaha Hadid, Rem Koolhaas and Daniel Libeskind are increasingly turning to landscape conceptualist outfits as collaborators on projects, as more and more architects who think as object-based designers recognize the importance of landscape, of what goes on outside their buildings. And increasing numbers of commercial companies and city councils are seeing in landscape conceptualism an opportunity to 'brand' their outdoor space by means of a narrative or set of interrelated symbols. Finally, landscape conceptualism is also functioning now as a useful corrective to contemporary ecological pieties. There is room for both attitudes in the built environment, but conceptualism will have to fight its corner ever harder in the face of politically expedient evocations of a romanticized ideal of the 'nature' which surrounds us as much in the city as it does in the country.

Atelier Big City Montreal

Trio of architects who play with concepts of scale, colour, volume, material and structure.

Randy Cohen, Anne Cormier and Howard Davies formed Atelier Big City as an architectural practice in 1987. The company's useful mission statement includes the following: 'Our work combines metaphorical [and] interpretative themes with innovative materials and construction. The projects are structured on a strong conceptual approach based on the interpretation of a programme and siting strategies. Of particular interest to the group is the notion of public space in buildings and the importance of the architectural promenade . . . In each project, we attempt to generate an architectural milieu of grand sensual stimulation through the use of very simple means: colour, volume, material and structure.'

All three partners work on each project. 'It really has to go through a wringer,' Davies says. 'I think our tendency is to refine the relationship between building and landscape in a spatial and topographical way. We don't really like flat things – we like people to move over things and under things.' Davies talks of the failure of the social-analysis moment in Modernism in the 1970s, and sees his own journey as 'a rebellion against Postmodernism and aformalism, to a rediscovery of Modernism in its Russian incarnation: lots of concrete and folded forms, struts and asymmetry. It is an abstract formalism, but it has its surprises and its subtleties that make it more fun.'

Skate Plaza

MONTREAL 2007

The brief here was to design a public space in which skateboarding was permitted. As Davies admits, this has led to an element of 'negotiation' between the young skateboarders and any others who wished to use the park. 'It's a mixture of public space and play equipment,' he observes. In light of this, the designers attempted to shift the skateboarders' emphasis away from single spectacular jumps and towards a sense of continuous movement through the space. As the company's statement puts it: 'Our work has consistently dealt with questions of scale, of infrastructure, and the role of the architectural project as "mediator" in the ongoing process of occupying marginal areas.'

The designers talked to the skateboarders, but as Davies states, 'They have very specific ideas and specific activities [or tricks] that need to be performed. It was a real battle to retain any kind of architectural expressiveness.' The plaza has been conceived as a folded plane with access points related to movement patterns across the space. The surface is bent up and down to respond to the particular acrobatic needs of the skaters, while at the same time creating a public place within the city. The site's contaminated soil was removed, creating a new topography, setting up skating runs and creating planted buffer zones between the skaters and passing pedestrians.

Head in the Clouds

MONTREAL 2004

This installation lasted for two years at the Jardins de Métis: in the first year the planting was all white, and in the second it was much more colourful. The idea here was to create a roof garden, but not as an extension of the interior environment. Instead, Davies describes this construction as 'an evolving architectural promenade'. The bent roof creates a variety of spatial experiences below it, while in the centre a ramp provides an ascent up to a private vantage point from which the flowered surface of the roof is visible. Davies speaks of one place in every project where the ideas become most intense – 'a Gordian knot'.

The flower selection also has a conceptual slant. The use of white flowers in the first year was intended to set up 'a playful relationship on the iconic whiteness of modern "heroic" architecture and the dreamlike potential of clouds'. For the second season, a decision was made to allow various colourful flowering plants to explode across the installation's tilted planes. These species included *Alternanthera dentata* 'Purple Knight', *Salvia farinacea* 'Strata' and *Diascia barberae* 'Red Ace'.

Lodewijk Baljon
Amsterdam

Analytical design with an emphasis on
elegance and a certain 'looseness'

One way of making sense of the mutability and diffuseness of gardens and landscapes is through methodical academic study, and Lodewijk Baljon has consistently pursued this approach. After graduating in landscape architecture in the early 1980s, he joined the Amsterdam firm B&B for two years (which included work on the Park de la Villette in Paris) before returning to university to complete a PhD. 'I wanted to get a grip on contemporary attitudes to landscape design,' he explains.

During this period Baljon began to design gardens for private clients, and to advise architectural firms about the landscape elements of their work. From 1990 to 1997 he acted as an advisor to the City of Amsterdam in the urban planning of a development of 5,000 houses, and his office has since completed a large number of commissions – public and corporate projects in the main, although Baljon designs two or three domestic gardens each year. 'Contact with plant material is the basis of landscape architecture,' he says. 'You have to be confident using soft and tender green materials.' This would have been a controversial message to impart to Harvard University's department of landscape architecture, where Baljon has lectured.

While his work at first glance appears Modernist in essence, Baljon confesses to a certain disillusionment with the functionalist aspects of this design creed, which came to the fore in the 1960s and '70s. 'My training was very pragmatic and oriented towards function,' he explains. 'No one was talking about the meaning of the garden or how people perceive it. For me, it was not elegant enough. I like straight lines, but I also know that there is a moment when you need to step back and add looser elements.'

Baljon did not find an answer in Postmodernism, which was at its peak when he graduated. Instead, his solution to the problem of style in a post-ideological design atmosphere was a flexible attitude which allowed for collaboration and compromise, an emphasis on elegant and often expensive materials, and a reliance on plants as decorative elements. 'The line of a concrete wall is different to that created by a green hedge,' he explains. 'Plants give us the opportunity to work with that balance between the straight and the loose.' Baljon cites his tutor Hans Warnau as a key influence, who encouraged students to take Modernist compositions and enrich them with an 'infill' of plant material (the opposite of the English tradition of gardening, in which plants set the tone).

Baljon's signature look is based on the concept of looseness, provided chiefly by plants, within a formal architectural context. 'I don't want to make it too severe,' he admits. The plantings do not exactly soften the Modernist lines, rather they create an enriching and dynamic contrast. He has been influenced by Piet Oudolf and the New Perennials movement in recent years, and cites the early Modernists, in particular Thomas Church, as an inspiration because they worked happily on a small scale and imbued their work with a sense of luxury, as opposed to the 'meagre form of functionalism' of his tutor's generation. 'With the addition of plants you can create that kind of elegance,' he says. 'In that sense it is an enrichment of Modernism.'

Key features of Baljon's work include plantings of roses with grasses intermixed, and fruit trees: 'If there is an opportunity, I try to create an orchard. As well as fruit there is an abundance of flowers, good autumn colour (if you choose well), and in a small garden you can introduce a sense of rhythm.'

ABOVE AND OPPOSITE In this award-winning design, a grouping of 'Golden Rain' trees (*Koelreuteria paniculata*) clustered in the southeast corner of the courtyard provides a softening counterpoint to the museum buildings. Rijksmuseum Twenthe, Enschede (The Netherlands) 1996.

Prins Residence

HAARLEM (THE NETHERLANDS) 2001

At this private residence, the problem was the small size of the garden compared with the substantial house (the result of the previous owners selling off land). The space available was essentially a strip of grass that encircled the property, with the added complication that it was 60cm lower than the level of the house itself.

Baljon decided to create a paved terrace of yellow stone, as the gregarious owner (a personal friend) 'likes to have a lot of people around'. But the problem of the strip of garden remained. Baljon decided to introduce one long and one short canal on different levels, linked by a cascade. The discrepancy in level between house and garden was dealt with by the addition of a 'floor' of clipped box hedge, while the perimeter, previously a yew hedge, is now marked by bamboo plantings.

In other parts of the garden, Baljon has used what he describes as 'rough plants': perennial plantings inspired by the work of Penelope Hobhouse, with whom he has collaborated. 'She has these huge plantings of perennials,' he says, 'most of them semi-woodland: hemerocallis, geraniums and grasses. Sturdy, tough things with long, narrow leaves.'

Thomas Balsley New York

Modernist landscape architecture with conceptualist tweaks.

Here is a professional who is disarmingly direct about the corporate and economic imperatives of a landscape practice built up in New York over the past thirty years, but which he feels has begun to reflect his true artistic sensibility only during the latter part of his career. 'I'm different to most of the other successful landscape designers of my generation – different in that I didn't go to Harvard,' says Balsley, who trained at Syracuse University. 'There is an old boys' club and it makes it more difficult for others. My practice has had a different ascent: first, it was all about trying to make a living (which meant no design competitions); second, it was about finding work in the private sector; and third, over the past fifteen years I have been learning to "fly", finding my real voice as a designer.'

Like his contemporaries, Balsley was reared in the tradition of Modernism, but (unlike some younger conceptualists) he has not rejected that legacy. 'Absolutely I call myself a Modernist,' he states, 'though I do have my dark side: a period of Postmodernism or stupid traditional projects. Our heroes at the time [i.e., at college] were Lawrence Halprin and Dan Kiley, plus Thomas Church and Garrett Eckbo to a certain extent. I've been following in the footsteps of Halprin: he preached social spaces but he was never able to build them.'

The social imperatives of Modernism have remained precious to Balsley, even as his work has developed along more conceptualist lines: 'For me, the concepts begin to emerge after a discourse with the people. The ground plan often begins from an architectural point of view, in that the landscape is a setting for the building. I like to think of Modernism as a beautiful brew or potage, but we need to add a little more spice to make it more digestible; I suppose the main spice for me is people.'

This social agenda informs all of Balsley's work, and the conceptual aspects of it arise directly from that engagement. As Balsley's corporate blurb puts it: 'Wherever we work – be it Tokyo or Portland, Oregon – we become acquainted with the local context, culture and microclimate conditions, as well as codes and policies.' This stance represents a practical fusion of corporate-speak, public sector-jargon and artistic conceptualism. Balsley prefers the term 'metaphor' to 'concept', however: 'You might see that some of our work (the waterfront parks, for example) is very Modernist, but it always celebrates history,' he explains.

ABOVE AND OPPOSITE This bold and simple design in the centre of Manhattan, with its grass berms and pine trees, was inspired by ideas taken from Frederick Law Olmsted and Dan Kiley. 'It's really about jogging a memory of nature in a city environment,' says Balsley. 101 Warren Street, New York 2007.

World Trade Centre

OSAKA 1995

Cosmos Tower is the centrepiece of Cosmo City, a mixed-use development along Osaka's harbour front. The tower's base is dedicated to public spaces, including a major retail centre that attracts visitors, office workers and shoppers. 'This was an invitation from a client who said, "Our architecture is frankly forgettable: you have the chance to be more imaginative",' Balsley states. 'Architects will often try to dominate our artistic intention. This was the client saying: ignore the architect.'

Balsley's greatest challenge here was the need to work around existing foundations and a series of concrete ventilators. He reshaped and incorporated these unsightly features into sculptural forms, whose random perforations allow light and steam to escape. Those in the North Garden have been transformed into a performance stage, while the six in the South Plaza appear as cone sculptures. Set in a mist pool and glowing red at night, these distinctive cones help to define the stylistic tone for the entire project.

Capitol Plaza

NEW YORK 2001

Capitol Plaza is located in the residential neighbourhood of Chelsea Heights, amid the weekend antiques markets and Flower District shops. This new public space, which connects 26th and 27th Streets just east of Sixth Avenue, features seating areas, a promenade and cafés. Curved walls slice through the plaza, organizing it into distinct areas with varying degrees of intimacy and enclosure.

Whimsical stainless-steel furniture provides a multitude of seating options, while the 18m-long metal wall draws the attention of passers-by on Sixth Avenue. Elliptical cut-outs reveal bamboo planted behind, while one of the cut-outs is the spout for a fountain. 'That wall is an inexpensive corrugated board,' Balsley states. 'The idea is that its colour will change: with a swipe of a paintbrush we could change that piece entirely. After all, in an urban environment everything changes all the time.' Of the cut-outs and bamboo plantings, Balsley explains: 'I wanted to break down the feeling of a wall – New York is all wall. With the bamboo, I can break that down without creating a fake natural environment. I can do it with metaphor.'

Julia Barton   Northumberland (UK)

Conceptualist artist working on large-scale installations using plant material.

English sculptor and installation artist Julia Barton has a particular affinity with plants and other natural forms, coupled with a fascination with technical and scientific advances and the minutiae of construction techniques and materials. This apparent dichotomy of interests is reflected in the basic theme of contrast which can be seen throughout her work, most clearly expressed in the use of vividly contrasting materials in individual pieces, though it can also be identified on a conceptual and imaginative level in the way that preconceptions about places or forms are ritually subverted in her work.

Barton came to wider notice after an exhibition of sculpture at Levens Hall, in Cumbria, entitled 'Phyto-forms' (see opposite). Eight sculptures married welded metal and plant material (alpines, annuals and succulents) to create elegant spiralling forms, intended to echo both Elizabethan dress patterns and topiary forms in yew – a reference to the history of the house and its famous 17th- and 18th-century garden. The metal armatures holding the works together were intended as a reference to whalebone corsetry, while on a practical level woven seed bags were incorporated into the framework to allow the plants to survive. Here, as in all of Barton's work, an original vision led to many technical challenges which had to be overcome with practical skill and imagination. Rubber hosepipe was repurposed to evoke black taffeta dress material, while flowering alpine plants introduced colour to the 'costumes' of the forms.

The relationship between inert materials (such as metal) and organic materials (such as plants, soil and the human body) is a constant thread in Barton's work. Her Northumberland studio has something of the character of a library or archive, while outdoors she nurtures numerous plants in polytunnels and on capillary matting. Current interests include sedums, liverworts, mosses and black ophiopogon grass; one present line of enquiry focuses on the similarities between our internal body organs and the systems and structures within buildings. Her interest in industrial fabrics and new building materials reflects a desire to collaborate with the construction industry more closely in the future.

LEFT This installation was created for the Chaumont Festival's 'erotic' year, a theme which brought out the best and worst in designers. Sexual forms were echoed by Barton using her characteristic palette of metals, industrial materials and massed plants. Paths of Seduction, Chaumont sur Loire (France) 2002.

FAR LEFT An evocation of the growth patterns inside tree trunks and the extraordinary columns of cells that transport food and water, this Westonbirt installation reflected Barton's scientific preoccupations. Plexus, Gloucestershire (UK) 2003.

LEFT AND BELOW Eight sculptures exhibited at Levens Hall echoed the shapes and fabrics of period dress. Phyto-forms, Cumbria (UK) 2001.

Resurrection

SAVANNAH (USA) 2005

This commission, Barton's most substantial work to date, was to create an installation in the derelict Chatham County Jail in Savannah, Georgia, a mixed facility dating from the 1870s which closed in 1979. The result is a meditation on the topic of incarceration, with redemptive overtones expressed through the medium of plants. 'It was a play on the idea of weeds and prisoners,' Barton explains. 'The name of the piece is taken from the Resurrection fern, a plant which seems dead but comes to life again.'

Barton was, of course, aware of the place's grim history, but constantly found herself drawn back to the idea of redemption and optimism. 'It's because the roof had gone and the plants were in there,' she says. 'It seemed to me

that the weeds had already made it a redeemed building.' She decided to honour the plants' colonization of the jail by re-creating a block of eighteen cells, using mesh walls on a scaffold base, each of which contained a single species of plant – such as goldenrod, morning glory, ragweed and saw palm – as an 'inmate'. Plants that died were left in situ in some cases. A long, straight walkway passed in front of the cell block, while on the other side was a more unruly 'free' area of native plants, including red and white mulberry, holly ferns and astragalus. The contrast between freedom and containment was thus made on a metaphorical and reflective level, rather than in an atmosphere of high emotion, recrimination and potential guilt.

BCA Landscape

Liverpool (UK)

Industrial and folk memories provide source material for inner-city conceptual practice.

This company, founded in 1984, has made the journey over the past decade from solid Modernist design in the corporate and public sphere to landscape conceptualism. It has been helped along the way by associate design partner Andy Thomson, who joined in 1991 and who lists Alain Provost and Groupe Signes, Kathryn Gustafson (p. 122), Martha Schwartz (p. 256) and Peter Walker as influences.

While some of their Continental and transatlantic counterparts utilize complex theorizing as a basis for creative work, BCA Landscape has developed a poetic and emotional approach that is founded in an appreciation of local history and an intimate understanding of the needs of the community. There is no jargon to be found in the public pronouncements of this company. Thomson studied landscape at Sheffield University, but avers, 'At the end I was frustrated with the limitations of the course. It was very scientific – all "form follows function". There wasn't much magic and creativity.' He cites film as a key influence, and speaks of the importance of 'meaningful design on a local level' and the creation of 'immersive, inspiring, three-dimensional places'.

BCA Landscape's schemes can be fairly intense. While much of the company's work can be slotted into the Postmodernist category of disrupted ground plan, use of colour and new materials, some projects are much more conceptualist in style, and in some cases (for example, Face of Liverpool, p. 28, and Burscough Bridge, opposite) clearly influenced by the work of Schwartz.

LEFT AND ABOVE This brownfield site in the Duke Street conservation area has been transformed, using a series of 'boxed' hornbeams and free-standing walls. Campbell Square, Liverpool (UK) 2001.

Burscough Bridge

LANCASHIRE (UK) 2007

This project is one of the most intense and sustained pieces of research on a locality in the entire canon of conceptualist landscape work. The result – in terms of the graphics produced by BCA – represents a mood board, a history board and an eco board of this small village near Olmskirk in Lancashire. The commission was to create environmental improvements around the main A-road, which thunders through the middle of the settlement and has made the village feel peripheral and unwanted. Thomson explains, however, that Burscough has always

been a transport hub, sited as it is was a day either side of Liverpool and Wigan by canal barge, and later in terms of its status as a railway interchange. The research process uncovered an amazingly rich history to the place, which is first recorded as a Viking settlement. Speaking to locals, Thomson became deeply immersed in the village's history and stories, incorporating themes from 'pace-egging' (a mumming play) to the World War II American airfield, the remnants of medieval Burscough Abbey to Martin Mere nature reserve and bird sanctuary.

Face of Liverpool

LIVERPOOL (UK) 2004

The project began almost as an afterthought for the planners, who commissioned the architects to make something of the 'in-between' spaces around a new complex in the city's docklands, on the site of an old eye hospital. BCA came up with a design that resonates with the site's history: the main triangular space acts as the apex of the design, with two walls (one of pre-cast concrete and one of Corten steel) and a large 'porthole' looking out to sea. The steel wall is engraved in heroic fashion ('Liverpool: Threshold to the Ends of the World'), while the concrete wall features a message in Morse code.

The impulse for the design was initially political, notes Thomson. 'We wanted to introduce the concept of the people of Liverpool into it,' he says. 'So we worked with PR and graphics companies and came up with a competition in which people would send in their stories about the experience of immigration to the city council's website. We took portrait photographs of some of these people and had their faces etched onto glass portholes, which we incorporated in the design. We even made a book out of it – Liverpudlians tell a lot of stories. So the site suddenly became very personal, not alienating at all.'

Garden of Light

LIVERPOOL (UK) 2006

BCA Landscape's creative intensity is occasionally lightened by Thomson and his colleagues, who can cut loose and create such fun and glamorous designs as the 'Garden of Light', part of a redevelopment of Liverpool's old cotton exchange into two restaurants with apartments above. Here, the open courtyard has been souped up and zipped up by the addition of glittering chandeliers, spirals of LED lights, ivy-covered pyramids and a sequence of seats in glass-reinforced plastic (GRP). The idea was to echo and honour the florid decorative exuberance of the building's 19th-century architecture by James Kellaway Colling. 'It was all about the idea of a decadent contemporary fantasy,' Thomson says.

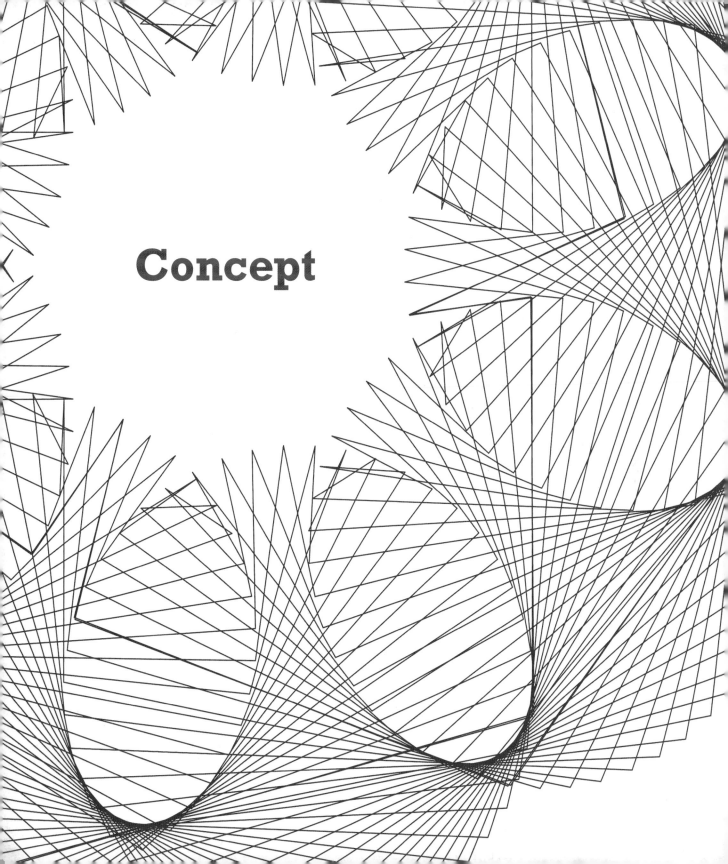

Concept

It was Martha Schwartz who first stated, 'A landscape can be about anything.'
This is perhaps the core idea of landscape conceptualism – the starting point –
for it also begs the question: how does a designer go about making a landscape
that is 'about' something, anyway?

Conceptualist landscapes are predicated on ideas rather than plants or the
architectural use of hard materials. Such spaces are underpinned by a single
concept, or visual motif, which informs every aspect of the design. The role
of the artist is therefore paramount, while the old idea of nature as a legitimate
guiding force for design is rejected. This is design in which the central idea
of the garden, inspired by the place's history, ecology or intended use, is
ultimately more important than its decorative appeal and planting. In nearly
all cases, however, a functional or social rationale is integral to the scheme
and must coexist with, and ideally nourish, the underlying concept. In the main,
conceptualist landscape designers are not creating stand-alone art objects; they
are making spaces which will be used by people and which will change and
develop over time. So while functionality never constitutes the whole conceptual
basis for this type of design, it is usually present as an essential component.
As Marco Antonini of Land-I has suggested: 'There is a certain level of
independence and cynicism in conceptual art which can make it seem
remote from society . . . In a garden, the conceptual process has a more
human dimension – there is always the sense of scale – and that makes it a
more "grounded" mode of expression.' There is no formal connection between
conceptual art and conceptualist landscape design: conceptual art does not
own the copyright on concept.

So in the sphere of landscape, what might these concepts be, in practice? Of course, a lot of design can be called 'conceptual' in essence – take, for example, the ancient Japanese tradition, or in the 20th century Edwin Lutyens' notion of the 'single idea, beautifully phrased': the one idea underpinning the design of a garden and which is extrapolated throughout, in every detail. A broad conceptual approach of this kind can often be characterized simply as good design. The difference with contemporary landscape conceptualism is that the central idea or concept is applied in a stronger and often more literal and obvious manner, so that it exists quite close to the 'surface' of the scheme and therefore quite close to the surface of visitors' consciousness.

There are a number of ways in which such concepts find physical form in landscape and garden settings. These may be categorized broadly as site-based, historical, visual and autobiographical. The majority of conceptualist designers tend to work within the confines of just one of these categories, and ultimately a designer's attitude to the realization of concepts effectively becomes their design methodology. This is because in order for a designer's work to develop and for their 'signature' to become stronger, it generally has to attain some kind of fixity or solidity.

First, the site-based approach: the traditional way of working with landscape spaces (especially those on a larger scale), is to 'consult the genius of the place', as Alexander Pope put it – that is, to soak up the natural atmosphere of the locale and somehow to work with it, designing in tandem with what might be considered the presiding spirit of the place, atmosphere or space-flavour. Several conceptualists – Martha Schwartz and Tony Heywood, for example –

reject this idea as inherently bogus and uselessly mired in the romanticism of previous ages. They revel in the heretical notion that their designs might erase or overlay all traces of what has gone before. It is a powerful polemical starting point for creativity. Other designers claim that their work is always inspired first by what they find on-site, and that they work with care to retain some vestiges of the space's former existence. One of the newer conceptualist outfits, Plant, practises this gentle and inclusive approach, always trying to ensure that some sense of the 'character' of the space is allowed to show through. 'Sometimes there are things on the site that we use, and sometimes we bring things to that setting,' Plant claim. These polarized attitudes to the idea of the inherent value of sense of place are equally valid as creative stances in the conceptualist milieu. In the world of design there is no reason why 'gentle and inclusive' should be better than 'confrontational and polemical'.

Among those designers who do not explicitly reject Pope's notion of the 'genius of the place', the most widespread attitude is to view this 'spirit' as a bundle of characteristics, some of which might be worth retaining or exploring in tandem with off-site research into potential concepts. It is not an empirical methodology in the Modernist tradition, but is tinged with the detected emotions of the populace and the highly personal reactions of designers. Mario Terzic of Trinidad inspiringly defines this self-referential quality of a landscape perceived in context, insisting at the same time on the 'double' nature of our attitude to history, existing as it does both in the past and in the present: 'Artists must rediscover the "genius of the place": vegetation, location, traffic, wind, surroundings, traces, springs, water, paths, the family catastrophes of the

owners, little erotic dramas, financial disasters, the battle against death and the fight for eternity. Only a comprehensive artistic analysis can bridge the gap between old and new. The present is the strongest force a garden has!'

Also contained within a site-based conceptualist attitude is a more ecologically nuanced stance. Many conceptualist designers explicitly include 'microclimate' as one of their guiding principles, while others (such as Ron Lutsko) go still further and insist on favouring native and preferably local plant materials as a key component in any design. All designers will work with and around existing architecture or stand-alone art pieces, but some conceptualists go further and make such material devices the conceptual cornerstone of their work. One example of this is Herbert Dreiseitl's use of water as a concept that underpins all of his work; elsewhere, pine trees have been favoured by several designers as a potent means of evoking natural landscape in urban areas. The urban environment itself, as opposed to concepts derived from nature and ecology, has also emerged as a source of inspiration for conceptualists such as Taylor Cullity Lethlean, who state: 'Parks and gardens in the past might have been considered as escapes or refuges from the city, but we try to create spaces that are totally integrated with the life of the city.' Some conceptualists (notably Karres en Brands, Philippe Rahm and Metagardens) have explored theories around the spontaneous, unassisted development of landscape, so that it becomes an organically defined entity in its own right, or have tried to harness climatic elements so that they might steer design decisions.

The second broad conceptualist category, and perhaps the most popular with designers, is the historical attitude (see also the essay entitled 'History').

A programme of research results in an appreciation of the site's industrial, agricultural or sociological context, primarily so that that designer can create a space which will seem to 'speak' to the people who are to use it, to stimulate the community of memory, and to provide a personality for the space in the future: a coherent 'space-flavour'. This objective is often pursued in terms of imagery and metaphor – for example, through the use of recognizable artefacts which might bring to mind memories of past industrial use or an activity which formerly 'defined' the town, city or region. Generally this refers to fairly recent history, though some designers follow the example of Land Artists and like to look to ancient civilizations for inspiration (Mario Schjetnan is one such), while others go back even further and follow geological precedent, looking at how it may or may not be expressed in the extant natural landscape. This historical interest can spill over into a biographical treatment of local people, as in BCA Landscape's 'Face of Liverpool' project. Or if the site is something which needs improving or finessing (a sewage works, for example, or an airport boundary fence), materials can be deployed in an almost euphemistic way to distract attention away from the true nature of the site and to lend it a new identity.

The contemporary identity of the site, as opposed to its historical context, can also be signalled with conceptual clarity: the landscape around a company headquarters might be devised so that it echoes the organization's ethos or atmosphere, perhaps. Kathryn Gustafson's 'feminine' landscape of the L'Oreal buildings in France was an early example of this. This kind of 'branding' – which might apply to corporations or local government equally – is potentially the key to the further worldwide take-up of conceptualist landscape design.

Finally, it is possible for this historical attitude to take on a mysterious or ambiguous character, in which an agglomeration of historically nuanced images might combine to create an overall sensibility without becoming over-directive. Meyer + Silberberg's 'After Maximus' project, an evocation of Roman tomb architecture, has a sense of mystery at its very heart, while many conceptualist designs contain clues or elements of narrative which are deeply buried and must be pointed out to visitors. Indeed, all conceptualist landscape design should ideally work equally well in the context of an 'open' interpretation – where the design is not correctly 'read' or understood by users – quite as much as in situations where visitors are actively engaged participants. Conceptualist landscape design must stand up to both scrutiny and indifference.

The visual approach to conceptualism (the third category) is in some places simply a matter of using repeated motifs or objects, an idea inherited from architectural Modernism. Martha Schwartz remains the designer who has explored this method most fruitfully, using lines, patterns and shapes to dazzling effect in numerous landscape designs. Other designers develop an interest with specific forms, which then become a kind of signature – Patricia Johanson's use of reptile imagery, for example, or Klahn + Singer's abiding interest in circular forms. Colour emerges as the strongest visual weapon in the conceptualists' armoury, often enhanced by artificial light at night, and the majority of designers do not shy away from using it as dramatically as possible. Particular visual motifs are favoured again and again by conceptualists. In recent years the barcode device has become something of a cliché, though in all cases the designers concerned claim that they came up with the idea

independently (and we should surely give them the benefit of the doubt).

The autobiographical strand in conceptualist landscape design applies most often in the work of designers who are operating in or quite close to fine-art genres, where ideas based around the integrity and imagination of the artist can completely supersede functionalist or social concerns. The work of designers such as Tony Heywood and Jean-Pierre Brazs is predicated on their own highly personal responses to specific landscapes, or else ideas around landscape and nature in general. The work is as much about the mind of the artist as it is about the space in which they are working; in effect, the two become indivisible. The work of Cao Perrot Studio is an interesting case in point because they use fairly specific conceptualist moves and ideas, which are often autobiographically based, to create a dream-like mood designed to transcend the specifics of literal meaning. 'Our work has always been about total environments,' they write, 'a blending of landscape and art to create a place for dreaming . . . We use [these] materials to create an environment that defies specific meaning, but invites the visitor into a contemplative world of colour and sensuality.' This kind of work is often more suited to the conceptualist garden festival than the urban square or plaza.

Beyond these formally categorized approaches to concept in landscape design, it must be averred that some designers (including Andy Cao and Xavier Perrot, and, most spectacularly, Ken Smith) explicitly decry the idea of specifiable meaning in their work. Thus Martin Rein-Cano of Topotek 1 talks of a conceptual 'looseness': 'Sometimes it's more about sensuality, a feeling, than a need to explain, or to refer to history,' he says. 'We often make that feeling quite

easy-going and loose – in a park, we don't want to make people feel oppressed.' But such specific feelings or emotions, if deliberately created by design, are themselves conceptually based.

Conceptualist designers do not work with 'concepts' alone as an end in mind: there is another, perhaps more subtle methodology pervading this kind of work, the result of designers' sensitivity to the 'qualities' of the materials and artefacts they are using. The qualities of objects, to borrow the terminology of contemporary neuroscience, are quite distinct from either their properties or their 'powers', in that they represent physically unquantifiable or relatively indistinct and mutable elements such as colour, texture, humour, tone – or perhaps simply a general feeling that objects in space might exude, singly or en masse. Landscape designers – all designers – must deal with such qualities on a daily basis. Qualities exist beyond 'form'. A manipulation of qualities in landscape or garden settings can help to create the overall tone or space-flavour of the place, as opposed to the more obvious literal or intellectual notions which are conjured up by concepts themselves.

The bald categorization of approaches to landscape conceptualism attempted in this essay should not lead to a reductive interpretation – if anything, the conceptualist approach widens imaginative scope and grants creative freedom. For someone working from such a standpoint, a landscape can indeed . . . be . . . about . . . anything . . . .

Petra Blaisse Amsterdam

Highly personalized cross-disciplinary
art projects.

Following a training in fine art in 1970s London and
Amsterdam, Petra Blaisse spent most of the 1980s working
in the applied arts department of Amsterdam's Museum
of Modern Art, where she designed exhibitions relating to
everything from ceramics to textiles to photography. This,
she says, was a particularly enriching creative experience:
'At the museum I learned how to use graphics and light to
affect the objects on show, to put them in a new context,
and also how to influence the gallery space.' In 1987,
Blaisse branched out as a freelance exhibition designer;
her most notable collaboration was with architect and
designer Rem Koolhaas. 'Designing the exhibitions, I was
automatically asked to advise on the interiors of their first
buildings,' she explains. This phase of her career – working
on projects such as the Netherlands Dance Theatre in
Amsterdam – put Blaisse on the map in the design world.

In 1991 Blaisse formed her own company, Inside Outside,
with the intention from the outset of uniting interior and
exterior design. Since then her company has completed
a range of commissions in Europe and the USA, including
the Dutch embassy in Berlin and the Toledo Glass Center in
Ohio. Inside Outside recently won the competition to design
a major new park in Milan (see right and opposite), for
which Blaisse enlisted the help of plantsman Piet Oudolf.

Blaisse concedes that the idea of uniting interior design
and architecture with garden space is nothing new – it is a
mainstay of the 20th-century Modernist tradition – but her
intention is more ambitious. 'What we aim to do is to make
that link more intriguing, to do something that architecture
alone cannot do,' she says. 'If you just have glass walls, for
instance, it can be terribly boring at night. So we might
introduce change, movement and softness. We want to play
with concepts of light and of time – it's all about movement,
not just in the materials but in the movement of a
person through the space, as influenced by the design.'

There are also elements of contemporary landscape
conceptualism in Blaisse's work. This is the habit of basing
a design on a single strong idea, which might be a pattern
or an abstract concept. But there is no autobiographical
element, as she explains: 'It's not about the "me, me, me".'
Blaisse's philosophy, like that of many contemporary
designers, emerges as passionately committed but non-
ideological; imaginative and innovative, but also rooted in
pragmatism, flexibility and teamwork. She happily admits
that the inside–outside commission is the ideal, but that
several of her biggest projects have involved interior design
alone. 'Of course, we are not going to turn those down,'
she says.

Softness and movement are the epithets most frequently
applied to Blaisse's work, as she aims for a tonal synergy
between interior and exterior. In the interior sphere, Blaisse
made her name with sumptuous designs for curtains

(including theatre curtains), dividing walls and decorative
floors. The glamour of the look attracted clients such as
Prada, which commissioned Blaisse to design the walls for
its New York store. But not everyone was so enthusiastic
about the Inside Outside idea. 'In the beginning some
people were very agitated and irritated,' Blaisse recalls.
'People said, "So you're called Inside Outside – what is it
that you do? Don't you want to specialize? Shouldn't you
just do curtains?"'

Outdoors, Blaisse aims to introduce serious planting
design into a Modernist landscape milieu that is still
essentially architectural and sculptural. 'I like gardening
and I am fascinated by plants and anything living,' she says.
An enthusiast for the New Perennials movement in planting
design (massed grasses and perennials), which was
pioneered in Holland and Germany, Blaisse is frustrated
that it has largely been confined to the domestic garden
sphere – hence her new collaboration with Oudolf.

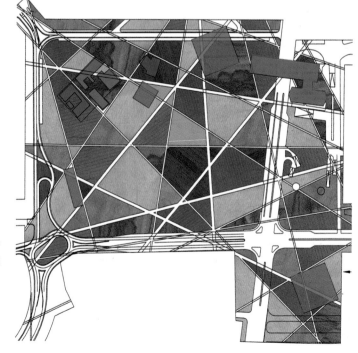

Chassé Terrein

BREDA (THE NETHERLANDS) 2001

The Chassé area of Breda is a 32-acre former military area now given over to housing and some office development. The well-known Rotterdam landscape outfit West 8 (p. 336) contributed most of the landscape design here, but architect Xavier de Geyter invited Blaisse to create the garden area around the bases of his five tower blocks.

'The towers stand quite close to each other, and it is quite a narrow space,' Blaisse says. In addition, a wide red driveway leading to each block was already in place, taking up much of the space. Inspired by the existing ground plan, Blaisse opted for a generic landscape setting that would add movement and softness to the uncompromising environment. She explains: 'We tried to concentrate on the materials and the colours, the wind, light and shadows.'

The in-between spaces were conceived as undulating grassy landforms forming knolls and hollows, planted with pine trees, wildflowers and naturalized bulbs, while the red driveway is edged with crushed white shells, a textural element that is continued 'inside' in that the glass façades are indented some way into the footprints of the buildings, forming a kind of porch. Long, wooden benches encourage residents to linger, and at night the translucent-roofed car parks which snake through the site start to glow.

De Plussenburgh

ROTTERDAM 2002

This garden lies in an urban environment between existing
and new apartment buildings for the elderly, which stand
with their 'feet' in a newly created water basin. The site
can be extremely windy, so Blaisse introduced a smooth
black asphalt surface (to easily accommodate wheelchairs)
with triangular incisions, out of which moisture-loving and
wind-resistant trees and grasses spring. Here and there,
wooden benches in the same triangular shape pop up.
A meandering path runs through the garden, while along
the water's edge a linear bench also acts as guardrail.
Inside the glass recreation space that hovers above the
water, a 'garden carpet' reflects the surrounding landscape.
Within the main building's lobby, the garden is continued:
two triangular cuts have been made into the black floor
surface, from which a bench and green plants emerge.

Jean-Pierre Brazs Paris

Site-specific land art and conceptualist sculpture.

Practising as a painter, sculptor and photographer since the early 1970s, Paris-based Jean-Pierre Brazs first turned to the topic of landscape in 1996. Brazs creates what he calls 'interventions' in the landscape, always site-specific and always conceptually predicated on what he finds in the place. Unlike other site-specific artists – such as Andy Goldsworthy, whose work Brazs's can superficially resemble – his preoccupation is not with natural materials found on site, but with the viewpoints it contains. Brazs has consistently explored the theme of the emplacement of the body in the landscape, a phenomenological perspective he shares with several other conceptualists, including Philippe Rahm (p. 230).

Brazs's methodology of deconstructing a landscape space according to its characteristics, and then reconstructing it again, has clear links with the deconstructivist literary theory made popular among his generation (he was born in 1947), and which later found an architectural correlative in Postmodernism and more recent deconstructivist disciplines. Brazs says that his first task in any setting is to explore its different viewpoints, and to extrapolate the detail of the piece from that basis. His is a visual response, which later becomes emphasized by careful material additions to the space. This concentration on the relationship of specific points in a landscape with one another, and with the potential routes and emotional responses of visitors, paradoxically introduces a strong sense of movement or flux in Brazs's work.

D'En Haut / D'En Bas

LE RAYOL CANADEL (FRANCE) 2006

A collaboration with landscape designer Gilles Clement, this piece was an installation for the Jardin des Méditerranées at the Domaine du Rayol botanic garden in the south of France. The garden's 'grand perspective' had already been decorated at each end by a pair of circular mosaics made by Clement, and Brazs decided to reference them in his own work by creating a circle of quartz halfway down the dramatic steps at the heart of the garden. For him, the quartz circle functions as a 'perfect form'.

The other element to the piece was a series of cuboid forms made from wire gabions, which seem to tumble crazily and uncontrollably down the steps when seen from above. Viewed from below, however, the cubes seem to be exhibiting an attraction to the circle, and eventually even coalescing with it. The apparent chaos visible from the top of the steps is seen to be ordered and resolvable when observed from below.

Le Chemin du Gaïac

NOUMÉA (NEW CALEDONIA) 2004

This installation was created around the Renzo Piano-designed Tjibaou cultural centre on the Pacific island of New Caledonia. It echoes some of Brazs's preoccupations with images of encirclement, unseemly invasions of cultural spaces and the disruption of natural environments. A long, sinuous line constructed from twenty-eight separate branches of the gaiac tree (native to New Caledonia) winds its way for some 180m through the forest surrounding the building, eventually entwining with the building itself. There is a sense of the natural environment somehow reclaiming the space where the state-subsidized building now stands, though this could be seen equally as either benign or threatening in its inferences.

Points de Vue

JUMIÈGES (FRANCE) 2005

This deceptively simple intervention at the abbey of
Jumièges in Normandy is the perfect summation of Brazs's
landscape sensibility. A stone staircase and its setting is
the theme of the piece. Brazs noted how the green apron
of lawn in front of the steps echoes the strident form of the
staircase, and the way that its central decorative feature –
a column – has been broken off near the base, and took
this compromised geometry as the basis of his inspiration.
The first 'point of view' is from the top of the steps,
looking towards the lawn, and then to the abbey beyond.
The second is from the foot of the steps, looking back. To
emphasize the strong shape of the stairs, Brazs introduced
a series of white-painted branches placed in the ground to
create a symbolic copse of trees. Crucially, there is a gap
in the centre, an echo of the absence of the column in front.

Le Jardin du Cercle d'Or

CHAUMONT SUR LOIRE (FRANCE) 2004

An installation at the Chaumont Festival, this project utilized gold paint for primary effect. A pile of broken branches evokes the natural tragedy and chaotic beauty of a fallen tree, while the ground plan forms a complementary ellipse. The climax of the piece is the golden circle painted onto the pile of branches, hinting at the redemption, redispersal and reconstruction of the elements of the tree, back into nature and the universe. The circle can be seen in focus from only one spot, however. Until one reaches that point, this sense of unity and resolution does not exist. In part, this is an evocation of the preciousness of any direct engagement with nature. Another installation of the same year, Obscure Clarté, also made use of gold paint. In that case, the gold colour echoed the play of sunlight of the smooth faces of the abundant natural rocks below the trees in its woodland location in Melle, in France.

Susanne Burger Munich

Outdoor conceptualist installations in functional landscape-architecture settings.

Initially trained as a ceramicist, Susanne Burger soon branched out into landscape design and has headed her own Munich-based practice since 2000. According to Burger, the basic tenets of her design methodology are: a clear structure; an atmospheric experience of space; clear use of forms; and a strongly worked-out relationship between the different materials and colours used in the scheme. She elaborates: 'All project planning focuses the plain formulation of the design topic, always in connection with the explorable, empirical definition of space. Design concentrates on a clear use of forms, implemented through a memorable use of materials and an awareness of and a sharpness of detail.'

What this means on the ground is that the materiality and detail of a Burger design is often one of its defining features. Rather than abstract notions or intellectual concepts, Burger allows the materials to shape the atmosphere of the space to a large extent, in communion with the presiding atmosphere she has detected at an early stage of the design process.

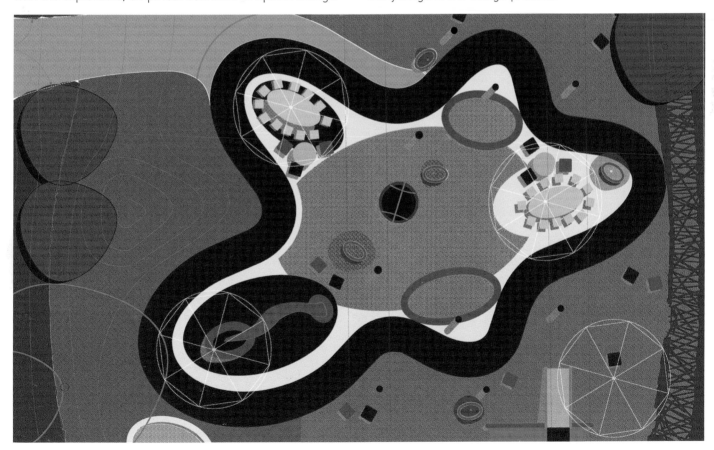

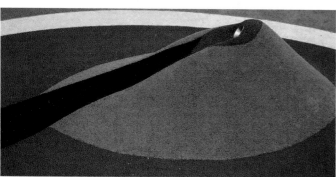

LEFT, ABOVE AND OPPOSITE Situated on an empty building site in the city centre, this relatively small and shady garden has to withstand constant exposure to children's games in all weathers. The edges of the playground are surfaced with wood shavings, cobblestones or grass, while fruit trees and berry bushes provide the green frame of the garden. Day-Nursery Garden for a European Patent Office, Munich 2005.

Susanne Burger **55**

Green Axis 13

MUNICH 1999

The Green Axis 13 of Messestadt Riem, a young community east of Munich near the former airport, runs from north to the south between residential areas. The 'axis' opens up towards the landscape park in the south, creating a link between the urban and non-urban landscape and connecting to the east–west promenade, which itself forms a link between residential areas.

A wide gravel surface, with trees planted at carefully thought-out intervals and forming a kind of loose green roof, stretches along the western edge of the axis. The solitary effect of the tree grove is emphasized by the exclusive use of plane trees. A main path made of durable macadam runs along the grove from north to south, and is connected to the residential areas via pathways which run east to west. Long walls with wooden benches integrated and scattered loosely throughout the grove present sunny as well as shady seating accommodation. The lighting follows the course of the main path.

Facing the tree grove, a wide and open meadow makes up an interesting counterpoint. It is divided into three areas by link paths. The 'Playground of Transversal Games' is situated in the southernmost of these green areas. Here, the orange rings modelled into the green surface appear like drops on a water surface that have formed circles and became fossilized in the process. In the centre of these wave-like rings, playing equipment for jumping, skipping, swinging and making caves can be found. The waves are made of concrete and playground surface, and have been modelled in various sizes; a ring-like roof offers protection from sun and rain.

The eastern edge of the green axis is lined by a hornbeam hedge clipped to different heights (200cm to 350cm). It runs the entire length of the grove and refers with its changing heights to the equally changing landscape of buildings adjacent to the axis. This varied and lively change of perspective creates new views and softens the relative roughness of the adjacent field.

In the north of the axis is the so-called 'pocket park'. Its square shape is trimmed by a circle of plane trees. Paths run from the axis towards and into the park, where seats tempt visitors to linger in this pretty spot. Again, a wide and open meadow forms a lively contrast. In the southwestern part of this park, a pavilion is situated; it has a lockable room for playing equipment and is intended to be the neighbourhood's meeting place for various celebrations and cultural events. The pavilion is framed by high hedges so that the spaciousness of the sports field is rounded off by a kind of closed green room that nevertheless is open to the sky.

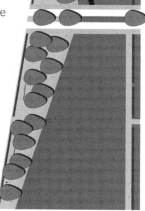

Five Courtyards

MUNICH 2003

The five courtyards are situated inside a block in Munich's old city centre, close to Marienplatz; they all have high walls formed by surrounding office buildings and shops. In a collaboration with architects Herzog & de Meuron, the whole block was restructured and given a new face, with a completely new layout and street façade, plus a variety of new shopping arcades, restaurants, courtyards and terraces. The open courtyard spaces were deemed essential to the plan. Burger explains: 'The design of the five courtyards was inspired by the two counterpoints [or contrasting characters] of the arrangement. The courtyards and terraces, places of quiet and of a homogenous character, contrast clearly with the variety of lures and displays in the busy shopping arcades. The courtyards, therefore, become a place of peace and tranquillity in the urban environment.'

Water, blossom, trees, the seasons of the year, light and shade have been translated into a simple and emphatic

language of forms. On a functional level, the clear visual differences between the courtyards' characters make it easier for visitors to orientate themselves in the bustle of the shopping arcades.

The Portia Courtyard, for example, is a simple, cobbled space shaded by magnolia trees serving an adjacent café. However, shoppers must use a stepping-stone to cross a pool to enter the space, which features a water curtain on one wall. The Promenade Courtyard features a long backdrop of different varieties of Japanese maple trees, vividly coloured in oranges, yellows, reds, purples and greens in autumn, while the tiny Garden Courtyard is filled with low clipped box hedges and yellow flowers. The Amira Courtyard features *Parrotia persica* trees (also brightly coloured in autumn) and moulded concrete seats, so that it presents completely different aspects to shoppers below and office workers looking down from above.

Cao Perrot Studio
Los Angeles, New York and Paris

Deeply personalized conceptual statements utilizing innovative materials.

Born in Vietnam, Andy Cao first came to the attention of the garden and landscape design world in 2000, with the Glass Garden he made at the rear of his house in the Echo Park neighbourhood of Los Angeles. Utilizing some 45 tons of recycled coloured glass pieces, which he blended together with great skill and discernment, Cao created a startlingly beautiful, autobiographical evocation of the salt mounds and agricultural landscape of central Vietnam. The glass also acted as a mulch through which plants could grow. This much-illustrated piece provided the springboard for his career, which has included commercial work in Los Angeles and Las Vegas, and the Prize Fellowship in Landscape Architecture at the American Academy in Rome. More recently, Cao has teamed up with Breton landscape designer Xavier Perrot, and they now work from studios in Los Angeles, New York and Paris.

The artists' prepared statement is unusually clear and apposite: 'At Cao Perrot Studio, our work has always been about total environments; a blending of landscape and art to create a place for dreaming. By drawing on diverse cultural backgrounds, we create work that adapts to a global perspective. All our projects require research on the properties of familiar, overlooked materials. We use these materials to create an environment that defies specific meaning, but invites the visitor into a contemplative world of color and sensuality.' Cao and Perrot prove that it is perfectly possible to make strong conceptual landscape works which are not underpinned by specific, describable ideas or narratives.

Their 2003 public artwork Cocoons (illustrated on the cover) – three spinning cocoons made of five miles of coloured monofilament and sited on a rocky point opposite the Golden Gate Bridge – contains no 'meaning' to be decoded, but nevertheless operates on a conceptual level as a profound mediation between art and nature, between the made and the natural. Similarly their work in high-profile urban environments often plays on ideas of history and place, but without making definitive statements and bringing in concepts and artefacts from other cultures (notably that of Vietnam) to reflect the artists' own engagement with the space. This can be seen in the way Cao floated yellow mimosa blossoms on the water of the Medici Fountain in the Luxembourg Gardens in Paris (an 'Eastern' reference), and in his Red Box installation at the American Academy in Rome (see opposite), an intensely worked piece which incorporated a twenty-panel suspended glass wall made from fused recycled medicine bottles, a grass wall, 9 tons of recycled glass pebbles and coiled incense from Vietnam, along with collaborations with music composer Derek Bermel, a Roman masseuse, and a performance artist.

Cao's initial coup was in the use of recycled glass, and this emphasis on unusual and innovative materials remains a hallmark of the work. 'Revealing inherent "imperfections" as beauty marks gives our work a spontaneous, hand-made feel,' the artists explain. 'Blending these qualities with environments that are functional, colourful and highly sensual has become a signature of our work.' The company also manufactures recycled glass tiles, aggregates and panels, which can be made to bespoke specifications. Cao and Perrot continue to operate in an interesting sphere that crosses the boundaries between commercial, artistic and residential work.

OPPOSITE After receiving the Prize Fellowship at the American Academy, Cao created this installation for its entry courtyard utilizing his trademark recycled glass chippings. Red Box, Rome 2002.

Lullaby Garden

SONOMA (CALIFORNIA) 2004

This installation for the Cornerstone Festival in Sonoma Valley was made from two hundred 1m-by-1m coloured nylon carpet sections, hand-knitted in Vietnam by sixty villagers, then sewn together and stretched over a 121m² rolling landform. The installation also included oversized zippers and polished coconut shells. A veil of clear fishing line was wrapped around the perimeter to create an 'invisible fence', which would sometimes disappear and, at other times, catch the light and form a shimmering wall around the garden. Vietnamese lullabies by contemporary Paris-based musicians Huong Thanh and Nguyên Lê completed the soothing environment. Visitors were asked to remove their shoes before climbing onto the installation, a gesture of collaboration which made the experience all the more intimate and transporting.

Kerpuns Garden

BRITTANY (FRANCE) 2004

Cao and Perrot continue to operate as garden designers as well as artists in both France and the US, and this landscape was created at a private residence in Brittany. In their garden designs, Cao and Perrot utilize simple, bold moves, such as the undulating grass berms used here, to create evocative spaces which evoke some of the 'dreaminess' they aim for in their art pieces. It is not the intense, fantastical dreaminess honoured in European Surrealism, but a more meditative feel, associated with relaxation and the drift in and out of sleep. Plant combinations are kept extremely simple in the duo's garden designs – generally broad swathes of textural grasses (such as *Stipa tenuissima*), complemented by one-colour plantings of lavender or osteospermum.

Jardin des Hespérides

MONTREAL 2006

This installation at the Jardins de Métis festival drew on the sounds, scents and materials of Vietnam, while simultaneously evoking the landscape of the St Lawrence River. (The design brief at Métis includes the need to make reference to the locality.) Paths of stark white seashells wind through a carpet of local green algae, vetiver grasses dotted with wild irises, and Himalayan blue poppies. In the centre of the garden, a saffron-coloured lantern looms, oversized and weightless, in a reflecting pond, where an orange grove mysteriously rises. The traditional Vietnamese lantern is made from lining fabric hand-dyed with Iranian Sargol saffron. Upon entering the lantern, visitors discover a unique fragrance inspired by scents of the sea, zest of seaweed crushed underfoot, and incense in a temple.

Paul Cooper Powys (UK)

Pioneering material experimentation
including use of exterior video.

As a garden designer who has worked chiefly for private homeowners (mainly in London), the conceptual aspects of Paul Cooper's designs have tended to reflect the personalities and requirements of his necessarily bold clients. Allied to this is a fascination with innovative technical materials, special effects and ambitious leisure programmes. Cooper listens to the needs of his clients and very often gives them much more than they originally asked for.

Cooper has also courted controversy with show gardens at venerable events by raising uncomfortable ideas. His 'Cool and Sexy Garden' at the Chelsea Flower Show in 1994 was partially censored: images of male nudity had to be removed. Only slightly less shocking for the British gardening establishment have been more recent Chelsea show gardens courtesy of Cooper, including a floating garden, an upside-down garden, and a laboratory garden. Many of the show gardens provided opportunities to try new methods including prefabrication with materials such as synthetic fabrics, alternative floor surfaces, out-of-ground planting systems, and gardens which are flexible, interchangeable or even portable.

Away from the festivals and shows, Cooper has built up a successful design practice distinguished by an emphasis on innovations such as films in the garden, atmospheric 'art lighting' and the use of stainless steel, plastic and fibre-optics. Cooper explains: 'The challenge of the urban environment, with its lack of ground space, has persuaded me to employ materials and methods of construction not traditionally associated with the garden.' His gardens represent a response to contemporary lifestyle, including 'twenty-four hour gardens' with specialist lighting and theatrical effects. Each one is tailored to the needs and interests of the clients in a conceptual manner which might be characterized as biographical: for one football fan, for example, Cooper produced a garden replete with painted crowd scenes and life-sized cut-outs of his favourite players. All of this places Cooper firmly outside the mainstream British gardens scene, but he has nevertheless garnered a sizeable popular following through the publication of four successful books, including *The New Tech Garden* (2001). Cooper has frequently redefined the garden, adding such adjectives as 'instant', 'portable', 'reusable', 'multistorey', and 'prefabricated' to the description.

Cooper began as an environmental artist, and in conversation is as likely to mention Klee and Kandinsky as an influence as any celebrated garden or gardener – which

ABOVE A multi-level, multimedia garden designed to make the most of a small, north-facing garden for a modern house in North London. The whole garden is constructed above ground and includes elaborate lighting effects. Golders Green, London 1992.

OPPOSITE At this installation for the Chelsea Flower Show, concealed pumps project a fine mist up into glass boxes to create a microclimate able to sustain the tropical marshland papyrus inside. Climate Cases, London 2003.

BELOW Inspired by drawings in an old biology textbook, this garden for the Jardins de Métis festival consisted of six pseudo-scientific experiments. As much art installation as garden, it was intended as a satirical reminder of our obsession with the desire to control nature for our own gain. Eden Laboratory, Montreal 2002.

is, again, unusual in Britain's horticulture-dominated garden scene. His early sculpture was highly influenced by plant form and structure, in particular the geometry and mathematics associated with leaf arrangement and the geology of the landscape. Gallery work led to invitations to create site-specific installations, culminating in 'Two Circles in a Stone Bridge', a dry-stone wall sculpture which signalled his interest in landscape design. Recent work has seen a fusion between garden and sculpture – outdoor installations that have included living plants.

Sensory and Interactive Garden

DARLINGTON (UK) 2004

Cooper has completed several gardens which represent a significant departure from his usual commissions: two have been for residential homes that care for adults with autism, and a third for a 'halfway' house for homeless young adults with alcohol or drug problems.

Commissioned by Castlebeck Care, the Sensory and Interactive Garden at Newbus Grange, near Darlington in Co. Durham, was designed to delight and entertain, but its primary function is to stimulate the senses and encourage social interaction. It is essentially a series of 'galleries', set within a formal layout. Each gallery is designed to highlight one of four main senses – touch, smell, sight and hearing – and contains statues, screens which act as paintings, and appropriate planting. The prism maze (a pathway which leads residents through a series of coloured, translucent acrylic partitions) is designed to engage the visual senses, while the screens and statues are intended to accommodate experimentation, allowing future introductions of other sensory experiences as part of the learning process.

Another of these projects, the Interactive Garden (2005) for Marissa House in Blackburn, Lancashire, differs from the Newbus Grange garden in that each element was created with a particular resident in mind. As a result, there is an outdoor puzzle, as well as spinning sculptures and noise-making contraptions. The design of each of the elements is garden-related: one of the spinning sculptures evokes an aviary; the 'Hearing Gallery' features bell sound statues set within *Miscanthus sinensis*; and another gallery mimics a pond complete with mechanical fish.

Claude Cormier Montreal

Exuberant, witty, no-holds-barred urban landscape conceptualism.

French-Canadian Claude Cormier is unusually well qualified: he has undergraduate degrees in landscape architecture and agronomy, as well as a postgraduate degree in the history and theory of design from the Graduate School of Design at Harvard University, where he was seconded to the office of Martha Schwartz (p. 256). After working for an architectural firm in Montreal for seven years, Cormier struck out on his own in 1995 and his office now employs seven full-time landscape architects. Most of his work has been concentrated in Montreal and Toronto, although he receives commissions in the USA and farther afield. Cormier's 'Blue Sticks' installation (p. 76) could be seen at Hestercombe in Somerset in 2004 (it is still in situ in 2007), and 'Blue Tree' at the Cornerstone Festival that same year.

Like his contemporary, the New York-based Ken Smith (p. 284), who also worked with Schwartz, Cormier is a leading second-generation conceptualist landscape designer. At the core of the conceptualist project is the idea that a naturalistic approach to creating landscapes is fundamentally dishonest since it denies the artificiality of the design process, as well as our complex and ambivalent relationship with nature itself. Like other conceptualist designers, Cormier bases all of his designs on a single idea which permeates every aspect of the plan on the ground, and this idea is often realized in a highly artificial or stylized way, using bright colour and artificial materials.

The habitual antipathy among conceptualists towards a romanticized vision of nature is if anything even more marked in Cormier. 'I grew up on a farm,' he explains, 'where the relationship with the natural world is very direct. We were making a living out of the land, so this idea of rural peace does not work for me. Nature bores me.

It is not the place where I get my inspiration.' Instead, Cormier is sustained by the wider culture and, in particular, the vibrancy and excitement of cities, and the wide diversity of the people who live in them.

He also has little time for ecologically based approaches to landscape design: 'Everyone is moving eco, but with eco we can also forget the idea of the made. It's the issue of artificiality. In our work we are honest about it,' he says. Bright colour and the innovative use of artificial materials is underpinned in Cormier's work by a serious commitment to exploring the history of the space. 'We have to ask, "How do we activate history and make it resonate well?"' he queries. 'There is always a reason for the design that is attached to the site conditions we are working with. It becomes contextual and specific.'

As can be seen with Place Youville in Montreal (see p. 72), Cormier's work is not always eye-poppingly challenging – the conceptualist aspect can be inserted in quite a subtle way. 'We basically follow the rules, but we tweak one thing to completely change the perception of it,' he says. 'We create a different way of looking at things. I like blurring the edges.'

OPPOSITE Cormier describes this tribute to Le Havre-born Claude Monet at the city's Hôtel-de-Ville as 'a basic palette of five colours distributed across thousands of strands of thin Christmas balls'. Grand Pergola, Le Havre (France) 2006.

Place Youville

MONTREAL 1999

Place Youville is a narrow residential plaza, about 600m long, in the centre of what is now becoming an upscale neighbourhood. Cormier's brief, in partnership with Groupe Cardinal Hardy, was to create a new public space without disturbing the archaeological integrity of the site; no excavation below the surface was allowed.

'The idea was to create a quilt of sidewalks that related to the 400-year-old history of the sidewalks in the city,' Cormier explains. 'We wanted to recycle history.' Wooden decking, stone pavers, limestone slabs and poured concrete were all used as materials for the several sidewalks which shoot off from the main walkway all along its length. The various materials relate to the nature of the buildings they lead to – residential, cultural or institutional. The fragmented ground plan is complemented by the textured shade created by gleditsia trees, while on summer evenings the plaza is filled with the scent and colour of massed dwarf lilacs.

Lipstick Forest

MONTREAL 2002

A forest of fifty-two bright-magenta concrete tree trunks
dominates one end of the vast, newly enlarged Palais des
Congrès convention centre. The colour is a tribute to the
city's cosmetics industry, while the idea of the tree trunks
was borne of the practicalities of making an indoor garden
and a reference to the street landscape of the city. 'It is
all about this notion of something that is artificial but not
false,' Cormier says. 'We were asked to create a winter
garden inside a convention centre, above a highway, in a
walled-in space. Yes, we could have used real plants, but
it would have been so false.'

   He continues: 'We had a terrible ice storm which
damaged all the silver maples. We could not cut any
trees down, so we thought we would use concrete trunks
painted to look real – the casts are life-sized and every one
is different.' And the decision to paint them pink? 'Montreal
is often grey and cold. But it is a very vibrant city, and we
have this cosmetics industry. So it looks artificial on the
surface, but what we have made is more true than if we
had used real plants. It's all about authenticity.'

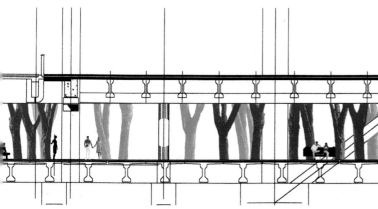

Blue Sticks

SOMERSET (UK) 2004

This piece is probably the most travelled conceptual show garden created thus far. It began life in 2000 at the inaugural Jardins de Métis at the Reford Gardens on the St Lawrence River in Quebec. Subsequently it was reinstalled at several other venues, until finally it was shown at Hestercombe Gardens, in Somerset, in 2004.

Blue Sticks was a response to the brief from Métis – that designs should somehow be inspired by the venue. The historic Reford Gardens were created in the early part of the 20th century by Elsie Reford, who followed the example of William Robinson, the gardening pioneer behind Gravetye Manor, in West Sussex, and Gertrude Jekyll. The blue poppy, *Meconopsis betonicifolia*, was a particular favourite of Elsie Reford, and has since become the trademark flower of Métis.

Cormier's installation consisted of hundreds of flat-sided sticks which were painted in very slightly differing shades of blue on two sides, and varying shades of red on the other two. Cormier's rationale was that in nature such variations occur naturally, even if they sometimes go unnoticed. The optical effect on the visitor was nothing short of startling, creating a sense of walking through pure blue, followed – upon turning round at the far end of the garden – by surprise at finding that the sticks have all turned bright red. It was a simple ploy – effectively a 'one-liner' – but it was also memorable, delightful and original.

Topher Delaney San Francisco

Complex and vividly realized garden spaces
that unite architecture and horticulture.

San Francisco-based Topher Delaney designs as many
gardens for private clients as she does for the public
and commercial sector. This makes her probably the
most successful conceptualist private-garden designer
worldwide. Such success, among a clientele which does not
necessarily see itself as part of an avant-garde movement,
belies the received idea among more conventional
designers and horticulturists that this mode of work is
somehow impractical, unpopular or undesirable in the
domestic realm. Delaney relishes personal interaction with
clients – with whom she often stays in contact for many
years after a garden has been installed – and all of her
gardens contain significant planting elements as well as
some of the most original architectural interventions to
be found anywhere. Indeed, some of them (such as the
Holland residence in San Francisco) pull off the near-
impossible trick of combining comforting floral
traditionalism with cutting-edge conceptual design.

In terms of horticulture, Delaney talks of 'the mixing
of colour and plant relationships in gardening – you start
piecing it together, like making a bouquet' – and this
collage approach can be seen in her architectural attitude,
too. From a basic central concept, which is often
articulated in the central feature of the garden or
landscape – in the shape or design of a swimming pool
or courtyard in a garden, for example, or on a larger scale
in the patterning of a plaza – Delaney develops a relatively
free symbolic rationale, so that the final expression of the
space never seems fettered by its conceptual basis. Every
aspect of the space is carefully considered in its own right
in these finely balanced conceptions. This makes Delaney's
designs seem fuller and more detailed than those of some
of her contemporaries, but paradoxically working on a
smaller scale can make detail seem more, rather than less,
appropriate. It is in the big-scale projects that large

LEFT In this blue garden overlooking San Francisco Bay, Delaney had
to come up with a design that accommodated the stringent building
codes of a roof terrace space, not to mention the myriad of skylights
and air shafts. The use of a single colour helps to unify the disparate
elements. Karam-West Residence, San Francisco 1999.

LEFT AND ABOVE Delaney's whimsical shopping-bag planters were designed specifically for the site. Among the different plants at the garden are Canary Island date palms (*Phoenix canariensis*) and rows of *Yucca flaccida* 'Golden Sword'. Central Plaza, Marin (USA) 2005.

landscape moves can be used to define the space, while in smaller spaces the details can be made to sing out.

At the Karam-West residence (see opposite), a roof terrace with views across San Francisco Bay, the conceptual theme chosen was blue: a blue garden to match a blue sky and a blue bay. The practical challenge was to reconcile a landscape design with the legal requirements of such a building: weight load factors, protruding air shafts, skylights and waterproof deck membranes which precluded the use of soil. As Delaney explains, 'The materials used in the garden reflect our interest in exploring the possibilities of products which are readily available off-the-shelf.' Bands of blue neoprene rubber (used for diving suits) were woven onto galvanized metal walls, while blue astroturf covered

the floor surface. Mass-produced waterproof boxes made of stainless-steel were used as garden seats.

Central Plaza (see above) in Marin, just north of San Francisco, is a shopping mall completely refurbished by Delaney. The central idea was recycling; Delaney says the mall itself has been recycled in her design. 'These malls have a certain life expectancy,' she explains. 'The materials wear out, but the vendors remain viable. Everyone loves this faux-Italian look, but I wanted something a little different.' Recycled plastic lumber now picks out a barcode message ('We Love to Shop'), while fibreglass 'shopping bags' double as planters for citrus, medicinal plants, herbs and edible annuals (references to some of the products on sale inside the mall).

Craford Residence

SAN FRANCISCO 2000

This extraordinary design is one of the richest conceptual visions yet realized in a private garden. It melds a wide range of materials and references to create a coherent space that responds to the undulating site's invigorating position overlooking Richmond Bay and Mount Tamalpais.

After progressing down a monumental path of pressed coloured concrete in grey and ochre tones, complemented by bands of river pebbles, visitors must cross a curved bridge over a square fishpond to reach the house, or proceed to the right and into a series of enclosed gardens that descend along the ridge. The ground surfaces of these courtyards are paved in intersecting arcs of coloured concrete, punctuated by trapezoidal, rusted-steel planters. Positioned at axial transitions are large slabs of stone, which are suspended vertically on thin armatures of steel. The pungent scents of rosemary, jasmine and citrus fill the air, with morning glory clothing the walls. The uppermost space is the 'music room', which is bounded by suspended bamboo trunks that slap against each other to form a drumming rhythm in tune with the wind's velocity.

A snaking path of granite setts descends to the front of the house, where the swimming pool (its bottom adorned with the barcoded message 'In Deep Immersion') is oriented below the main living room. Variegated box forms in tubs, spiky red phormiums and groups of fastigiate beeches provide more structural intrigue. The overall rationale of this series of garden spaces spilling over into each other creates a sense of forward motion throughout the space. Delaney's skill here lies in using diverse materiality that is united in tone.

Garden Play

SONOMA (USA) 2004

This elegant installation at the Cornerstone Festival was themed around the concept of play. Billowing white curtains part to reveal a Surrealist space defined by ball shapes and a series of silver birch trees. The floor, strewn with silver petanque balls, is made from crushed oyster shells, while large balls of coiled marine hawser rope extend the metaphor of the rolling sphere. There are hidden messages here, too. Delaney asks: 'Do we understand the embedded messages within the physical environment? What is the effect of encrypted cultural texts upon our comprehension of the physical environment?' The grid of trees is arranged formally north to south, and informally east to west. Meanwhile a striped black and blue text panel, made of recycled plastic lumber, is not abstract but utilizes Delaney's trademark barcode motif. The encrypted language here spells the words 'Game Play'.

University of San Francisco

SAN FRANCISCO 2000

A substantial flight of steps brings the visitor up and into an exhilarating courtyard hidden behind the university building. The main body of the space is taken up by a massive sinusoidal projection map of the world in green and blue rusticated terrazzo, with trade routes picked as grey lines. The barcode pattern beneath running across the terrace and into the student lobby reads 'Ex/Change', while black and white stone benches echo the barcode, each embedded with two opposing inscriptions on the topic of trade ('Supply' and 'Demand', 'Credit' and 'Debit'). The planting is designed to echo the local agricultural economy, with fruit trees thriving on the terraces next to the descending steps.

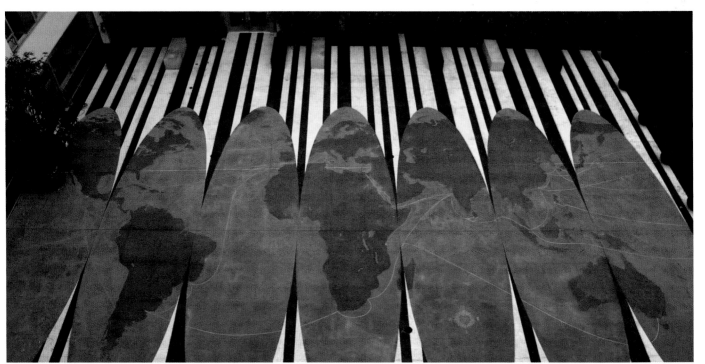

Hurley Residence

SAN FRANCISCO 2001

Delaney created three new garden spaces (plus a small balcony) at this house with panoramic views from its roof terrace across San Francisco Bay towards Alcatraz and the Golden Gate Bridge. The visitor first enters a contemplative space which acts as the shady front garden, the floor made of Haifa limestone and its walls a soothing abstract 'painting' made up of twenty-four interlocking plaster (mixed with marble dust) rectangles in different shades of

blue. The theme is continued in the kitchen and toy-storage area on one side of the garden, hidden behind sliding steel doors. Recycled turquoise glass pebbles diffuse the fibre-optics and fluorescent lighting which lie at the base of the walls and subtly alter the colour tones. In the centre of the space is a limestone 'chadar' from India, a textured slab over which water continuously flows. 'It's like the Alhambra,' Delaney states. 'You don't need a huge amount of water, just

an evocation. They have this huge amount of water in front of them, this sort of chaos, the blue chaos of the sea, and then in here it's this very controlled, manicured blue garden.'

The roof terrace features recycled plastic lumber decking, diachronic glass panels and a stainless-steel kitchen area, but is otherwise unadorned. 'Who wants to look at sickly plants up here, when you have this view?' Delaney asks. The rear garden (which replaced a Thomas Church design) has been conceived as a play area for the owners' young sons. A rubber 'safe-deck' describes an abstract pattern of red and orange circles on black, which echoes the pattern of the mini-golf course embedded in the plan. There are slate drawing walls, a pink sandpit, a cauldron roundabout and a basketball hoop, but the main feature is a moulded concrete boulder which can only be accessed through a hole in the top, via a rope or ladder.

Herbert Dreiseitl
Überlingen (Germany)

The world's leading conceptualist water designer,
a maker of liquid narratives.

It was in 1980 that Herbert Dreiseitl founded his landscape-architecture practice, and from the outset he decided to specialize in water. 'I was working as an artist before then,' he explains. 'But it was the challenge of water, and the low quality of existing work, that attracted me to it. I decided that in my professional life I would focus only on water.' Over the past quarter-century Dreiseitl has built up an international reputation, and has often collaborated with architects such as Norman Foster and Renzo Piano. The range of work undertaken is impressive: as well as town-centre landscapes, Dreiseitl has designed water playgrounds for children and large-scale water sculptures, diverted rivers, created ecologically friendly water systems, and even introduced a water recycling system for the Zurich Zoo, with purifying reedbeds in the bear enclosure.

Dreiseitl has a profound personal affinity with water, which is expressed scientifically as well as aesthetically. 'One of the reasons I decided to base my practice at Überlingen,' he explains, 'is because it is close to the various research institutes which specialize in water.'

The latest research into the inner structure and rhythmical movement of water has been a strong influence, and Dreiseitl has worked closely with scientists from such establishments as the Institute of Liquid Science.

Science aside, Dreiseitl also believes that water gives people a special contact with nature. 'Even in city centres people have a real desire to connect to what I call the "lost environment" or "lost nature",' he says. 'Water is a very emotional agent for this.' All this is a long way from the traditional vertical, single-jet fountain which so bored Dreiseitl at the start of his career: 'This is just one element and it did not interest me,' he says. 'What did was the movement of water and its interaction with light. If you design with water, you have to design with light, too.' In practical terms, there is an important emphasis on cleanliness, safety and reliability in all Dreiseitl's design work. Throughout garden history, water features have been notoriously difficult to build and maintain successfully, and Dreiseitl's technical expertise – born of his single-minded specialism – has been the key to his reputation.

ABOVE, TOP AND TOP LEFT The variety and invention of Dreiseitl's career-long relationship with water as a design material can be seen here – crucially, the way that hard surfaces can alter the appearance of water (top left), and also the way that wind or underwater sounds can conspire to create mist or unusual surface patterns from water.

OPPOSITE Sheets of water create liquid curtains in this typically innovative Dreiseitl scheme. Heiner-Metzger-Platz, Neu-Ulm (Germany) 2005.

Town Hall Square

HATTERSHEIM (GERMANY) 1993

The small town of Hattersheim, near Frankfurt, was
looking for a way of making itself an attractive proposition
for newcomers to the economically thriving region. The
area between the town hall and a public park was an
anonymous space, so a competition for its redesign was
launched. Dreiseitl's practice won the competition with
a design focused on a new set of steps up to the building,
carved in two by a cascade of flow-form granite basins
that reflected new, scientific ideas about the rhythmical
flow of water.

'With those curved steps, you must imagine the water
moving from side to side in a figure-of-eight at a constant
rate,' Dreiseitl explains. The stylized stream travels
underground a little way before emerging as a meander
punctuated by plane trees at the edge of the square, and
then reaches a pond at the edge of the square where it is
cleaned. The stream then flows into a naturalistic pond in
the park, and is finally pumped back up to the top of the
town hall steps.

The project typifies the eco-Modernism of Dreiseitl's
practice, in which the non-naturalistic aesthetic of the
Modernist look is partnered with environmentally friendly
functionalism: 'I began involving ecological factors in my
work almost twenty years ago: how to capture and reuse
rainwater, how to avoid flooding, how to clean water, the
principles of slow-release into rivers to avoid erosion.
I want to bring them into modern design and modern life.'

DS Landschapsarchitecten

Long-established art-based conceptualist practice characterized by clarity of vision.

Amsterdam

In design it can take more confidence to aim at simplicity as opposed to complexity, but this truism does not faze Maike van Stiphout, director of DS Landschapsarchitecten of Amsterdam. The company message talks about a 'clear answer' to 'complex problems', and that is exactly what is provided: the clarity of her vision is outstanding and leads to finished commissions that brim with panache. The company was founded in 1988 when van Stiphout was in her early twenties, which makes it one of the longest-established conceptual landscape outfits. Singularity of vision is what defines the work. The team at DS Landschapsarchitecten spend a long time circling a project and the concepts which arise from it – but when the plan is decided, there is a sure touch at work.

Van Stiphout comes from an art background, but there is no sense that she is striving to insert some of that experience into the landscape discipline. Rather, she integrates these interests. 'I have never viewed my landscape work as some kind of installation,' she says. 'I use the same methods as artists, but where an artist does it for herself, we do it for society.' This communitarian attitude is at the heart of the ethos of the company, which mainly undertakes public work. Van Stiphout draws on her experience as a member of the board of art and public space in Holland. 'We like it when public art is integrated,' she explains, 'art which gives meaning to a space. We want to stay away from this modernistic idea that it is all about function, not meaning. We have got more soul.'

The other key idea behind the company's work is continuity. 'Things always change in the landscape, but I like to emphasize what continues,' van Stiphout explains. 'It can be ecology, or a city's history. We always go through processes, stepping backwards and then forwards. We go from the concept straight on to the detail.' The emphasis on detail at an early stage also marks out DS Landschapsarchitecten from most other companies. 'People ask a lot about the meaning of the place, but I like it when the detail is part of the concept,' van Stiphout adds, noting that it can be difficult to find materials (such as street furniture), as well as practitioners, that measure up to the vision for such elements.

Clarity of expression does not necessarily lead to a dour minimalism, however, and colour plays a major role in many of the company's designs, such as the vivid orange used for a play area at Nicolaas Beetsplein (see opposite) in a run-down part of Dordrecht. 'We use a lot of colour,' van Stiphout says, 'but not a lot of colours, so you never get this fantasy-land look. It remains abstract in that sense, although it is all part of giving the piece meaning.'

LEFT This artificial oasis in the 'new town' of Almere is sited within a masterplan by architects OMA. Van Stiphout and her colleagues also designed a 'city scenario' and pavement for the town centre. Waterplein, Almere (The Netherlands) 2000.

LEFT AND BELOW This project, a collaboration with NL Architects, incorporated a baseball field into a hill and brought new life to a neglected part of the city. Nicolaas Beetsplein, Dordrecht (The Netherlands) 2005.

RWZI Amsterdam West

AMSTERDAM 2002

This large sewage works and water purification plant
in a harbour area of Amsterdam is surrounded by sand
dunes and stands out starkly in the landscape. For DS
Landschapsarchitecten, it was not simply a matter of
masking these industrial buildings with their slightly
unpalatable role – the aim was to transform them into
a virtue of the site. 'We were fascinated by these tanks
and wanted to make something just as impressive,' van
Stiphout says. 'We thought of a pine forest, so we took two
materials: pine trees (*Pinus nigra*) and a 1km-long chalk
pavement alongside, which will attract plants from outside
the fence.' This one big, simple idea complements the
scale of the site and its built components. 'The plant is
enormous, with this repetition of the white tanks,' van
Stiphout says. 'We didn't want to scale it down at all.
We said: this is landscape already.'

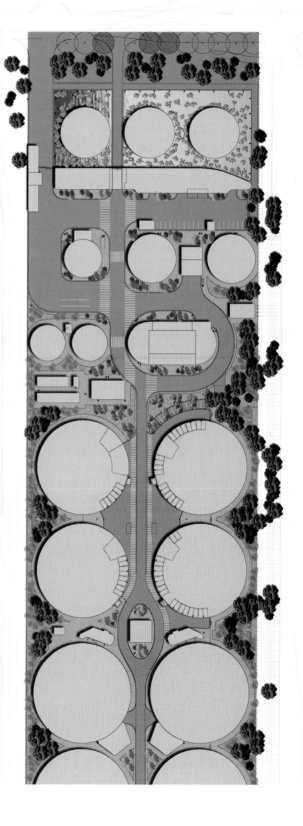

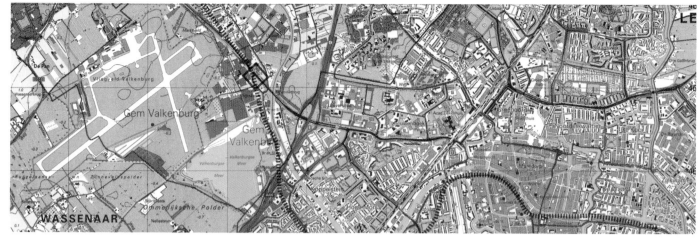

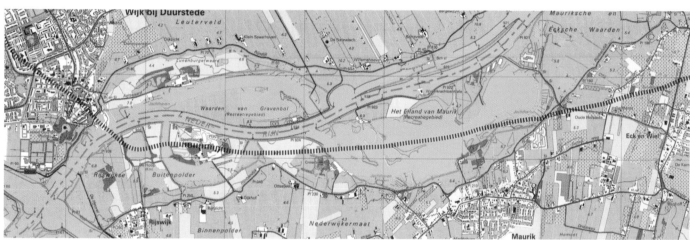

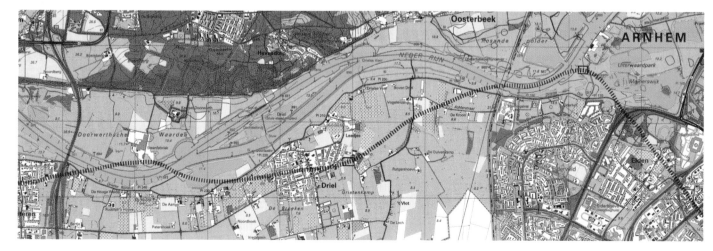

The Limes

THE NETHERLANDS AND GERMANY 2006

'The walk is the art,' says van Stiphout of this project, which retraces the line of an old Roman road through Holland and Germany, known in ancient times as *Limes* (not referring to the tree, but related to the word 'limit', meaning border). The road marked the northern border of the entire Roman Empire, and stretched from the Black Sea to Scotland.

'It followed the old stream of the Rhine and ran from Katwijk aan Zee via Utrecht and Arnhem to Germany,' van Stiphout explains. 'The border was defended by watchtowers and forts, and was connected by a road. Now what's left of the sites are only traces of piles from the watchtowers. And on the sites of the forts, cities are risen (amongst others Utrecht, Alphen aan den Rijn, Woerden). The road has sunk into the ground, been ploughed up or washed away. Lots of people who live on the site now are unaware of this historic relic in their back gardens.'

The piece initially took the form of a walk along 6km of The Limes in 2006, with the findings then communicated to the local community via lectures, school visits, exhibitions and contact with local history groups. The project is now being expanded, and a book is planned. 'It's about things which are invisible,' van Stiphout says. 'By walking the route you make it visible. It's not archaeological in any sense – we say you have to awaken the road, not rebuild it.'

History

An ignorance of history has long been a hallmark of mediocrity in the avant-garde of any medium. A dismissal of history from a position of knowledge is something else, the result of a critical and emotional engagement with historical themes. Despite an often aggressively modernistic stance, and a tendency to deny the power of the past over their own creativity, it is a paradox that conceptualist landscape architects can generally be seen to be obsessed with history, to a greater or lesser extent. Many conceptualist landscape designers have a somewhat tortured and paradoxical relationship with history, on one level dismissing it as irrelevant to their artistic aims, but in many cases using it as a stimulus for creativity. This deep connection with the unseen or invisible elements of a site immediately raises their practice above that of the many landscape architects who remain fixated on 'design problems' alone for the duration of their careers, and who often show hostility to this type of work – perhaps because it represents a living critique of their own lack of vision.

The importance of history to conceptualist landscape design first became clear while I was writing a monograph about Martha Schwartz, effectively the 'founding mother' of this putative school or movement. (This means, incidentally, that the other designers in this volume are Schwartz's 'sons' and 'daughters', despite the fact that a number of them are older than she is – a form of biological conceptualism?) Despite the fact that Schwartz was initially eager to debunk historical attitudes to landscape design, after just a few minutes' discussion about particular projects it emerged that she was deeply concerned with concepts derived from the history of the site.

'History' in this context means a sense of the site's ecological, social,

cultural, topographical and functional characteristics, which have already been developing over time before a designer's appearance on the scene. Such a timeframe could be thought of as relatively finite (the character of a busy urban plaza during the past decade, for example), long-term (the 19th-century industrial legacy of the place, perhaps) or almost timeless (the geological and climatic characteristics of the area as historical or present-day wilderness). Each designer selects a different historical timeframe for each site, depending on their perception of the place's inherent powers and potential needs.

This intimate relationship with the meaning of the place, usually derived from formal research into the various 'histories' of the site, is the principal means by which most conceptualist landscape designers add richness, meaning and emotion to their designs. Plants and trees, concrete and stone, plastic and artificial light may be used in a design, but they function as materials which work to an end; it is only meaning which remains an inviolable characteristic of conceptualist landscape design.

The metamorphosis of the concept from an abstract idea into physical form is at the core of the conceptualist project. Some designers like to produce designs which relate clearly to, or are grounded in, particular ideas: the landscape as metaphor. Other designers are less comfortable with this approach, preferring a more opaque and elusive (often allusive) sense of meaning. The attitude to history of a particular designer is often a barometer of their attitude towards conceptualism – how specific those metaphors or that framework should be, how close to the surface of the design they should operate. What results is a creative relationship with history which is in its way

an even more intimate relationship than that experienced by historical landscape consultants, who look to restore a site as 'authentically' as possible. There is also a comparison to be made with literature, in terms of the process of translation. A literal translation of a text may seem to be 'truer' or more authentic, but a freer, 'creative' translation (to use Ezra Pound's formulation) may well be a) more revealing of the text and its author's intentions, and/or b) more powerful itself than any literal translation of the original could ever be. On an avowedly 'historical' site, it takes guts on the part of both the artist/designer and the patron/commissioner to go down this route.

The relationship between conceptualist landscape design and history is well illustrated in the work and writing of Mario Terzic, founder of the Vienna-based group Trinidad. His polemics on this topic, which amount almost to a manifesto of landscape conceptualism, clearly demonstrate the vital difference between an anti-historical and an anti-historicist approach, in that the former is based on prejudice and ignorance while the latter is founded in knowledge and a belief in the power of newness in art.

'Every art garden is based on a central idea,' Terzic writes. 'It is almost always centuries old, may have been a model of the world, a political scheme, a theatre of the gods and man . . . it has paled . . . Historians can give it a name but not new life . . . It is a real challenge for artists to evaluate the fragments, to improve the site, to make the entire structure legible again and to set the scene anew for an exciting art form. In addition to preserving the substance, it also needs a core idea drawn from the present. This must be strong enough to meet existing artistic, social and financial demands.'

Even new landscape commissions can be treated in the same way as the 'historic' gardens described here, because every site has its own rich history: every landscape space is an historic site, even if it is not billed as such or appreciated as such. The conceptualist landscape process is all about 'evaluating the fragments', to use another of Terzic's phrases.

Every designer or design team must create its own personal and idiosyncratic rationale, and the stated methodologies of two other conceptualist designers are perhaps worth outlining here. The ecologically inspired conceptualist Patricia Johanson has produced one of the pithiest descriptions of landscape conceptualism in action. 'I never design until I have discovered the meaning of the place,' she states. 'Each place has a unique set of conditions, and we need an intimate understanding of what it has been, is now, and will become in the future, in order to create a design that is more than a wilful act.' The challenging notion that a shallow form of conceptualism constitutes merely a 'wilful act' is useful in determining the worth or value of conceptualist landscape design.

The stated rationale of Land-I, the Rome-based conceptualist outfit, is more theoretical but praiseworthy for its jargon-free exactitude. Part of their mission statement reads: 'Our first step is to observe the landscape, an aesthetic and cultural approach necessary to interpret the site and intervene on it. A site is never new, and in our designs we acknowledge that it always hides traces of a previous state, a potential waiting to be discovered, creating opportunities for a new start.' Land-I's designers respond to these historical nuances in different temporal schema – either referring to the actual history of the place, to

inferences arising from its prevailing atmosphere, or even importing
a sense of place from elsewhere.

'History', for designers, must also refer to design history, since this is
the area of life with which they are generally most passionately engaged. The
professional development of a number of the 'older' designers in this book
(though none are particularly old!) represents a trajectory from an education
and early career steeped in architectural Modernism – either 'Continental',
'Scandinavian' or 'American/Californian' – which then underwent a profound
change in the 1990s or 2000s towards a more conceptualist outlook. A handful
of designers have stuck so rigorously to core Modernist tenets that their work
has effectively 'become' conceptual because of this very purity of focus (Ulrich
Singer's devotion to the spatial precepts of Danish Modernism, which he first
experienced some forty years ago, is the best example of this). Elsewhere it
is possible to discern the almost wilful abandonment of Modernist precepts
such as functionalism, a geometric ground plan and a dependence on neutral
colours, while some designers hold on to certain of these tenets as precious
and inviolable aspects of their own design outlook.

Numerous practitioners, particularly those schooled in the 1960s and 1970s,
complain of the functionalist slant of their design education, though it is also a
preoccupation of some of the most recently qualified conceptualist designers,
such as Andy Thomson of BCA Landscape in Liverpool, who regretted the
lack of 'magic and creativity' in his design education. There is a feeling that
imagination was deliberately reined in by tutors and other mentors, as if design
should arise only as a result of rational and quantifiable research processes

in place of more old-fashioned creative notions based on 'inspiration' and free association. For many designers who have had such experiences, a conceptualist approach has been enormously liberating. If Modernism is pure, then conceptualism is dirty.

The social role of public space is probably the Modernist tenet which has endured most strongly in landscape conceptualism, perhaps because it is its most humanistic, not to say passionate quality. This can be seen in the attitude of San Francisco-based Ron Lutsko, for example. While he criticizes what he calls the 'streamlined, minimal, technical, efficient and soulless' aspects of Modernism, he holds on to the ideal of creating 'places that have a relation to people's lives now'. This stance is echoed by Thomas Balsley in New York: 'For me the concepts begin to emerge after a discourse with the people.' On the other hand, some conceptualist designs can be read as almost a burlesque on the functionality of Modernism, utilizing mock laboratories, for example, or fake elements of officialdom, as a way of satirizing civic or corporate culture.

Martha Schwartz provided the example early on when she took classic elements of Modernist design and 'tweaked' them by scaling them up, colouring them vividly, or otherwise compromising them in a sometimes mischievous manner. Perhaps the most obvious way that architectural Modernism has been 'attacked' by conceptualist landscape design is in the wilful disruption of a geometrical ground plan of long, straight vistas and subtle changes in level. Again and again in conceptualist landscape design, it is possible to see such ground plans disrupted or compromised, sometimes in a graphic or violent way, as the linear ground plane appears physically

destroyed, as if by an earthquake or bomb. Humour is another important aspect of landscape conceptualism which can be seen to be signally lacking in architectural Modernism: it is quite possible for a conceptualist landscape design to be based on a visual or literal joke, though as in everyday conversation the successful 'telling' of these jokes is a skill which not every designer has acquired.

Modernism is also criticized by some conceptualist designers for its lack of sensitivity to more nebulous or emotionally derived ideas of the sense of place. Its rational, functional basis is seen as lacking in humanity and imagination, as well as an appreciation of the 'genius of the place'. Mark Rios of RCH Studios in Los Angeles argues: 'Pure Modernism is devoid of the concept of site – its expression comes out of the way things are pieced together. Our work is the opposite: we use the sense of place. It comes out of a connection with memory, the place and the culture.'

Some designers were influenced early on by Land Art, Pop Art or Conceptual Art – which can be seen to be echoed in their landscape design – while others derived their landscape inspiration from the development of their own art practice in different media, such as sculpture, printmaking or textile design. (This latter 'trajectory' has been achieved almost exclusively by female designers, which is perhaps illustrative of the gender bias in different areas of the arts.) Several designers – but only a handful – explicitly make reference to architectural Postmodernism as an influence or stimulus. Martin Rein-Cano of Topotek in Berlin, for example, observes, 'In the end it was the Postmodern movement which brought forms and colours back to landscape design', while the Lützow 7 team claim that Postmodernism was a crucial phase in their own

artistic development. Some designers are critical of Postmodernism, however. Lodewijk Baljon states, 'What went wrong with Postmodernism was that it was a mixture of different shapes with no attention given to meaning.' There is a feeling among some conceptualists that architectural Postmodernism was ultimately limited in its terms of reference and that its relationship with history was burdened by over-literalism and a vocabulary of stock features and treatments. The resultant Postmodern 'style' is intimately associated with the 1980s and early to mid-1990s, and can almost be reduced to a catalogue of reusable features. Conceptualism, as potentially the landscape correlative to architectural Postmodernism, though arriving a decade later and developing quietly and at a slower pace, can operate more as a design attitude with a wide variety of physical expressions, so that the 'look' does not date quite so palpably.

Finally, it can be observed that an historically nuanced yet stridently contemporary approach to landscape in the public realm can often be popular with local people and regular users of spaces, for whom the landscape's narrative or metaphor can reclaim or reconfirm their sense of ownership of the space. At its most effective, an historical/conceptual response to landscape can inspire a whole new relationship between the space itself and the people who use it, live next to it or pass through it. History is consciously used to activate the contemporary meaning in a landscape, garden or park setting.

Monika Gora Malmö (Sweden)

Strident forms and ideas which blur the boundaries between art and design.

After training in landscape architecture and setting up her own practice in 1989, Monika Gora now combines this work with a successful career as an artist. She specializes in conceptual works that play with ideas of artificial light, amorphous shape, the meaning of nature and the value of rubbish (among much else). Almost all of her work exists outside traditional gallery settings, mostly in public spaces.

Whether stand-alone objects or series of objects, Gora's artworks always respond to a particular landscape setting in a meaningful way, as one would expect of a designer with these twin interests. There is even perhaps a sense that the objects she produces exist as landscapes in their own right – apart from, but somehow integrated with, their settings. Her predilection for brightly coloured, artificially lit objects makes her work appear paradoxically organic and elemental in character. Gora describes her artistic work – which also embraces ceramics and drawings – as Surrealist in its overtones. There is also a strong vein of humour which she attributes to her engagement with this movement.

Gora operates at the border between conceptual art and landscape – in effect, blurring or negating that border – and she traces this interest back to an early reaction against her education as a designer. 'When I trained, the approach was more naturalistic than it is now,' she says, referring to the Swedish tradition of naturalistic Modernism pioneered by the Dane, Carl Theodor Sørenson. 'My own approach is more about distinct shapes.'

LEFT AND ABOVE Designed in collaboration with lighting designer Lars Bylund, this temporary sculpture was powered by three sulphur lamps, which lit up the 30m-long white balloon from within. A Volume of Light, Vienna 1995.

LEFT AND BELOW At this installation for the Chaumont Festival, 195 fishing rods were covered with climbing plants and presented as a 'new kind of cultivation support', requiring the plants to acclimatize themselves to inhabitual conditions. Vertical, Chaumont sur Loire (France) 1994.

Common Ground

UMEÅ (SWEDEN) 2002

This intriguing installation was sited adjacent to and partly inside the University Hospital's blood donation and laboratory wing – hence the colour of the armchairs, some of which were made of polyester and some of fibreglass. Lit up at night (and the winter nights are long this far north), there is something of a Magritte quality about the piece, with the glowing chairs ranged around two grassy areas planted with birches, pine and alder flanking the glass passageway that links the new blood-testing department to the main hospital. Several small, paved terraces allow patients to survey the landscaped areas.

Gora says that there is no specific meaning embedded in the design, that it is not just about blood, or even chairs. She points out some of the subtleties which become apparent to patients over a short time: 'The shape of the chairs looks a little like a heart, or perhaps a flower. The red is less like blood and more of a magenta; there are flowers in the north of Sweden of that colour. In fact, there are different amounts of pigment in each chair: some are pink, and some are more red. The black chair is made of granite and is more permanent than the others.' Despite the slightly disturbing overtones of the piece, its effect is primarily humorous and uplifting, a tension used to good effect by a number of conceptual landscape designers.

Garden of Knowledge

MALMÖ (SWEDEN) 2001

This temporary installation was made for the 'Bo 01' housing exhibition in Malmö, one of several such projects sited in a young willow plantation. Tall watchtowers marked the entrance to this area, while Gora's own installation, which she termed a 'labyrinth', was intended to act as a voyage of discovery for children.

The structure was made from indigenous timber and partitioned into five main 'rooms', each defined by a single concept: wood, stone, plants (grasses and pumpkins), animals (geese: 'they ate everything'), and one which was 'forgotten', incorporating a well of memories (recorded sounds emanating from the ground, including the cries of someone trying to get out). Five smaller rooms contained features such as a water-spitting machine and, in the 'sky room' designed for contemplation, a tiny working lavatory. Children were encouraged to discover each space and its theme for themselves. 'They soon extended the labyrinth by making enclosures in the willow,' Gora recalls.

Glass Bubble

MALMÖ (SWEDEN) 2006

'In a way, it's like creating another world. The glass is so thin it's exciting,' is what Gora says about this conservatory, overlooking Malmö's harbour. It has been built next to a residential building for the elderly which Gora describes as 'boring to the point of ugliness'.

'The shape of the glasshouse was determined by the space available,' she continues. 'I had different solutions. This was the most daring one.' The result is a building which works as a sculpture, an organism and a paradise, compounded. The form of the Glass Bubble is 'soft spherical', constructed of clear glass. Inside, the climate is Mediterranean, and tree ferns, camellias, citrus and magnolias grow. In an exposed and extreme environment, the structure becomes a transparent bubble of warmth and a membrane against the raw climate outside. In the darkness of the winter, it is a big, lightened volume.

'This place close to the sea is stormy, extremely barren and exposed,' Gora states. 'The only thing that separates the inside from the outside is a partition wall made of thin glass. The function of the glass is like a membrane. The inside becomes a bubble filled with warmth and life. Full of light and space, protected and quiet.'

The residents' courtyard outside is paved in Norwegian slate, with the walls of the flower-beds constructed of the same material – shading from rust orange to green black due to the iron content – a theme which continues within the glasshouse. Between the flower-beds winds a meandering path, a secluded and exclusive route. Only a few plants survive in such harsh conditions, making the contrast between the climate inside and the barren courtyard grow in strength: while the plants outside act as a reminder of the forests of northern Sweden, the interior evokes memories of warmer climes. This is a site situated between the rugged north and the milder south.

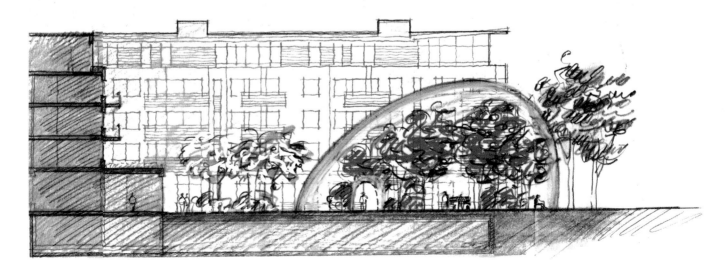

Gross.Max Edinburgh

Colourful and imaginative public-space solutions which address the complexities of the urban environment.

Founded in 1995 by partners Bridget Baines and Eelco Hooftman, who were joined by partner Nigel Sampey (from West 8; p. 336) six years later, the Edinburgh-based company Gross.Max has received numerous commissions despite the challenging and theoretical nature of their work, which ranges from public parks and plazas to large-scale urban regeneration.

Like West 8, Gross.Max is unusual among conceptualist design outfits in that it has the confidence and expertise to take on city-scale urban planning in all its complexity. This demands an approach to masterplanning which is not reducible to a single concept, but involves the integration of a wide variety of discrete spaces, each with different functions and user expectations. The challenge is to create linked spaces which nevertheless boast their own identities.

The company's design integrity and habit of sticking to its guns has also earned it the attention of some high-profile collaborators, including the American artist Mark Dion (see Vertical Garden; p. 118). An ongoing association with London-based architect Zaha Hadid has produced the ambitious rejuvenation of the Zorrozaurre area of Bilbao (see p. 120), 64 hectares of former docklands along the River Nervion. Here, the main theme is porosity – in the open areas between the buildings, and in the matter of opening up the potential of the riverside to users through the creation of a wide variety of spaces for recreation.

Bullring

BIRMINGHAM (UK) 2003

One of Europe's largest city-centre retail regeneration schemes, the Bullring is the latest in a sequence of newly created public spaces in Birmingham. It takes advantage of the natural slope by creating streets and open spaces on different levels. The architecture of the commercial buildings is a mixture of the ordinary and the sublime, with the new Selfridges store by Future Systems an iconic landmark. Its 'Yves Klein blue' façade is clad with 15,000 anodized aluminium discs, inspired by the chain-mail dress designs of Paco Rabanne; the reflection of the changing sky on the curved outer skin is arresting. Opposite is the

historic St Martin's Church, which has gained a new, more prominent position at the bottom of the square.

St Martin's Square is determined by its dramatic topography, the prominent position of the church, and the curvilinear building façade of the retail development. An arresting combination of cascading water walls, reflecting pools, steps, terraces and sculptural trees negotiate the approximately 8m level difference. Illuminated in slowly changing hues of pink, yellow and blue, the water sculpture acts as a visual break between the limestone terrace areas to the east and the sloping, granite-paved square to the west. The top water flows into slate-clad pools at the base of each cube, and is continually recycled and released through a concealed tank. The sequence of different terraces forms part of the cascading ensemble of steps and level areas and allows for flexible use, while the overall configuration could also be utilized for large-scale events and performances.

Central Street, in between St Martin's Square and Rotunda Square, is paved in two contrasting granites. The street is lit by catenary lighting, allowing ample space for pedestrian circulation and an uninterrupted view towards the church spire and a repositioned bronze statue of Nelson. At night, circles of colour are projected onto the floorscape to animate the street when the busy crowds of people are gone. Rotunda Square, at the top of Central Street, is strategically located at a crossroads of routes, a position celebrated by a dramatic sculptural landmark designed by Peter Fink of Art2Architecture and based on Gross Max's conceptual idea of three 'lightwands'. The wands feature rotating 'leaves' of stainless steel which limit the degree of movement in the upper parts of the mast to a gentle swaying. Internally lit, the wands echo the lighting theme used in the water sculpture in St Martin's Square.

Potters Field Park

LONDON 2007

Located adjacent to the Norman Foster-designed Greater London Authority (GLA) building on the south bank of the Thames, Potters Field Park has open views towards some of London's most iconic monuments and its ever-changing skyline, and forms part of a series of new developments along the river. One of the most challenging aspects of the regeneration is to reconcile the different user groups on a relatively small and intensively used space. Gross.Max's office credo – 'to reveal the different layers of the landscape, not unlike the sensuous act of striptease' – has resulted in an extensive historic survey of the site.

The design consists of an intimate neighbourhood park facing the residential areas along Tooley Street, gradually opening up towards the river with a series of stepped terraces. A new entrance is marked by two ornamental cast-iron gates (one fixed, one sliding) and an extended hedge to allow for safe transition between park and road crossing. The sliding element allows the entrance to be enlarged for special events, or closed off in its entirety. The park is to be planted with a spectacular variety of herbaceous plants and grasses designed by Piet Oudolf, while hedges will provide structure and a veil of birch trees will soften the presence of the GLA building.

The public frontage of the park contains a variety of designed elements: a long strip of pavement with Delftware patterns (a reference to the local 17th-century porcelain trade) cuts through the grass, while a playful cluster of periscopes of various heights allows for views across the river. Blue Irish limestone is to be used along the river walk and between the park and the neighbouring More London development site, and flexible paving (Clearmac) for the pathways. White granite has been selected for steps and low retaining walls and as a surround for the lawn areas. The paving strip will form a continuation of this granite edge, enhanced with a laser-cut inlay pattern of limestone.

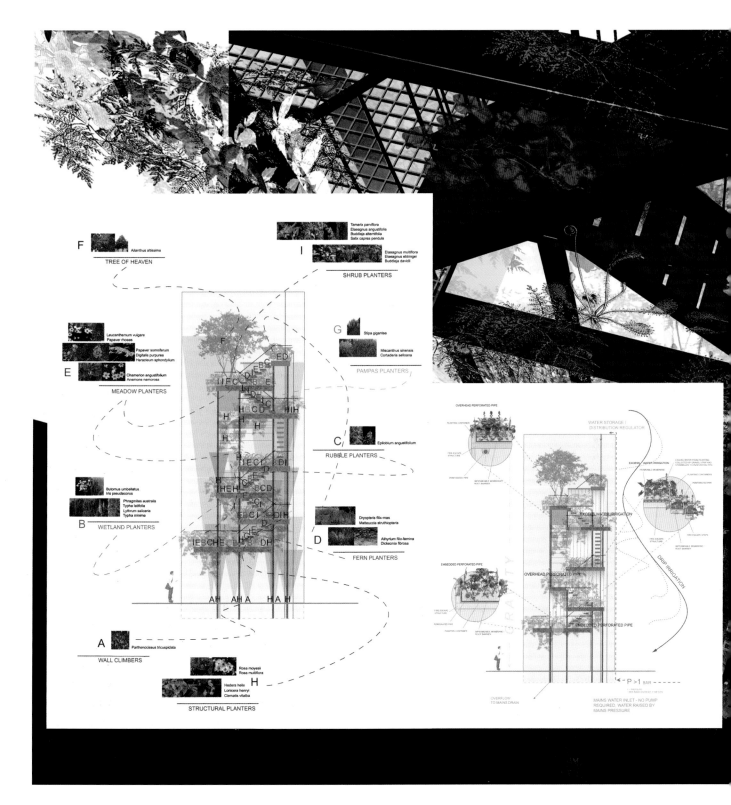

Vertical Garden

LONDON 2005

Vertical Garden is the second collaboration between Gross.Max and Mark Dion, and incorporates the end gable wall of a block of tenements built in the 1890s, located along a busy road leading to Tower Bridge. The proposal is to install a salvaged fire escape alongside the wall as support for a vertical garden, which will contain a multitude of native and exotic plants selected for their vigorous growth, cultural value and attraction to wildlife. Different planters represent different soil types, from sandy soil to heavy clay, as found as sedimentation along the Thames in Central London.

The selected plants range from butterfly bush to London rocket, the so-called 'fireweed' which has thrived in building rubble after such disasters as the Great Fire of 1666 and the Blitz. Reference to the local breweries is provided by a hop plant winding up the fire escape, while other plants represent the import of herbs and spices during Britain's imperial heyday. The vertical garden is punctuated by a solitary Tree of Heaven. All plants are watered by means of a simple drip irrigation system and occasional shower curtains of perforated down-pipes. Fine nozzles will spray the ferns and mosses, creating a microclimate not unlike the famous fog of London itself. Occasional artefacts such as bird-houses and oil drums for rainwater collection complement the overall structure.

Zorrozaurre Masterplan

BILBAO 2003

Perhaps Gross.Max's most ambitious collaboration with Zaha Hadid is the rejuvenation of the Zorrozaurre area of Bilbao. At the heart of the plan, an elegant system of building blocks functions like a set of 'tiles', allowing the ground formation to respond to the curving spine of the river, the street grid, and the shifting orientation of buildings from upstream to downstream. In this way, the tiles give an overall unity while allowing the differentiation of districts and clusters. The platform level of the tiles establishes the critical level of defence against floods, while also creating space for underground parking. By linking this critical level to the development of building clusters, the waterside promenade can dip closer to the normal level of the river, allowing visitors a closer engagement with the water's edge. Meanwhile, above the platforms, the buildings are turned perpendicular to the long axes of the river, opening the building fabric so that the pathways and views may be enjoyed by all. The rich pattern of public

and private spaces can be achieved through the subtle differentiation of levels, promoting a balance between the needs of privacy and the pleasures of community life.

The overall structure of the area is established by three long axes, crossed by local streets and pedestrian paths, and permits a densely built environment to accompany the fabric's strong feel of porosity. Waterside promenades, parks, the tree-lined central avenue, small squares and public gardens – all link together to create a textured setting for urban social life. A new sequence of bridges will become an exciting element of this landscape. Raised decks open towards the activated waterside of both river and canal, and composed vistas onto the waterfront and beyond direct views and provide orientation. Green spaces weave through the urban fabric and integrate buildings, while a series of interlinked water elements animates the public space, modifies the microclimate, and forms part of an integrated system of surface water run-off.

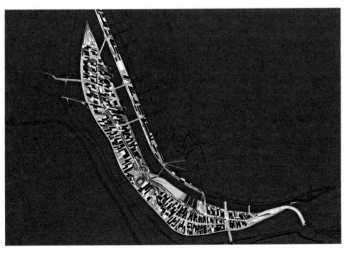

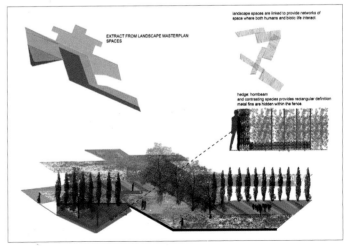

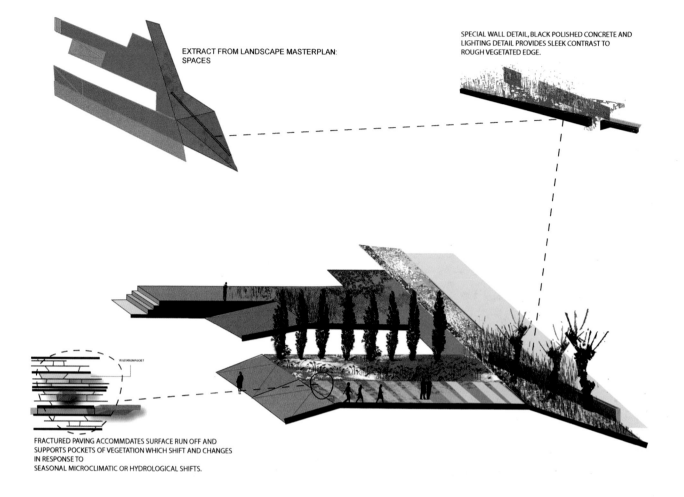

EXTRACT FROM LANDSCAPE MASTERPLAN: SPACES

SPECIAL WALL DETAIL, BLACK POLISHED CONCRETE AND LIGHTING DETAIL PROVIDES SLEEK CONTRAST TO ROUGH VEGETATED EDGE.

FRACTURED PAVING ACCOMMDATES SURFACE RUN OFF AND SUPPORTS POCKETS OF VEGETATION WHICH SHIFT AND CHANGES IN RESPONSE TO
SEASONAL MICROCLIMATIC OR HYDROLOGICAL SHIFTS.

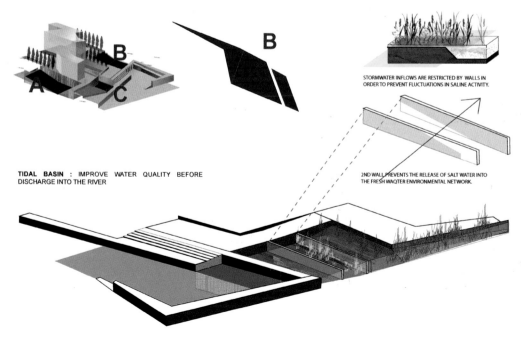

STORMWATER INFLOWS ARE RESTRICTED BY WALLS IN ORDER TO PREVENT FLUCTUATIONS IN SALINE ACTIVITY.

TIDAL BASIN : IMPROVE WATER QUALITY BEFORE DISCHARGE INTO THE RIVER

2ND WALL PREVENTS THE RELEASE OF SALT WATER INTO THE FRESH WAQTER ENVIRONMENTAL NETWORK.

Gustafson Porter

Elegantly sculpted, coolly uncluttered public-space design.

London and Seattle

Seattle-born Kathryn Gustafson started out in fashion design before graduating from the École Nationale Supérieure du Paysage in Versailles in 1979. She initially made her name as a solo landscape architect in France with her work for corporate clients such as Esso, Shell and L'Oreal, for whom she designed landscapes of undulating grass berms and striking Modernist architecture. Her key early work was the landscaping of a large park area above the small town of Terrasson in the Dordogne, where she explored especially a fascination with water and its capabilities.

In 1997, Gustafson founded Gustafson Porter in London with Neil Porter, who trained and taught architecture at the Architectural Association in London and then worked with architects including Will Alsop and Bernard Tschumi. Like Gustafson, Porter is an original thinker who allows spaces to spark conceptual ideas, thematic or visual, that form the basis for a more rigorous theoretical and practical treatments. In 2004 Gustafson and Porter were joined by a third partner, Mary Bowman, previously a partner at architectural firms Foster and Partners and Walters and Cohen. As a result of the fiasco surrounding the Diana Memorial (see p. 124), Gustafson Porter has become one of the best-known landscape firms in the UK. Gustafson also has an office in Seattle, the city where she is based.

The approach is unashamedly artistic and intuitive in the first instance. Gustafson is well known for her method of creating clay models of the desired topography of the designed space. It is this which so often gives Gustafson Porter projects a feeling of clarity and wholeness, because this basic shape, usually formed by grassy expanses, is generally uncompromised by the budgeting and construction process. Porter describes the genesis of many of their projects as 'a conversation' – sometimes conducted transatlantically – in which thoughts about the space and its functions gradually take visual form. It is really an updated take on the 18th-century idea of the genius loci, or spirit of place. 'They can be just words,' Porter says of these initial concepts. 'There's almost a Dada quality to it, where you have these words which conjure up an atmosphere or a mood about the character and quality of a landscape.'

But Gustafson Porter is not rigorously conceptual – for some projects, the functional or problem-solving needs of the space are the chief influence on its final appearance. Conceptual elements are always encased in the work but they are worn quite lightly, often emerging as details rather than as one grand, overarching formula. 'I feel happier with the slightly ambiguous, less strident interpretation which we are doing now,' Porter explains. 'It is quite a pared-down, ultimately rather cool take on Modernism. It's meant to pass the test of time, it's not meant to be a provocative statement that lasts just a few years.' Porter is referring

LEFT AND OPPOSITE Gustafson Porter's solution to a large, sloping rectangular space just off the busy Swiss Cottage traffic interchange in North London was its trademark simplicity, using large panels of smooth turf, terraced where it descends to a diagonally aligned central pool, and substantial perimeter plantings. Despite its size, this is a surprisingly intimate space. Swiss Cottage Open Space, London 2006.

obliquely here to those conceptual landscape outfits – such as Martha Schwartz (p. 256) – who are perhaps more influenced by Pop Art and the potential of new materials.

As with many of the best landscape firms, the work of Gustafson Porter is often instantly recognizable. Trademarks include the sculptural form already mentioned, terraced or marked by dips and pools, plus an emphasis on the power of open space and the calm expansiveness of horizontals. A large water feature very often forms the focus for the design, which is never symmetrical or stridently geometric, but incorporates curving principal axes or paths through the space. These characteristics have in the past led to a description of the work as peculiarly 'feminine', an idea that Gustafson has not discouraged. It is becoming increasingly difficult, however, to justify critically such gender stereotyping. The work is also dignified by a relatively limited palette of materials, in terms of the stone used, as well as trees, shrubs and other plants. Practicality is another watchword: key features are often reversible (a pool, for example, might be drained to create a party terrace) and the designers are careful to provide a range of potential experiences for different user groups (such as the old and the very young). 'Despite our reputation in the press, most people see us as quite sensitive to people's needs,' Porter says.

Diana, Princess of Wales Memorial Fountain

LONDON 2004

A cascade of flowing and bubbling water on a sculpted slope overlooking the Serpentine, this controversial project was marred at the outset by maintenance and safety problems. After several visitors slipped and fell soon after its opening, the fountain became a cause célèbre in the newspapers and closed to the public. Having reopened with a substantial security presence, a crude fence was erected around the perimeter. Gustafson Porter now express a wish that the fence might come down and the fountain be allowed to 'bed down' in the life of the park. It has certainly proved popular with many visitors, who enjoy watching the way the engineered granite base of the channel creates a fascinating variety of effects and moods, from bubbling cauldron to swooshing smoothness.

The memorial aspect of the Diana Fountain was a difficult challenge for the designers, but Porter says the way the fountain radiates outwards yet draws people in mirrors the character of Diana, and adds that the various qualities of the water also reflect aspects of her life. From a landscape perspective, much of the criticism of the feature's 'starkness' should have been offset by an understanding of the way the trees (*Cladastris kentuckea*) planted around the fountain will grow up to form a glade that will provide a coherent setting for it. People will always come to see the memorial,' Porter says. 'In five or ten years, it will look like it has always been there.'

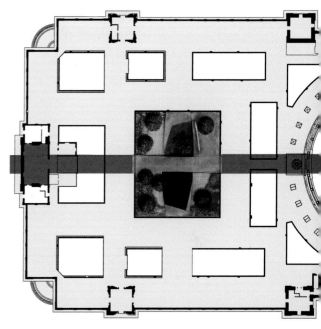

HM Treasury Courtyards

LONDON 2002

Gustafson Porter designed twin courtyards (not open to the public) that were previously lightwells in the offices of the Treasury and the Inland Revenue in Whitehall, with 10 Downing Street on one side and St James's Park on the other, and collaborated with Foster and Partners on the creation of a new axis from the west to the east courtyards via the main central 'drum' courtyard of the building.

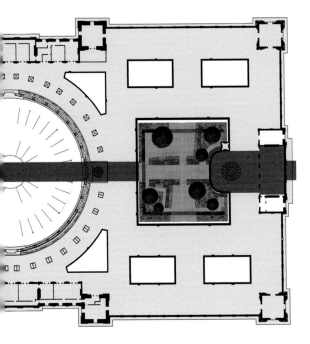

The first space to be designed was the west courtyard (see opposite), conceived as a quiet space, with a footway spanning a pool and flowers in blue and white overshadowed by magnolias and liriodendrons for shade. A trench marks the perimeter of both courtyards and provides the only artificial light. The east courtyard (right) is a more formal yet more gregarious space, with contrasting clipped hedges in yew and box, 'pocket' gardens in each corner, acers for colour and bark texture, and a raised rill surrounding the whole. 'It's almost like creating a fragment of parterre,' Porter says. 'Looking down from the offices above, it's as if you have caught a glimpse of a little bit of Villandry.'

The choice of materials here was inspired by a tour of the Treasury offices: 'We observed these cellular offices with these English gentlemen in their bespoke suits with slightly eccentric or colourful linings,' Porter recalls. 'So we chose a Welsh grey slate which was very conservative, laid with a narrow strip in it, like a pinstripe. And then there is a bright silver lining in the rill at the perimeter of the slate.'

Cultuurpark Westergasfabriek

AMSTERDAM 2004

The Westergasfabriek is a partially dismantled industrial site – a gasworks – with vestiges of its layout intact. The existing buildings are monuments to the Industrial Revolution. The park acts as a contemporary exploration of this change and its impact on landscape types and forms. This kind of rehabilitation of industrial sites has become a genre in itself in Europe and is particularly prevalent in Germany, where Peter Latz and others have led by example.

Here, the use of the park is twofold: a green park environment and a cultural centre with indoor and outdoor activities. A central promenade, 'The Axis', links the town hall with the Cité des Artistes and a variety of spaces between. It serves as a central vertebra that carries the park's functional requirements. The adjacent spaces give it a varied ambience. A great field slopes into a stone-lined lake, which can be drained for large events and festivals, and a mix of native plants and selected varieties express a dynamic between human needs and natural order.

Fritz Haeg Los Angeles

Provocative horticultural installations in suburbia.

Fritz Haeg is an artist, architect, teacher, activist and gardener, and Gardenlab (the name a satire on the idea of the computer lab) is one of several ongoing projects in his portfolio of work. 'American colleges have invested a great deal in "technology" to support the curriculum,' Haeg explains. 'Computer labs are always a priority. Meanwhile, the principles of the natural organic cycles of our ecology that define the world we live in, and upon which we all depend, go unnoticed. The designers and artists who will shape our future environment need to understand the complexity of the natural world they will be affecting.'

The Gardenlab manifesto reads: 'Inspired by the garden as metaphor and laboratory, Gardenlab initiates ecology-based art and design projects. Gardenlab seeks to fundamentally shift the current self-reflexive culture of art and design, where formal novelty, hermetic discourse and the latest software dominate. The Gardenlab provides a balance to these forces by provoking thought on the interdependent relationships that define our communities and environment.' The ecological activism of Gardenlab is so strongly focused that its physical incarnations effectively tip the work over into the realm of conceptual design, even though Haeg's impulses and ambitions are quite different from those of most other designers featured in this book.

The most successful Gardenlab projects have been the Edible Estates at Salina in Kansas and Lakewood in southern California (opposite); another is being constructed in metropolitan New York, and a further eight are planned countrywide. Edible Estates are agit-prop artistic

RIGHT Haeg orchestrates a wide range of activities from his headquarters, a geodesic dome in a garden setting that serves as both studio and schoolhouse. Sundown Schoolhouse, Los Angeles 2004.

statements about the redundancy of the American lawn, in that the front lawns of two suburban plots have been taken up and replaced by vegetable gardens. 'I dislike the idea that plants grown for food are ugly, while the lawn is beautiful,' Haeg says. In brochures printed to accompany the Edible Estates initiatives, Haeg writes stirringly of his mission: 'Edible Estates is an attack on the American lawn and everything it has come to represent. Why do we dedicate so much land to a space with so little function, but [which] requires the consumption of so many precious resources and endless hours of maintenance while contaminating our air and water?

'The American lawn is almost entirely a symbolic gesture. Exactly what it represents has shifted from its ancestry in English estates to today's endless suburban carpet of conformity. The lawn divides and isolates us. It is a buffer of antisocial no-man's land that we wrap ourselves with, reinforcing the suburban alienation of our sprawling communities. The monoculture of one plant species covering our neighbourhoods from coast to coast celebrates puritanical homogeneity and mindless conformity. The lawn devours resources while it pollutes. It is maniacally groomed with mowers and trimmers powered by the two-stroke motors responsible for much of our greenhouse-gas emissions. To eradicate invading plants, it is drugged with pesticides which are then washed into our water supply with sprinklers and hoses, dumping our increasingly rare fresh drinking water down the gutter.

ABOVE This Edible Estate project is the prototype garden, located in a Los Angeles suburb. Planted over Memorial Day weekend in 2006, the garden was the basis for the Machine Project exhibition later that year. Edible Estate, Lakewood (California) 2006.

Edible Estates proposes the replacement of the American lawn with a highly productive domestic edible landscape. Food grown in our front yards will connect us to the seasons, the organic cycles of the earth and our neighbours. The banal lifeless space of uniform grass in front of the house will be replaced with the chaotic abundance of biodiversity.'

Haeg views this initiative as a way of reconciling two big problems facing the West: land use and food production. 'To some people [the idea of growing your own food] is shocking. In the US we have become profoundly disconnected from our food.' The relationship between humans and the Earth's ecology represents the conceptual core of all Haeg's activities. He adds: 'The garden is the perfect example of how we as humans can learn to occupy the planet in a more thoughtful way. The garden is what humans make to feed ourselves. Where we grow food, it's scary, industrial, there are chemicals and machinery. But when you eat out of your garden, you don't dump things in it that you don't want to eat. It's very direct: you understand the connection. The more disconnected we become from the garden, the more reckless we become with the way we occupy the planet.'

Paula Hayes New York

A distinctive artistic vision melded with horticultural curiosity.

Based in Manhattan and coming from a background in sculpture, Paula Hayes has carved out a niche for herself at the boundary between the art and garden worlds. Some of her earlier works, in the late 1990s, had a savour of agit-prop, or else worked as a satire on attitudes to nature: the 'Plant Packs', which she marketed to the fashion- and style-conscious, were backpacks that contained living plants, enabling harassed city dwellers to get their 'fix' of nature while on the move without compromising their urgent urban lifestyle.

In private garden-design commissions, Hayes has continued to explore the sculptural possibilities of plants and an artistic engagement with concepts of nature and landscape, and likes to mix up the highly artificial with the extremely natural and earthy: pink plastic-moulded chairs next to stripped logs or hedges of evergreen trees; delicate flowers creating unlikely redoubts on downtown high-rise roof spaces with dramatic views of the Manhattan skyline. 'I try to create an ecological feeling, but one that also includes people,' she says. 'I would also suggest that industrial materials are not inherently evil. In every project you are forced to contend with complex, unharmonious elements. I try to bring those elements together in my work, to interweave all that complexity.'

Away from the city, Hayes has recently designed a number of large gardens which utilize a native-plants palette integrated with sculptural elements, notably the coloured silicone planters (see opposite) which have become one of her trademarks. Hayes talks about addressing the 'particularities' of a place in her work, and then drawing out a basic conceptual framework from that. 'I like to match the creative temperament of the client and the microclimate of the site,' she says, neatly summing up, in a conceptual manner, this traditional aspect of the role of the garden designer. The work is characterized by big sculptural moves – whether created by the planters, drifts of native plants, trees, or the architecture of the house itself – which are carefully planned so that they seem to complement the surrounding natural ecology. The result is a palpably sculpted landscape. Hayes explains: 'In combination with all those things which are uncontrolled, all those random interactions, I try to create extremely considered arrangements which function almost like large-scale ikebana. It's a combination of the natural and uncontrolled, with the highly crafted.'

LEFT The designer's silicone planters have become something of a trademark. The material is a type of rubber used for mould-making: 'Its most useful characteristics are durability and stability, but it also has this translucency,' Hayes explains. 'Light comes through the silicone and transforms the look of the root ball – mosses and lichens grow all around it, and you can see it all quite clearly.' Silicone Planters, 2005.

OPPOSITE The 'Terrarium' series of planted-up glass tanks function as practical growing spaces, borrowing the 19th-century technology of the 'Wardian cases' used to transport plants by sea, and as 'primary aesthetic experiences [and] statements about beauty'. Terrariums, 2006.

Paula Hayes **133**

Garden for a Private Residence

EAST HAMPTON (USA) 2004

The aim with this design was to blur the boundaries between the garden spaces and the natural ecology of the surrounding Long Island dunelands. Hayes used a native palette that included pennisetum, blue-stemmed grasses and shore junipers to create a sense that the garden was simply bleeding into its surroundings. 'It's very open and natural, with these large curvilinear beds,' she explains.

However, nearer the house, silicone planters were used as sculptural moves and the drifts of grasses and banks of low-growing seaside plants were carefully arranged so that they directed the visitor's route through the space. A serpentine 'green driveway' of concrete pavers interplanted with these low-growing plants contributed to the sense that the man-made garden was treading lightly on the space.

Private Garden

SANTA FE (USA) 2004

'My natural inclination in a high-desert situation [such as here in New Mexico] was to preserve water, but the owners wanted all these specimen trees, like weeping Sequoias and cedars,' Hayes begins. The owners of this fine modern house of concrete and glass are ardent collectors who display the eclectic aesthetic which typifies Santa Fe style; they collect not only minimalist contemporary art, but also ceramics, folk art and unusual plants. A water-harvesting system was installed to make the collection of trees more ecologically sustainable, and Hayes created a basic framework of native plants – mainly grasses – suitable for the starkly beautiful environment. But she resisted any attempt to 'naturalize' the alien trees. 'I decided to put these specimen trees directly into the natural setting – some of them in silicone planters,' she explains. 'It wasn't a typical attempt to naturalize but more a way of emphasizing the "unusual neighbour" element. I think the garden became very magical as a result.'

Tony Heywood

Dramatic landscape installations, massive writhing forms and botanical minutiae.

Operating at the boundary between conceptual art and landscape design, Tony Heywood has built up an impressive body of 'horticultural installation art' during the past decade that encompasses large-scale outdoor works. Beyond its potential role as public art, none of his work is conceived in a functional way, a key area of difference between his practice and that of most conceptualists. Heywood suggests that the difference between a design concept and an artistic idea is that the latter is intangible, while the former is a means to an end, usually with a functional component.

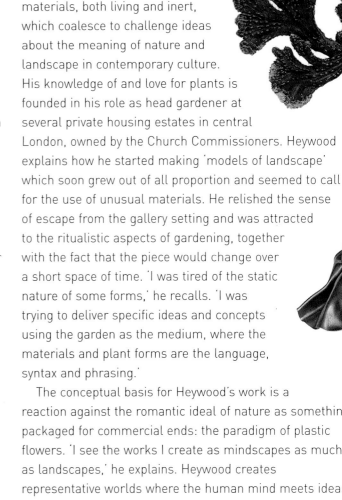

The writhing, colourful forms of Heywood's sculptural works utilize a rich variety of materials, both living and inert, which coalesce to challenge ideas about the meaning of nature and landscape in contemporary culture. His knowledge of and love for plants is founded in his role as head gardener at several private housing estates in central London, owned by the Church Commissioners. Heywood explains how he started making 'models of landscape' which soon grew out of all proportion and seemed to call for the use of unusual materials. He relished the sense of escape from the gallery setting and was attracted to the ritualistic aspects of gardening, together with the fact that the piece would change over a short space of time. 'I was tired of the static nature of some forms,' he recalls. 'I was trying to deliver specific ideas and concepts using the garden as the medium, where the materials and plant forms are the language, syntax and phrasing.'

The conceptual basis for Heywood's work is a reaction against the romantic ideal of nature as something packaged for commercial ends: the paradigm of plastic flowers. 'I see the works I create as mindscapes as much as landscapes,' he explains. Heywood creates representative worlds where the human mind meets ideas of landscape, ideas which may be idealized or romanticized, or – just as likely – tinged with fear and apprehension.

The mutable aspect of garden art – the fact that living, changing organisms are involved – is something that

LEFT, BELOW AND OPPOSITE Heywood's smaller-scale, gallery-bound work includes the series 'Superbotanics': tiny, intricate and rather beautiful model gardens which are a collage of plants, mosses, fungi, and all kinds of man-made detritus. Superbotanics, 2006.

Heywood welcomes: 'I like the idea of the artwork being changed over time,' he says. 'I see the garden as a context – I'm not finding a "design solution". Even where there are no plants in my work, I think of it as a representation of a living environment. Where I do use plants, I use those that are spectacular, because they are living things and have to grow like that to live. It's an in-built genetic structure that creates an odd but perfect form.'

The Calling/The Echo

KINSALE (IRELAND) 2005/BELFAST 2006

This piece was first installed at Charles Fort, in Kinsale, as 'The Calling' (left and below), and subsequently at Belfast Botanic Garden as 'The Echo' (opposite). Heywood explains: 'At Charles Fort, the bejewelled anthropomorphic forms appeared to invade and occupy all areas of the stronghold, as they emerged from the sea and crawled over the ramparts until they formed a central garden installation. An electronically manipulated soundscape added to the sense of an alien presence as the sculptures emitted haunting sounds . . . I want viewers to think about the piece and become aware of their own reaction to it. That is why the form is so important: it makes you position yourself in the world and ask, "What is landscape?"'

Kinki Kensho

CHAUMONT SUR LOIRE (FRANCE) 2002

This installation at the Chaumont Festival was a response to that year's theme: sex. Heywood explains the conceptual rationale: 'All gardens are sexually charged areas. Fertility, pollination, interbreeding and fruitfulness are terms in daily use among gardeners and visitors to gardens. Yet the garden culturally carries an oddly desexualized meaning.' He points out that the Japanese garden of raked gravel, with its spiritual and contemplative aspects, seeks to help viewers transcend their bodies in some way. With this piece, he was attempting 'an aggressive juxtaposition' of that tradition with erotic sculptural forms. 'Kinki Kensho takes note of the fact that the garden of contemplation and erotica share an attribute and then asks a question: what happens when they collide?' This confrontational approach is a consistent theme in Heywood's work. 'I want people to have an experience where they feel unsure,' he says. 'Most landscape has to do with the ground and other "components" of landscape. I am trying to present a different way of looking. It's like super-nature, or super-landscape. In a way, it's so real it's almost obscene.'

Helter Skelter

LONDON 2001

This piece is located at the corner of two busy streets in Central London: Sussex Gardens and Edgware Road. The urban setting appeals to Heywood's artistic sensibility: 'I see the "new landscape" as hoardings, car lots, buildings – urban life,' he says. 'I do see that as a landscape. I'm trying to find a new language.' A mixture of inert and vegetative forms – including agave, titanium, lead, moss, pine, slate and pumice – create a wide range of textures in the piece, in which a landscape appears to tip and tumble towards a molten glass pool: 'I was using various pieces of landscape to create an entirely new landscape, using speed and movement to explore the way we experience the world.'

Nature

Conceptualist landscape designers have been unfairly caricatured as wishing simply to replace plants with plastic artefacts – always favouring the artificial above the natural. This generalization is not only misplaced from a conventional perspective, but is an irrelevance to many conceptualists, for whom any 'natural' intervention or material used in a landscape – if it has been through the hands or mind of a designer – must be considered to be to some degree man-made and artificial anyway.

The fundamental difference between the conceptual and ecological attitude is that ecologists instinctively believe in the moral and redemptive value of 'natural' man-made landscapes, while conceptualists maintain that to suggest a man-made landscape is ever going to be 'natural' is at best optimistic and at worst a con. For conceptualists, an authentic reaction to a site is not to create some kind of wilderness fantasy in the space, but to take inspiration from the historical and ecological context and to make something relevant to its end users. This is particularly important in urban settings, where conceptualists habitually attempt to honour and celebrate cities as opposed to creating 'refuges', 'escapes' or little pieces of countryside for urbanites stereotyped as morally and physically diseased. This embrace of urbanism can become almost tribal among conceptual landscapists. It is no coincidence that most of them are city-based.

As always there are exceptions to this 'rule' about conceptualists reacting to nature in such a way: Danish designer Helle Nebelong works conceptually, but believes in the moral value of her natural playspaces, Ron Lutsko's work seems equally freighted with the Modernist, ecological and conceptualist outlook,

while a designer such as Michael Van Valkenburgh mingles a quasi-evangelical ecological attitude with a conceptualist aesthetic, with no loss of integrity. The most pragmatic conceptualist landscape designers, and many of the youngest, view the rise of eco as an artistic and business opportunity rather than as a challenge or problem. Janet Rosenberg states: 'The next step for our profession is to forge successful relationships with architects, and I think the ecological and environmental movement will enhance those possibilities.'

In fact, the conceptualist and ecological attitudes can be seen to be the two most exciting and innovative attitudes blazing a trail in early 21st century landscape architecture. Architectural Modernism (which could just as easily be called 'corporate Modernism' in most cases) utilizing patterns and materials familiar throughout most of the later 20th century, is still the dominant mainstream option, with the eco component increasingly being 'bolted on' to that aesthetic in the form or recycling or irrigation facilities, or in the use of select 'native' plants. (The use of quotation marks here indicates the inherent absurdity of the concept of 'native' plants in large or climactically diverse countries such as the US and Australia; in the latter instance, William Martin has constructed an entire horticultural–conceptual polemic around the fallacy that a plant from Western Australia might be 'native' and therefore appropriate on the opposite side of the country.) A conceptual attitude is a more demanding and commercially more daring option than an 'ecological' sensibility, which is perhaps why it is still very much a minority interest. But landscape conceptualism has been growing apace during the past decade or so, and it is to be hoped that this volume might help accelerate its progress.

One major contemporary scheme can be used to illustrate the ecological trend in landscape: the High Line project in Manhattan, due to be completed in 2010. This derelict elevated railway was constructed between 1929 and 1934 to serve the warehouses along the Lower West Side, but by 2001 it was scheduled for demolition – a large area of open space above the city streetscape which was completely inaccessible to New Yorkers. After pressure from residents, the city council reversed its decision and pledged instead to resurrect the overgrown trackway as a 7-acre park-promenade through the Meatpacking District and West Chelsea – at an estimated cost of $65–$100 million.

Following an open design competition which attracted 720 entrants, a partnership between New York architectural firms Field Operations (which has also secured the huge Fresh Kills project on Staten Island) and Diller, Scofidio & Renfro was appointed. The mantra of their proposal is: 'Keep it simple, wild, quiet and slow' – epithets rarely applied to Manhattan. Over the course of twenty-two blocks, the rejuvenated High Line will be realized as a meandering boardwalk of undulating concrete, surrounded by naturalistic plantings of various types: mossland, wetland, meadow, woodland, mixed perennials. Field Operations, which undertook an ecological survey of the High Line site, came to the conclusion that the 'otherworldly' atmosphere and ecological character of the overgrown railtrack was worth keeping. So this is not going to be a narrative experience of discrete episodes, but rather multiple variations on ecological themes, with areas such as a 'vegetal balcony', shade garden, a sumach woodland, river overlook, butterfly garden, grassland preserve, sundeck and a large outdoor event space. There will be twelve

different entrances, each with its own character, while pedestrians at street-level looking up, or office workers looking down, will encounter a tree canopy floating 15m above ground level.

The structural aspects to the scheme are conventionally Modernist in character. Ever since Le Corbusier, the received wisdom among Modernists has been that the best landscape complement to such work is naturalistic or even untouched landscape – either a woodland setting, an orchard, a park up to the house in the English tradition, or else swaying grasses and perennial flowers offsetting the crisp lines of the architecture. (The precedent can perhaps be traced as far back as Palladio, whom Modernists have tended to admire.) The problem with this approach in the linear context of the High Line is that there is no architectural focus, while a narrative or episodic quality to the scheme has been ruled out. The idea is that the various eco-spaces will flow into each other seamlessly. The architects put it like this: 'A unified but flexible design permits shifts and gradations of environment and experience without segmentation.'

This is easy to say, but difficult to achieve in practice. It assumes, for example, that the different ecological zones will segue together seamlessly just because they are . . . well, ecological. The naturalistic fallacy – that a 'soft' landscape is somehow less artificial than other man-made solutions – has nevertheless emerged as a good way of winning design competitions. In the case of the High Line, it was quite a coup: what Field Operations and Diller, Scofidio & Renfro have sold to the jury is a glorified wasteland, which they call 'agri-tecture' or 'wildscape'. For the purposes of the competition, at least, they are taking their design lead entirely from nature. It would be difficult to imagine

a design methodology that is further away from conceptualism.

But there are good programmatic reasons for 'following nature'. It is an open secret in landscape circles that 'eco' sells. Any proposal which is tricked out with feel-good references to natural habitat, birdlife, sustainable irrigation systems, tree planting, recycling and havens for butterflies can be sure of a sympathetic hearing, especially if a jury is low on landscape expertise – as it was in the case of the High Line competition, notwithstanding the presence of Bernard Tschumi. Politicians, business representatives and local residents often feel that they can more easily understand and evaluate the ecological rather the aesthetic components of a proposal. 'Eco' is a balm to the conscience of civic and corporate leaders in the face of our apparently deteriorating planet. Thus we have seen over the past decade an increasing number of landscape firms making ecological awareness and sustainability a key aspect of their work – to the disgust of many conceptualists. This is not to suggest that Field Operations has cynically adopted an ecological pose; it is doubtless genuine. But its success with the High Line proposal is symptomatic of a wider trend.

The apparent 'rejection' of nature in conceptualist landscape design is probably its single most controversial aspect, though as so often with this design attitude any statements should be understood as in part polemical. It is not in fact a rejection of nature in its entirety, rather a specific version of it: the romantic, naturalistic tradition of Western garden design since the 18th century. The nadir of this for many designers is represented by what is often described as the English landscape park of 'Capability' Brown and others. American and European conceptualists will often display a broad-brush and somewhat

aggressive attitude to this tradition, which can often be accredited to a form of post-colonial anger, or 'cultural cringe'. Among conceptualists one often comes across a blithe and supremely confident conflation between pastoral fantasy and the English landscape park, which fails to take in the detail and value of that particular tradition. In fact, in its earlier phases, the English landscape movement exhibited many of the qualities now associated with contemporary conceptual work. Such factual cavils aside, the caricature has proved a useful stimulus for a number of conceptualist designers. Tony Heywood, for example, deliberately 'fictionalizes' his garden spaces or installations by exaggerating their qualities in the most extreme ways, in order to point up the inherent artificiality of all human interactions with the natural world.

This robust attitude to Romanticism in landscape is heresy to more conventional designers, who tenderly manipulate the site or landscape and 'work with nature, not against it'. Also controversial is a limited use of living plants and a reliance instead on materials that are obviously artificial, such as plastic and glass. There is also a subversive and sometimes sarcastic use of plant material, which can also enrage horticulturists and gardeners, for whom plants must self-evidently be the raison d'etre of any garden.

As a conceptualist attitude towards nature, that of Montreal's Claude Cormier is perhaps most bracing. 'I grew up on a farm,' he explains, 'where the relationship with the natural world is very direct. We were making a living out of the land, so this idea of rural peace does not work for me. Nature bores me. It is not the place where I get my inspiration.' Instead, Cormier is sustained by the wider culture and, in particular, the vibrancy and excitement of cities

and the wide diversity of people who live in them. He also has little time
for ecologically based approaches to landscape design: 'Everyone is moving
eco, but with eco we can also forget the idea of the "made". It's the issue of
artificiality. In our work we are honest about it,' he says.

On the other hand it is possible for conceptualists to construct their work
around a genuine relationship with natural landscape, if that is what truly moves
them. Melbourne-based Taylor Cullity Lethlean, for example, find much of their
inspiration in the natural Australian landscape. 'It informs all our work,' Perry
Lethlean explains, 'the patterns, the forms, the materials, the colours.' What
results is something akin to Outback Modernism, with a savour of the
surrounding natural world introduced in a non-naturalistic way. Germany's
Herbert Dreiseitl believes that the water he utilizes in all his designs gives
people a special emotional contact with nature. 'Even in city centres people
have a real desire to connect to what I call the "lost environment" or "lost
nature",' he says. 'Water is a very emotional agent for this. Even a single drop
of water contains the potential for all life – it is the start of life.' Dreiseitl's
landscapes are not natural-looking, and frequently comprise smooth edges,
precise measurements and clean lines – 'a lot of people try to copy nature
in their design, and it is a little bit kitsch,' he says. 'Modernism is not abstract
and intellectual. It is an honest statement: this is man-made; this is not nature;
we have changed things; we respect nature more by reinterpreting it.'

Perhaps there is a generational aspect to these differing attitudes among
conceptualists to nature. Quebec's youthful Nip Paysage displays a genuine
engagement with ecological issues. Anyone who went to school in the 1990s

could hardly emerge without some sense of impending ecological disaster, and Nip Paysage display none of the belligerence towards nature and natural forms which can be a driver to creativity among a (slightly) older generation of conceptualist designers. Michel Langevin describes how he and his colleagues will often turn to natural materials instead of concrete, plastic or asphalt. At the Unity apartment block in Montreal, for example they opted for large expanses of Canadian cedar decking to create an exterior 'dance floor'. Langevin recalls: 'We said, "Let's not use paving and concrete and asphalt. Let's do something more homey, using wood."' The conceptual element is there, in this case, in the way the angles of the wooden planks continue the lines of the building's footprint.

Conceptualist landscape can exhibit a somewhat fraught and contradictory relationship with nature, ecology, and the concomitant moral role of landscape designers. But, of course, such tensions can also be a source of memorable and challenging design. It may even be that conceptualist designers are exhibiting a more ecologically responsible attitude than their naturalistically inclined contemporaries, by questioning the honesty and authenticity of a methodology which seeks to replicate nature while never acknowledging that it cannot truly replace or repair it.

Patricia Johanson

Buskirk (USA)

Ecologically inspired organo-conceptualism
from Korea to Canada.

Patricia Johanson, based in Upstate New York, is unusual among conceptualist designers in that her work is informed by an abiding concern for environmental issues. She has been working in this spirit since the early 1970s, when ecology was considered a fringe interest. Today, of course, an eco-sensibility is de rigueur in the commercial mainstream. Her very first design – at the invitation of *House and Garden* in the late 1960s – featured a snaking waterway for a park, with forms resembling stems and leaves sprouting from it. It was considered too radical to publish at the time, but all of her work since has followed this basic premise: that the ground plan of a large-scale design might describe recognizable forms found in nature.

Those forms are generally taken from the world of plants or are inspired by snakes and other reptiles. They always have a relationship with a particular site, and in this sense Johanson follows the typical conceptualist methodology of researching the history and ecology of a place before embarking on the design process. 'I never design until I have discovered the meaning of the place,' she states. 'Each place has a unique set of conditions, and we need an intimate understanding of what it has been, is now, and will become in the future, in order to create a design that is more than a wilful act.'

There is a painterly quality to Johanson's striking designs, a sense of sweeping openness and fluidity coupled with a fearless love of colour and movement. In the use of overlapping and repeat patterns, Johanson has suggested some link with the programmatic music of her friend, the composer Philip Glass, in whose honour she once designed an urban park. But more important than this visual component is her conviction that landscape design is a medium which can fuse social, artistic, ecological and functional concerns in a way appropriate to our age. She believes in the transformative power of landscape; her own survival from cancer has, she says, lent this conviction further piquancy.

Johanson is dedicated to reintroducing a sense of connection with ecology and the universe, and has claimed that she wants to eradicate the idea of the artist and the design, so that what is left is simply the visitor and the place. Ultimately, her work posits an escape from the conundrum of the Earth's deteriorating ecology. As she says: 'Each of my projects is a model for an inclusive, life-supporting, self-sustaining world.'

LEFT This transformation of a derelict and stagnant lagoon adjacent to an art gallery and natural history museum was Johanson's first large-scale project. A pioneering act of environmental restoration, here she masterminded the purification of the lagoon and the replanting of the habitat, including tall grasses and reeds along the shoreline. Fair Park Lagoon, Dallas 1986.

Endangered Garden

SAN FRANCISCO 1988

Uniting some typical Johanson concerns, this commission was for the beautification of a sewer along the banks of Candlestick Cove in an ecologically sensitive but degraded area. After an initially fraught relationship with the engineers, Johanson's plan for an underground sewer with a walkway roof was realized.

The unifying concept here was the form of the local garter snake, an endangered species, which dictated the shape of the walkway itself, though the ecological imperative was to attract butterflies back to the habitat. 'This is a very windy area,' Johanson says. 'By building the head of the snake as an earth mound, I was able to create an area protected from wind so that butterflies could fly there.' The coiled tail section of the walkway winds itself up as a seating area, and near here Johanson created a series of raised paths in the form of ribbon worms. These paths form rock pools at high tide.

Johanson explains: 'The sculpted worm echoes the larger baywalk snake, as well as the tiny ribbon worms found at the site among the mussels and barnacles. Similar forms are formed by underwater currents and repeated incessantly underfoot. This fusion of form, function and ecological system, and its pervasiveness from microcosm to macrocosm, often lie along a mucky path.'

Patricia Johanson **155**

Karres en Brands Hilversum (The Netherlands)

Uncompromisingly high-concept public
park design.

The Dutch team of Bart Brands and Sylvia Karres, in partnership since 1997, is idealistic, experimental and socially collaborative. Both designers worked at the large Amsterdam firm B+B for a number of years before striking out independently. 'We see ourselves as an omni-force,' Brands says. 'We like to work on all scales, from masterplanning to the little details.' Their conceptual methodology is collaborative: 'It's not like we have one basic idea and the plan comes from that,' Brands explains. 'If we start a project, we start as a team and we attack it from all sides. Initially these streams are quite independent, then we see what the oppositions are and what fits. Then we split it up again. In the end, we have a clear idea – but I need to be able to say to the client that we have tried all these different paths.'

One of their more radical ideas is for 'spontaneous urbanism' – by which they mean a town which grows organically and dynamically in a manner dictated by its inhabitants. The basic concept here – or 'framework', as they prefer to term it – is that of individuality. This idea has

been realized in their plan for the post-war new town of De Draai in Heerhugowaard, north of Amsterdam, where the city's initial brief was for 3,000 new houses, following a set of different typologies. Brands recalls: 'I said that it was impossible. Can we not make a neighbourhood that grows very slowly, as they used to do, to create a grown richness, or spontaneous urbanism?' The idea is for house design to be dictated by topography and factors such as soil type, so that individuals can specify their own ideal home. The town will gradually grow up around a central park, which runs down the spine of the town (the site of the national gas line).

Brands wants to talk about his failures, too, as a way of illustrating the method. At Park de Hoge Weide, a new suburb near Utrecht, the idea was to transform a former refuse tip and chemical waste dump into a public park, not by creating a design in the usual way, but by opening the space and seeing how the public would use it and responding to that. Thus the design would be dictated by its future users. Huge mounds of earth created by the adjacent building were formed in the space and stone paths introduced, made from recycled stone taken from Utrecht's streets. 'Everyone was excited,' says Brands, 'but the manager left and staff changed. The maintenance teams said they couldn't work there because it wasn't finished, when the idea was that the design, build and maintenance would all happen at the same time. It was three years of fighting and in the end it didn't work – it was a mess.'

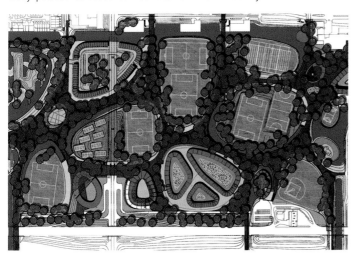

LEFT This was a competition entry for the redesign of a park in the southeast part of Amsterdam. Karres en Brands created a simple and logical framework based on the existing walking paths, with adaptable egg-shaped and oval enclosures, and colourful walls. Bijlmerpark, Amsterdam 2002.

Hoeg Biezen Park

IJSSELSTEIN (THE NETHERLANDS) 2002

This highly unusual park design was dictated by the
dimensions of the site: a 2km strip flanked by 5,000 new
houses on one side and the old village of IJsselstein on
the other. 'The park is so small and thin that it is not really
a park at all; it is more of a connector,' Brands explains.
'We decided to borrow its qualities from the surroundings
because there was not enough body in the space itself.'
A series of islands connected by one long bridge running
the length of the park, north to south, was created; the
vertical poles along the edge are the only 'detail' of the
design. The strips going across are paths linking the new
houses with the village; each path is focused on something
on the skyline. 'You can walk the length of this bridge from
the town centre to the fields,' Brands says. 'The park is
different in every season. The water is all newly created
and filtered – half of our design is under water.'

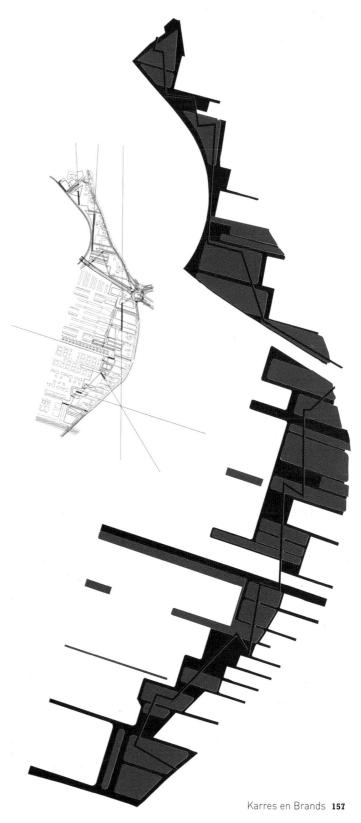

De Nieuwe Ooster Cemetery

AMSTERDAM 2003

'We always start with a basic framework,' Brands explains. 'With the cemetery, for example, it was a spatial framework based on the form of a barcode and an idea about societies and cemeteries.' In this cemetery – the largest in the Netherlands – two extensions to the original area were added after 1915. There was a clear historical hierarchy in the oldest section, in which the rich were buried near the curving paths and the poor in the open fields. The second section was more uniform and less class-organized, while in the last section the methodology had completely broken down, giving the cemetery a fragmented feeling. It was this last section which received the most attention from Karres en Brands; the basic idea was to create a space with no hierarchy of income or class, a series of narrow, rectangular sections inspired by the image of a barcode.

'We understand that everyone wants a choice, and we have built in variety,' Brands says. 'Every stripe of the barcode is different – some are wider, some have hedges, or flowers, or water. You can be expressive – there is no description of what each stripe should look like.' One walkway is lined by a row of tall basalt blocks, monumental fixtures designed to hold urns, while a simple black reflecting pool crossed by low bridges produces a sense of variety. Karres en Brands have also designed a monumental curving wall filled with a grid of niches: a columbarium for ashes.

Responding to the suggestion that the barcode image has capitalistic and retail overtones which might be deemed inappropriate for a cemetery, where money and possessions (let alone shopping) no longer have meaning, Brands states, 'The barcode is for us a symbol of individualism. People understood that. This is the biggest cemetery in Holland, and it is also a business. They have "clients" in the same way a shop does.'

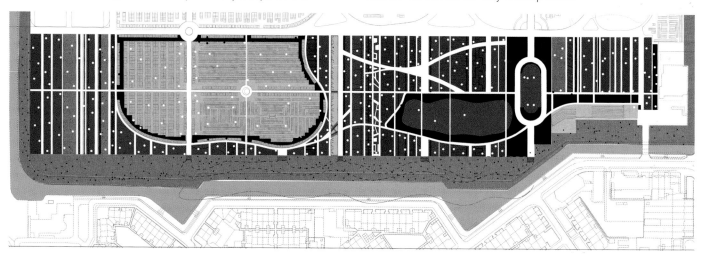

Klahn + Singer

Karlsruhe (Germany)

Horticultural and architectural formal
experimentation go hand in hand.

Founded in 1968 and therefore almost forty years old,
Karlsruhe-based Klahn + Singer is truly a venerable
company in the world of landscape design (let alone
conceptual landscape design). Ulrich Singer and Jurgen
Klahn met while studying landscape at Kassel in Germany,
but only formed the company several years later, by
which time Singer had completed a two-year diploma
in landscape at Copenhagen Academy of Arts, where
he studied under Sven-Ingvar Andersson and also got
to know Carl Theodor Sørenson. The Danish experience
made a lasting impression on Singer's style and attitude
to landscape; there is certainly something of Sørenson in
his sculptural treatment of space, in his consistent use
of the circle motif, and in his confidence with a feeling
of openness. Singer and Klahn were joined by partners
Clemens Appel (in 1997) and Klaus Veiel (in 2000) before
Klahn's retirement in 2002. They specialize mainly in public
spaces and landscapes for schools and old people's homes,
though they do take on the occasional residential garden
project.

'In Denmark, the greatest compliment to a designer
is to say that something has been kept simple.' Singer
asserts. He achieves this in his design by concentrating
above all on the spatial qualities and potential of a site,
what he calls 'the integrity of the space'. On the ground,
this makes for designs characterized by large, sweeping,
emblematic landscape gestures featuring plenty of open
space. This does not necessarily signal austerity, since
favoured motifs in Klahn + Singer's work include circular
patterns and the use of bright colours (even pink!).

Singer believes, however, that his style is not
fundamentally any different to the way it was when he
began practising some forty years ago. 'We have always

done simple things, using just a few plant species in any
project.' he says. 'It must not be cheap, but it must be
simple. First of all, it has to be about space. And space
means emptiness. Of course, many people will not accept
emptiness – especially gardeners.' While there is no
narrative structure or clear metaphorical underpinning
to the duo's designs, the work becomes conceptual in
the sense that the manipulation of space itself is the
overriding theme, and is perfectly discernible to viewers.

ABOVE AND OPPOSITE Two distinctive wavy lawns and a simple grass plat were introduced as a preface to this castle, the most important building in Karlsruhe, restored in the 1980s and now a music school. Here and elsewhere, the beginning and end of Klahn + Singer's design methodology is spatiality, with function not even a major consideration. Castle of Gottesaue, Karlsruhe (Germany) 2003.

ENBW Zentrale

KARLSRUHE (GERMANY) 1997

Klahn + Singer designed three inner courtyards for the head office of an energy company in Karlsruhe. Planting and weight levels were limited because the landscape spaces were situated above the underground car parks (as is often the case in contemporary office blocks). The watchwords of simplicity and spatial awareness were clearly to the fore here, as the designers endeavoured to create spaces that were redefined and made elegant by simple geometric moves using the medium of plants.

The first courtyard is focused on a grid of sixty poplar trees, underplanted with ivy as groundcover. 'It's surprisingly windy in there,' Singer says, 'so you have the sound of the wind in the leaves.' The second courtyard is divided diagonally by a row of four lime trees, which create a glade setting and diffuse a pleasing green light through the space in sunshine. Here, as in the other courtyards, substantial curvilinear beds of ivy soften the contours of the space and the utilitarian office block, while also providing orientation for the emergency vehicles which may require access through the space. Black pumice has been used as a ground material.

The idea of splitting up the space is used for the third courtyard, as well, but this time the split travels diagonally from the ground to the upper storeys; steel wires stretch to the roof, along which blue wistaria grows. Electrical isolators were used on these wires as a useful way of stopping the wistaria sliding back down the wires. Since ENBW supplies electricity, this constitutes a subtle metaphorical moment. But on the whole, Klahn + Singer avoid discernible narrative or metaphorical clarity.

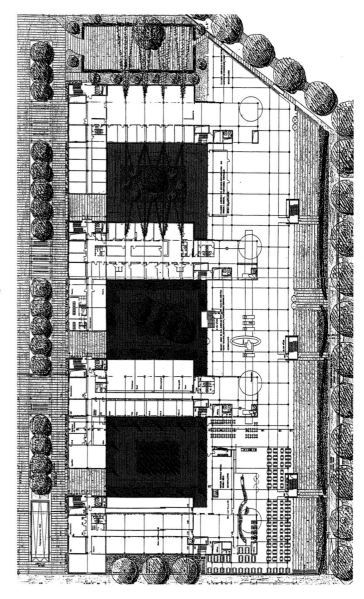

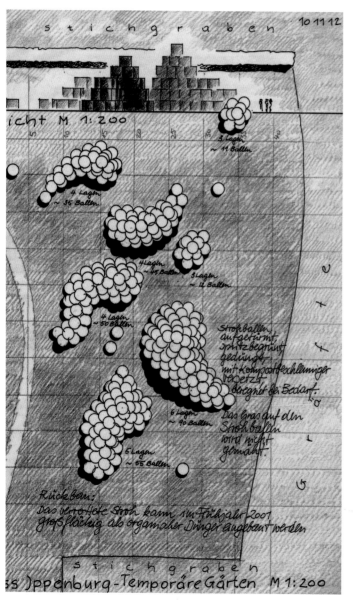

Garden of Babel

BAD ESSEN (GERMANY) 2000

This installation in the grounds of Schloß Ippenburg in Westphalia was a play on the biblical idea of the Tower of Babel, and specifically Pieter Breughel the Elder's fantastical painting of the subject, in which the tower resembles a high-rise version of the Colosseum in Rome. Klahn + Singer's idea was to create a version of this image using straw bales as the material. The symbolic theme of the Tower of Babel story is that of the overweening pride and ambition of humankind. In that sense, the eminently perishable material of straw was ideal.

The bales were piled up to create huge forms, the largest being six 'storeys' high and containing some ninety bales. The architectural mass of these edifices provided a satirical counterpoint to the castle in the background, in that all such undertakings are ultimately 'temporary', and the processes of natural change and decay were harnessed to emphasize this, as the bales either collapsed because of waterlogging or grew a green covering of grass. In spring, the bale structures looked crisp, brown and architectural; by summer, they were greened all over and losing their shape; and by the autumn they were decomposing.

'I am very interested in the concept of development in landscape design.' Singer adds. 'You can see this in the Babel garden – it had to reach its full development in a relatively short space of time, six months.' Klahn + Singer's 'sequel' to this installation at Ippenburg was a structure made using burned and blackened straw bales planted up with lilies and other bright flowers.

Land-I Rome

Art collective who construct highly worked-out landscape installations.

This Rome-based trio of young landscape architects – Marco Antonini, Roberto Capecci and Rafaella Sini – met at the University of Rome in 2000 and scored a success with their very first collaborative project, a temporary garden for the Chaumont Festival (see below). A loose partnership, sharing office space but also working on individual projects, Land-I has nevertheless carved out an international reputation as the outfit which is perhaps the most

sophisticated and successful in the genre of temporary gardens. They have participated at the Cornerstone, Jardins de Métis and Westonbirt festivals, as well as at Chaumont.

Spokesman Antonini is aware of the limitations of the temporary garden form, but believes that shows such as Chaumont have revitalized the garden scene. 'This movement in temporary gardens might reach saturation point in coming years,' he says, 'but Chaumont came about after several centuries of the romantic garden. It had all come to a standstill. Temporary gardens are not experimentation for the sake of it – I think this blurring of the threshold between art and architecture can somehow survive in permanent landscape commissions.' Land-I's work often seems 'fuller' conceptually than that of their contemporaries, many of whom view temporary work at shows as an opportunity for experimentation rather than as an end in itself. On the other hand, Land-I has not yet had a great deal of opportunity to complete permanent gardens or landscapes.

The Land-I philosophy is founded on conceptualist principles. Their mission statement has at its heart the following points: 'Our first step is to observe the landscape, an aesthetic and cultural approach necessary to interpret the site and intervene on it. A site is never new, and in our designs we acknowledge that it always hides traces of a previous state, a potential waiting to be discovered, creating opportunities for a new start.'

The designers respond to these historical nuances in different temporal schema – either referring to the actual

LEFT This show garden for the Chaumont Festival is entitled 'Mente la-menta?' (or 'does mint lie?'; the question mark is deliberate), and was designed by the trio who teamed up specifically for this show. Mente la-menta?, Chaumont sur Loire (France) 2000.

history of the place (Metropolis; see left), or inferences arising from its prevailing atmosphere (Ombre, Jardins de Métis, 2002), or even importing a sense of place from elsewhere (Stone's Throw; see p. 169). The very name 'Land-I' is a conceptual motif: the 'I' stands for Italy, for 'idea', and also as the first-person singular, 'which puts the person at the centre, with the landscape as the central means of expression'. Land-I now also use a 'semi-cryptic' name – Archicolture – in certain contexts, such as their website identity. Antonini explains: 'It puts together "architecture", in the sense of the meaning of a space, with "culture", or the sensitive use of plants.'

Antonini is one of the deepest-thinking of conceptualist landscape designers, acknowledging the debt to Land Art ('its minimal approach, its relation to context and the temporary quality'), as well as what he sees as the comparative limitations of conventional, gallery-based conceptual art. 'There is a certain level of independence and cynicism in conceptual art which can make it seem remote from society,' he explains. 'There is no need to confront people in terms of the way they experience the place. In a garden, the conceptual process has a more human dimension – there is always the sense of scale – and that makes it a more "grounded" mode of expression.'

LEFT AND ABOVE LEFT A series of wooden crates contained and confined plants sourced from every continent in this temporary garden for the Westonbirt Festival. The plants in each crate were carefully labelled, creating an immediately readable meditation on the business of collecting and importing plants from all corners of the world. Metropolis, Gloucestershire (UK) 2003.

Insabina Yoga Centre

ROME 2003

This permanent landscape for a yoga centre, set in rolling hills amid olive groves, is a good illustration of the Land-I methodology – thoughtful, witty, uncompromising. Antonini explains: 'We designed a yoga platform with a canvas roof, but the client wanted some sort of natural garden. Instead of transforming this landscape in a typical way, we put twenty metal boxes on the wide lawn, each raised 20cm above the ground, and then seeded wildflowers and grasses beneath them. It was aesthetically convincing, and we felt we had not contaminated or suburbanized the landscape. The boxes confined the changes that had been made in an obviously retraceable way. In a way, we were denouncing our own contribution to the landscape. We did not want to be mimetic or mingle with the landscape. It was an almost ironic reaction to the client's request: we felt we had responded to her desire for a "natural" garden.'

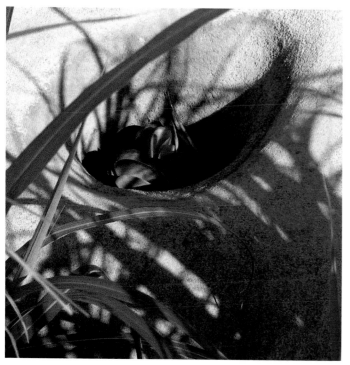

Stone's Throw

SONOMA (USA) 2004

Land-I demonstrated their flair and originality with
this temporary garden at the Cornerstone Festival in
California. 'Throughout garden history, there is the theme
of miniaturization of the natural landscape,' Antonini
explains. 'We took this concept and turned it around,
using a single stone we found on a beach in Italy. We
took this object and reproduced it millions of times, so
that it became a landscape in itself. Conceptually speaking,
we "threw" this stone across the landscape, and the world.'
Antonini points out the similarities of this idea to those
used in Pop Art, in which an object might be blown up
to surreal dimensions. Here, however, it is not a familiar
mass-produced object, but an arbitrarily chosen yet unique
element of a specific landscape, in this case a beach on
the Mediterranean.

Die LandschaftsArchitekten

Structural minimalism offset by extensive plantings and conceptual humour.

The partnership of Die LandschaftsArchitekten was set up in 1995 by Petra Bittkau and Friedrich Bartfelder, both of whom lecture in landscape at the University of Applied Science in Wiesbaden. They first met in Berlin some five years previously, when Bittkau was freelancing as a landscape architect and Bartfelder was working in nature conservation, eventually going into business together when Bartfelder came to Wiesbaden. 'We like to work in competition,' Bittkau says. 'We have separate rooms in our office.' Bittkau specializes in the horticultural aspects of design, and particularly private gardens, working four days a week, while Bartfelder's area of expertise is in landscape and public-space planning – he works just one day a week at present, but this is changing from next year when he leaves the university to concentrate on the practice. The pair have already completed an impressive number of commissions in Germany, a mixture of large private gardens and public or institutional projects.

Bittkau and Bartfelder come from a European Modernist tradition – they cite the Swiss designer Dieter Kienast as a key influence – in contrast to the other principal school in the German garden scene: the New Perennials planting movement pioneered in the public parks system. While plants are an important element of the duo's style, they are not used in a pseudo-naturalistic way. Bittkau explains: 'Organic forms are not our way of working. We think that the plants we add to our designs are themselves organic. That's enough – the plan does not have to be organic, too. So you have a flower-bed with perfectly straight edges, and the plants and flowers within it grow just how they want.'

The minimalist, functional, reductionist creed of Modernism is another integral part of their approach; their gardens appear refreshingly simple at first glance, with clear architectural lines and broad statements in terms of planting. 'We want to design gardens with just a few principal elements,' Bittkau explains, 'but we want those elements to be of the best quality – better to have just two perfect features rather than a number of average ones.' Lest this sound somewhat serious-minded, it is worth noting that Die LandschaftsArchitekten are not averse to a conceptualist strain of humour in their gardens, whether that be in the form of topiary shaped as 'soldiers' or the disarmingly cute basis for their Daisy Garden (see p. 172).

All the work of Die LandschaftsArchitekten highlights the contrast between geometry and nature: a linear and geometric plan, with plenty of stone and concrete and strong shapes in topiary, is offset by luxuriant and carefully planned planting schemes. 'We think that nature becomes more interesting when you set some geometric elements in the landscape,' Bittkau says. 'Then you see the difference between the natural landscape and man's intervention in it – the point where they meet.' The plantings are not designed to 'soften' the strong linearity of the plan, but to complement it in an equally powerful way by utilizing the green forms of leaves and the shapes of plants and trees. The result is a garden look which is uncompromisingly Modernist in structure, but which is given a sense of abundant life and variety by its planting. These are gardens designed to be enjoyed as well as 'used'.

LEFT AND BELOW The brief here was to create a private space in which relaxation was the paramount consideration. It is an overwhelmingly green space, hemmed in by mature rhododendrons and old trees. Next to the rectangular ornamental pool is a large area of abundant green planting for form and foliage, defined by effective groupings of hostas, *Alchemilla mollis*, ivies and hydrangeas. The most Modernist feature of the garden is a line of clipped yew cubes by the top pool. Private garden, Frankfurt 2000.

Daisy Garden

GLOUCESTERSHIRE (UK) 2004

'They called us the "daisy people",' says Bittkau, recalling the reaction of many visitors to this memorable exercise in garden conceptualism, shown at the Westonbirt Festival. 'Most people like daisies, but they don't know they like them,' she explains. 'The daisy is a weed, but it is not really considered a weed – it's a plant for children.' The basis for the garden was the children's game of 'he loves me, he loves me not', chanted while pulling petals off a daisy, coupled with the meaning of the flower's Latin name *Bellis perennis*, or 'lasting beauty'.

A wide cedar deck leads the visitor along under a line of three huge daisy parasols with green 'stalks' (stitched together by a Wiesbaden tailor), to turfed 'love seats' designed for two people. The magenta insets in the seats were made of a special material: a mixture of concrete and recycled wood pulp that is very hard but can be sawn into pieces. The garden was enclosed by hurdles obtained from a Somerset maker, a form of fencing the German designers had never seen before. 'We loved the hurdles – very natural but also architectural,' Bittkau says. 'They enclosed the garden so that you were alone with the daisies, and with your love.'

Ron Lutsko — San Francisco

Botanically and ecologically nuanced
conceptual landscape design.

Born and bred in California, Ron Lutsko's career trajectory
as a designer and gardener has encompassed formal
training in botany, horticulture and landscape architecture.
After graduating in horticulture from the University of
California at Davis and running a design practice in
San Francisco, Lutsko realized he needed a grounding
in landscape architecture and enrolled for another
undergraduate degree at UC Davis, where he was also
asked to teach. Throughout the 1980s, Lutsko combined
a teaching career with his landscape practice until in
1988 he decided to take a Masters' degree in landscape
architecture at UC Berkeley, effectively writing his own
curriculum because he was now well versed in the
practicalities of the job. In 1990 he gave up academia
and concentrated on the landscape practice, which has
employed about ten people ever since and has a 60/40
split between public and residential work, plus commercial
projects at wineries.

Lutsko comes out of a rich tradition of mid-century
Modernism in California, and counts the designer Garrett
Eckbo as a seminal influence. As with many 'true-believer'
Modernists today – such as Christopher Bradley-Hole
in England and any number of designers in Germany –
Lutsko argues that Modernism is still a relevant attitude.
He criticizes what he calls the 'streamlined, minimal,
technical, efficient and soulless' aspects of the approach,
and instead refers to its ecological and social applications.
'Modernism means that you are trying to create places that
have a relation to people's lives now,' Lutsko explains.
'Poverty, environmental preservation – merging people's
lives more with nature, if you like. It's about letting people
get in touch with what is keeping us alive on this earth. It's
not that I'm interested in simply "putting nature" into the

site.' Lutsko is probably the most botanically knowledgeable
Modernist landscape designer in the world.

The key to the Lutsko look is Modernist minimalism,
melded with an acute awareness of the ecological context.
Lutsko is careful to point out that he is not 'strictly'
ecological in the sense that he would never ban the use
of plants which are not endemic or native to the region, but
aims instead for a palette that responds to the locale in the
most beautiful and practical way. 'There are native plants
and local materials,' he explains, 'and there are honourary
native plants and honourary local materials. I make sure
that the materials are compatible with and kind to the
environment.' Lutsko's method can be characterized as
a generous and naturalistic use of plants, sometimes in
single-species groupings, complementing a core structural
ground plan of hard materials.

ABOVE, RIGHT AND OPPOSITE This garden design in California consists of four distinct zones, which refer to the way nature becomes integrated into human culture. The most natural zone also serves as a comment on the idea of an untouched fragment of nature presented as a conserved museum piece. Private garden, Santa Clara County (USA) 1991.

Oak Savanna Vineyard

LOS OLIVOS (USA) 2004

At Oak Savanna, the commission was for a multiple-use landscape space amid the Californian vineyards and depleted native forests of the private winery. 'We used this old irrigation pond at the centre of the site and made it into a formal pool bounded by two big, 5m-high curving walls,' Lutsko says. The space is used for family gatherings, corporate hospitality and charitable fund-raising events, so the challenge was to create a design that would function equally well as a spot for a dinner for two, a dining area for 120, or a party venue for 300. The decked platform extending over the pond provides an intimate outdoor dining room (as well as an informal diving platform for the pool), while the surrounding crushed gravel terrace is functional and hard-wearing. An integral part of Lutsko's plan was the rejuvenation of the surrounding oak woodland – mainly the native evergreen *Quercus agrifolia* – and the replanting of native 'bunch grasses' (nasella and festuca) and bulbs.

Sustainability Gardens

REDDING (USA) 2003

The town of Redding is situated 200 miles north of San Francisco, and is ringed by no fewer than four mountain ranges. 'It's one of the most complex ecosystems in the world,' Lutsko asserts. The new Lutsko-designed sustainability gardens here take up a 10-acre parcel of a 275-acre wildlife preserve and park, with several buildings performing an educational function. The celebrated architect Santiago Calatrava designed a bridge that links the gardens with the rest of the park. With this design, Lutsko has moved into conceptualism, as have many Modernist designers in recent years. The stepped terraces which accompany the meandering rill that forms the focus of the garden refer to the ecology of the region – the way that vast amounts of water drain off the mountain ranges in winter and help irrigate California. A mount and cascade in the middle of the garden reflect this aspect of the ecology. Every winter the basin-shaped gardens experience considerable flooding, and Lutsko's design accommodates this. 'The clumped deer grasses (Muhlenbergia) next to the stylized river will take a level of water saturation,' he explains. 'We're actually inviting flood waters into our site – a lot of landscape architects would say we are out of our minds! But I'm looking forward to the first really wet winter.'

Lützow 7 Berlin

Long-established deconstructivist practice
promoting a visionary conceptual outlook.

Cornelia Muller and Jan Wehberg studied landscape
together in Berlin and were collaborating even as students
in the 1970s. They won several competitions in the 1980s,
including the International Building Exhibition in Berlin
in 1985, when they worked with an English architectural
team on a design for the new Tegel Harbour. Throughout
the 1990s, and especially after reunification, they designed
courtyard spaces for government offices, businesses
and hotels, and entered (and won) a number of design
competitions. They formed Lützow 7 in 1997 (the company's
name refers to its address in Berlin), parting ways with

a third partner at this point. There followed successful
competition entries for a public park and an urban quarter
in Dusseldorf, though, as Wehberg admits: 'None of these
parks were built – we survived on residential commissions,
housing projects.' In 2002 came the highlight so far, the
design for the Platz der Republik (below) in front of the
Reichstag in Berlin, which is clearly Modernist in inspiration.
'Our work is not an anti-Modernist statement,' Wehberg
states. 'We have made many designs that are strictly
minimalist and linear.

'We came in as young people growing up in the 1970s,
all the hippies and so on.' he continues. 'I even saw London
in '69. We were critical of the modern architecture of the
time. We were pretty ready for Postmodernism. It was not
perhaps so serious, but it was a frank and beautiful look
back to the ancients. We had no problem getting along with
Postmodern architects. People had been caught in the cage
of Modernism, and our work was definitely Postmodernist.
What you call conceptualism came later. Early on, though,
we didn't really think about style. We just thought about
single projects. We always had a single detail or part of the
design from which everything else came. We tried to look
at the unique spirit of the place. And when Daniel Libeskind
and Zaha Hadid started deconstructivism [in architecture],
we said, "Yes!"'

In their writings, Wehberg and Muller argue that the
aesthetic conception, developed in garden and landscape
architecture by abstraction, should not be weakened by

LEFT The designers maintain that this project is to be understood
as 'a reaction of garden architecture and open-space planning to
the urban development of the new government district, in interaction
with the Reichstag in the Spreebogen (a bend in the Spree River)'.
Platz der Republik, Berlin 2002.

LEFT AND ABOVE Lützow 7's courtyard for these government buildings is a study in geometry: the linear arrangement of the vertical windows is echoed in the horizontal patterning of the square lawns and water basins. Federal Ministry for Employment and Social Affairs, Berlin 2002.

'opportunistic conformism'. 'The variety of the single element is the simplicity of the composition,' they say, which is an avowedly conceptualist stance. Most of their work on the ground, however, complies with familiar Modernist ideals: lines of trees, straight axes of paths, geometric water features, cool rectangles of limestone, an asymmetrical ground plan, a functionalist rationale.

The conceptual streak is worn quite lightly; their argument is that public landscapes and parks are all too easily overlooked by residents, and that 'new symbols are needed to revitalize such spaces and connect them again with their users'. To formulate these new symbols, Lützow 7 utilize what Wehberg describes as 'analogies, words,

poems, pictures or simple images related to the city'. They are also comfortable with the use of natural materials, unlike some of their Modernist predecessors: 'Look back,' say Wehberg and Muller. 'The beauty of nature and human interventions are not irreconcilable contrasts.' They also talk of 'the recovery of sensual design theories and the neutralization of the contrast between aesthetics and utility in garden and landscape art'. This is a gentle and commercially palatable brand of landscape conceptualism, not too far divorced from Modernist certainties to scare away potential clients, commissioners of public spaces and architect collaborators.

Jewish Museum

BERLIN 1999

Taking its lead from Daniel Libeskind's intricate web of allusions which related the museum complex to space, time and history, Lützow 7's design conceptualizes the museum's surrounding garden spaces. The theme is the history of Berlin: a courtyard dedicated to Paul Celan is an interpretation of a typical inner court in a Berlin apartment building, while the garden dedicated to the writer and civil servant E.T.A. Hoffmann contains forty-nine cubes planted with oleander, 'implying a multitude of symbolic meanings'. A small play area is dedicated to the writer Walter Benjamin and relates to the architecture of the museum itself and the surrounding urban context. The 'Paradise Garden' is a small forest of robinia trees, growing out of the rubble of war. This is 'a symbol for the potential to reverse the meaning of the Garden of Eden today, and also an image of the undiminished force of nature'.

Wehberg explains how Libeskind's graphic 'micro-megas', pinned to the office wall, provided a conceptual starting point. 'They opened your mind to fantasy and new inspiration. I didn't want to use the micro-megas only, though, so I took photos all around Berlin and then made a collage of them. That collage was photographed, then I made a lot of copies and overdrew them. It was not an organic process: it was a grid. It started as a net of lines relating to places in the city. Those lines start to bend under certain conditions. What results does not constitute a ground plan, but it creates structures that make you free of linear thinking.'

Neanderthal Museum

METTMANN (GERMANY) 2002

This project constitutes one of the most ambitious and complex conceptualist landscape projects undertaken to date by any company or individual. The multimedia museum is situated on the site of the discovery in 1856 of Neanderthal bones in the Kleine Feldhofer cave. As Wehberg points out, 'The challenge was to re-create a sense of place, and to connect visitors with something which happened some four million years ago. We thought that there is still something in each of us from the Neanderthal period: how do we activate that? After all, like the Neanderthals we all have nature and we all have an idea of paradise. So we made a time–space axis: visitors make their own way to their own time, in real time.'

This axis is a walkway which proceeds past metal waymarkers, with a notice at the end of the route suggesting that visitors turn around. 'Visitors then feel they have travelled a huge distance through space and time,' Wehberg says. A 'lounge' of outsized chairs is situated next to the time–space axis, and a field of red-and-white poles relates to the exact grid reference of the cave itself.

'You can ask why landscape architects in public spaces have to tell so many stories: we have come from nature, from the forest,' Wehberg explains. 'It's almost a primal idea, an emotional, not an art-historical point.' He says that paradise has been forgotten in landscape architecture, and that it can be found in the forest, in the desert and in the water. 'In one way, this is a mystical and faraway topic, about how early man came up from Africa,' he concludes.

William Martin
Noorat (Australia)

Individualist garden-maker melding sculptural
artefacts and botanical know-how.

William Martin is a highly idiosyncratic gardener, who
has spent the past decade developing a garden called
'Wigandia' on three isolated acres in rural southern
Victoria. To complement his carefully structured plantings,
Martin fashions rusting corrugated iron and odd pieces of
wood into benches, fluted columns and other objects in an
invented style that he calls 'Bunyip Classicism', after the
mythical bogeyman figure of the Outback. This is partly
intended as a satirical jibe against all the Australians
who aspire to an English garden. For Martin, this kind of
Anglophile pastiche is as out of place in the Antipodes as
the bunyip is in the 21st century. 'Australia has never lived
through a classical period,' Martin observes. 'This classical
period I have invented never existed, and the bunyip is a
mythical creature. Corrugated iron is like the marble
of our world. "Bunyip Classicism" will rust and fall over.'

The conceptual core of Martin's garden is precisely this
bloody-minded, angry rejection of the legacy of colonialism,
and what he sees as the complacency and snobbery of the
modern Australian garden scene, orchestrated by a cadre
of haute bourgeois based in Melbourne. Martin says he
feels snubbed by this gardening establishment, and points
out that Wigandia was mysteriously excluded from the
recently published *Oxford Companion to Australian Gardens*,
even though he was interviewed for it. Ian Hamilton Finlay's
combative garden at Little Sparta was a decisive influence:
'It was the first garden or outdoor space that sat me down
and shut me up,' he recalls.

Wigandia sits on an exposed knoll beneath the green-topped Mount Noorat, a dormant volcano responsible for the thin, free-draining, reddish-brown ash that counts for soil here. Martin acquired an old outbuilding from a nearby estate and reassembled it on the summit of the knoll. He then set about creating paths in the surrounding scree. Superficially, the garden looks a little rough-and-tumble, but in reality everything is carefully worked out. 'Whenever I plant anything,' he says, 'I think about how it connects with both the immediate area and the wider landscape.'

Favourite plants include succulents of all sorts, echiums,

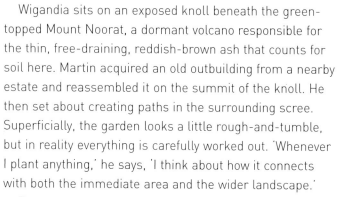

grasses, cordylines, phormiums and sculptural subjects such as trachycarpus palms and *Melianthus major*. He has no truck with specimen plants – 'More gardens have been destroyed by that than anything else. I'm not interested in rarity; it's composition above all else' – and is equally dismissive of colour. 'If you garden for structure and get that right, the colours just seem to work,' he says. Martin says that his carefully structured pictorial compositions start from the bottom up: 'I practise a layering effect. Get the lowest level right and build on that: it's simple but it works. I'm also obsessed with pairs of identical plants. It's not about rooms or enclosures like you have in Britain; that's so easy to do. It's much more of a challenge to create a garden that connects all these subtle changes.'

Martin is also scathing about 'ecologically correct' gardening using only native Australian plants, a contemporary trend. 'I've yet to see native plants used as well as they could be,' he says. 'Many people think that with natives you can use a relatively unstructured context. But I believe every garden needs a structure. And remember, this country is bigger than Europe: to me, plants from Western Australia might as well be from outer space.'

Accordingly, the garden at Wigandia is filled with specimens from all over the world that are united by one criterion: they all thrive in the dry conditions. 'It's a simple equation,' Martin says. 'You have a plant – an agapanthus, say – and it does well. So you look at where it comes from and target the plants of that region. You can't go wrong.'

Shunmyo Masuno
Yokohama (Japan)

Classical Japanese design meets contemporary landscape conceptualism.

Shunmyo Masuno pursues an unusual dual career as a Zen Buddhist priest and internationally acclaimed landscape gardener. He has completed some forty projects since setting up his design company, Japan Landscape Consultants, in 1982 – mainly domestic gardens, but also high-profile commissions such as the Canadian Embassy in Tokyo (1991), and a number of big projects in Germany and Canada. He is a regular speaker at universities worldwide, and in Japan also acts as a professor at Tama Art University. Shunmyo graduated in agriculture from Tamagawa University in 1975, and spent the rest of the decade serving a garden apprenticeship under an acknowledged master. He began his Zen training in 1979, qualified as an assistant priest in 1985, and was finally made head priest at Kenkohji Temple in 2001.

As might be expected, Shunmyo's design philosophy is rooted in Zen principles and the tradition of *Ishidate-so*, the brotherhood of Zen priests who were also landscape gardeners. He has been particularly influenced by two teachers: the 13th-century thinker Muso Soseki, who emphasized a personal, psychological, and therefore conceptual approach to garden design; and the 15th-century priest Ikkyu, who was influential in the formulation of the Japanese tea ceremony. Zen priests have traditionally sought out artforms – such as calligraphy, ikebana, or rock placement in landscape gardens – where it is possible to create 'an expression of oneself', of one's inner being. Shunmyo sees a successful garden as being a kind of other self, a mirror of the mind, which speaks directly to those who experience it. In this sense, a garden can be viewed as a spiritual training ground for a religious sensibility.

Like all Japanese garden designers, Shunmyo's work is defined by the strong native traditions of classical design philosophy and horticultural method. Given the length of time it takes to become qualified as a landscape gardener in Japan (up to a decade), it is not surprising that most designers are rooted in tradition. While some of Shunmyo's work is overwhelmingly classical in tone – with an emphasis on rock placement, raked gravel, framed views, trained shrubs and trees, and a traditional plant palette – he often introduces a frisson of Modernism into his designs. This takes the form of stonework cut smooth and arranged 'unnaturally' (geometrically, or in linear fashion, and in contrast with other stonework); a sinuous, abstract ground plan that is not dependent on episodic order; and unusual sculptural motifs, such as cones of gravel or perfectly circular pools. There is often a sense in his work that the shards or monumental fragments of rock are references to the human psyche rather than the natural world, and this emphasis places his work as much in the tradition of Modernist designers, such as Carlo Scarpa, as it does in that of classical Japan.

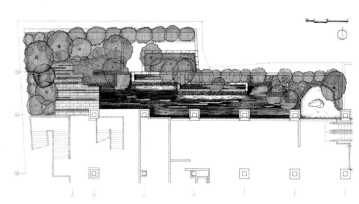

ABOVE AND OPPOSITE Tranquil planting and a gentle waterfall help to bring the serenity of the outdoor garden into the bustling hotel. Hotel Kohjimachi-kaikan, Tokyo 1998.

Hofu City Crematorium

YAMAGUCHI (JAPAN) 2003

Here, the plan was to create a landscape setting for bereaved families and friends attending the funerals of loved ones. As Shunmyo explains: 'The great leaders of religion, land and man have not been able to escape death. It is something that we all inevitably face, experience, and finally accept.'

The two principal garden spaces at the core of the plan divide the main building from the crematorium itself, and are intended to invoke different moods for consolation and contemplation. The first, and larger, space is a viewing garden called *Tabidachi no niwa*. It consists of 'pools' of raked gravel, low evergreens, a few sculptural trees, and a variety of rocks arranged to echo the shapes of natural mountain forms in time-honoured fashion. However, the abundance of rocks, their shape and their distribution give this garden a contemporary savour. The second garden space, *Shokha no niwa*, is centred on a still, circular pool dignified by a single, large rock at its edge, and is intended to be experienced after the cremation. Shunmyo explains: 'The water in the basin represents the sky, and the scenery reflected represents the uncertainty of things not remaining as they are. Seven rocks set in and around the basin express the process by which Buddha became Buddha, forty-nine days after death.'

Another substantial area is a dry garden called *Shizume no niwa*, where the mourners bid the deceased goodbye before the cremation. This calm and quiet space is intended to evoke images of the topography of Hofu City and its district. Shunmyo's unusually ambitious conceptual scheme for this most sensitive of spaces appears to face the actuality of death through landscape, rather than trying to soothe it away.

Suifu-So

LAKE KASUMIGAURA (JAPAN) 2001

A complex of buildings on the edge of Lake Kasumigaura comprises reception areas and individual guesthouses for a company. It was designed in tandem with the landscape and entirely subsumed into it. Shunmyo's intention was to create a total aesthetic experience that honours Japan's natural landscape and the passage of the seasons. The place of water was particularly important, as the site is filled with streams and ponds, as well as three dramatic waterfalls. Some of the interior spaces were designed with the reflection of water in mind.

'The layout of each room was devised to create specific scenes for that particular space,' Shunmyo explains. 'The positioning of the windows and the interior and exterior grades [the shape of the ground plane] were crucial tools used to obtain this effect.' The idea here was to create an environment that encourages a refreshingly simple frame of mind, far from the complexities of modern life. As Shunmyo comments, the name of the project (mushin-tei) refers to 'the practice of attaining detachment of your mind. This does not mean to draw a blank, but to focus on a task, such as breathing a breeze over the garden to create a feeling of coolness.'

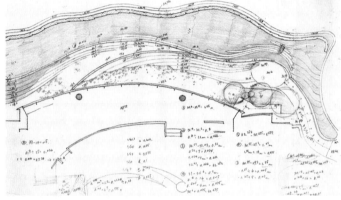

Garden for Cerulean Tower

TOKYO 2001

This narrow garden of steep terraces encircles the sunken lobby of a hotel and completely dominates the interior. Shunmyo says that he wanted to create the traditional sense of interior melding with exterior in Japanese domestic design, though as with all of Shunmyo's work, he manages to update the concept so that it seems stridently contemporary. 'The famous gardens of Kyoto are beautiful,' Shunmyo has stated, 'but it won't do to simply copy them and paste them onto modern urban spaces.' Here, a simple palette of materials has been used: grey stones and curved stone slabs to define the terraces, creating an almost marine feeling of movement and a glamorous and stylish environment for hotel guests.

Metagardens London

Organically morphing and growing garden
and building structures.

Fernando Gonzalez's Metagardens is the youngest landscape
company to be profiled in this book. A Spaniard based in
London since 2000, Gonzalez graduated in garden design at
the University of Greenwich in 2005. To date Metagardens'
work exists in plan only, as a series of exciting computer
graphics illustrations. But that does not make the work any
less relevant in a conceptual sense: even if these designs
are never realized in actuality, the ideas base behind them
will remain useful and relevant. As this book goes to press,
Gonzalez has won through the competition stage of both
the 2008 Jardins de Métis Festival in Quebec and the
conceptual gardens section of the 2008 Hampton Court
Flower Show. So the work is, in fact, about to transcend
the virtual sphere.

The Metagardens method is to create computer-
generated garden plans, which respond to unpredictable
criteria based on the vagaries of nature and the amorphous
fecundity of the botanical world. The resulting designs
have uncontrollable, bacterial qualities, while at the same
time existing solely as products of man-made technology.
Thus at all levels they combine elements of both wild
nature and the very latest technology. Gonzalez refers
to 'the challenges established by the digital age, when
the boundaries between the artificial and the organic
are more blurred than ever before'.

Typically Gonzalez will put objects or existing plans into
transformative programmes, see what comes out, and then
layer the result on the roof of a skyscraper, a suburban

LEFT This project, claims Gonzales, is 'a step forward into the evolution of gardens'. A machine is created using a biodegradable plastic skin attached to a steel skeleton, in which any kind of exotic or unusual plant can be grown. EvoTerrarium, 2006.

OPPOSITE Using a parasitic protozoa as its model, this installation 'infects' and transforms its 'host', the roof of the building to which it is attached. Parasitus Imperator, 2006.

back garden, or some other space which apparently needs improving by means of avant-garde design. It is Gonzalez's contention that 'our cybernetic culture' renders a romantic or pastoralist attitude towards nature, and our artificial evocations of it, even more inappropriate than ever. 'We live in a post-human environment,' he claims, 'where the relationship between the biological and the machine, the born and the made, is more of a symbiosis than a contradiction. The cyborg, genetics and cyberspace, among others, are our current symbols.'

Such cyborgian sentiments may be familiar to the point of cliché in the early 21st century, but Metagardens' mode of expression is refreshing. The Parasitus Imperator project

(see opposite), for example, typifies Gonzalez's preoccupation with concepts of mutation and biological spread. The specified location for this parasitical landscape is 'any skyscraper', and the idea is that the roof garden will infect and transform the habitually dull roofscapes of such buildings: 'Parasitus Imperator acts as a catalyst which injects life, sensuality and richness, exploiting weakness and opportunities. The rooftop is colonized through a skin made of red Corian panels and warm-coloured timber, all computer-cut, that provides a path and a terrace through the movement of the grasses and waterlilies. The planting plan is completed with architectural cordylines encapsulated in pods hanging outside the walls.'

Aerial

SPECULATIVE DESIGN, 2005

Metagardens' contention here is that roof gardens are generally characterized as a collection of plants in 'an enclosed and static orthogonal space'. For this design, Gonzalez utilized a computer technique known as a 'displacement map', which creates a bumpy texture on a previously flat surface, as extrapolated from the texture of a real artefact – in this case, a piece of wood.

Gonzalez states that it is the 'dynamic characteristics' of wood that made it appropriate as a textural starting point: 'It arrives at its final shape through an expansion and contraction process due to changes in humidity and temperature, creating a porous and permeable material.'

The resultant textural model provides the basis for an extension of the roofspace over the building's lip, a soft skin made of fibreglass panels which acts as the framework for a display of architectural plants.

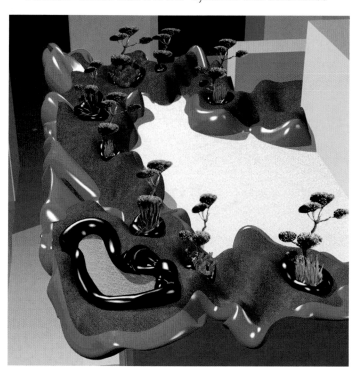

Shime-Nawa

COMPETITION ENTRY (JAPAN) 2005

The title of this work, an entry for a competition in Japan, is a term which refers to the rope delimiting a sacred area or holy object in a Shinto temple. The design itself is a dynamic computer-assisted exposition of the celebrated Ryoan-ji garden of rocks and grey gravel in Kyoto. The dynamic geometric shapes refer to the power contained within the sculptural objects (principally the fifteen carefully placed rocks) within the garden's rectangle.

Gonzalez points out that in Shinto philosophy the inanimate objects used in garden design – the rocks, ropes, gravel and water – are in fact believed to be the residence of the gods, and are thus possessed of great power or 'gravity'. Gonzalez explains that his virtual space 'is composed of ten force lines affected by the different gravity forces represented by the virtual stones. After running several dynamic animations, the outcome is a fluid and flexible garden where stones made of red fabric and black fibreglass ropes interact with the solemnity of cypresses and the movement of sago palms.'

Meyer + Silberberg Berkeley (USA)

Elegant, understated Modernism with unexpected conceptual twists.

David Meyer and Ramsey Silberberg have an impeccable pedigree as landscape conceptualists: both worked at Peter Walker and Partners in the mid 1990s, with Meyer also partnering Martha Schwartz (p. 256) and Ken Smith (p. 284) for a brief but frenetically fruitful period (1990–93). However, since joining forces as Meyer + Silberberg in 2001, the pair have sought to place some distance between their own work and the more exuberant style of Schwartz, et al. They say that theirs is a more relaxed take on the ideology of conceptualism, defined by a self-conscious seriousness and a certain solidity in the work. They do detail, certainly, but their work is never ornamented and never frivolous.

Meyer states: 'When Pete and Martha joined forces in the mid-1980s, that was an exciting time. What is interesting

for us now is that there is a counter to doing things Pop for the sake of doing it Pop.' (This can be interpreted as a 'pop' at Schwartz.) 'I feel differently today than I did when I was working with Martha,' he continues. 'The use of materials in a creative way was interesting, but it's not the main drive in finding what's beautiful about an area. Personally, I like elegance and simplicity.'

Both Meyer and Silberberg place great emphasis on the experiential rather than the pictorial aspects of landscape. They explore the use of light, space and progression as a means of influencing the emotions of the user. 'We try to absorb the atmosphere of the place,' Silberberg says. 'It all depends on the site. We have more urban sites than anything, and those historical ideas are always in there. We look at a place and try to decide what is special about it.'

Overall, then, Meyer and Silberberg have not allowed the Modernist precepts which have shaped their development in the late 20th century to be over-compromised, as they would see it, by modish conceptualist ideas. Meyer praises the process of editing as a key aspect of design, and decries landscapes which are 'overstuffed with narrative'. Silberberg points out that they both grew up in very simple agricultural landscapes, Meyer in Iowa ('a sensual landscape characterized by change and geometry') and herself in New England. 'The beauty of those places impacts on our sensibilities,' she says. 'A lot of designers try to redo the landscape of their childhood in their work. In a way, it is about revisiting the sensibility of childhood.'

LEFT During his scholarship year at the American Academy in Rome, Meyer created an installation from hundreds of tiny cypress cuttings, taken from cemeteries throughout Tuscany. Based on the concept of a memorial, the design referred to a missing cypress in the courtyard of the Academy. Cypress Vigil, Rome 2001.

Limelight

GLOUCESTERSHIRE (UK) 2003

This popular installation at the Westonbirt Festival was comprised of nothing more than an existing tree and a sculpted earthwork surrounding it. The designers allowed the tree simply to be a tree, a near-perfect conceptualist statement. 'We were able to pull off our philosophy here in a very powerful way,' Meyer says. 'When I looked at some of the other gardens [at Westonbirt], I could see they were pulling every trick in the book.' Silberberg adds: 'It's the difference between creating as opposed to decorating a space. We tend to work very elementally at the initial stages of design.' Meyer: 'Limelight allows natural elements to speak for themselves – it's a celebration of a tree' (in this case, a humble sycamore). Envisaging the space 'remotely' from the US, the designers initially drew out idealized versions of trees and then hit upon the idea of the earthen medallion around it – an encircling amphitheatre.

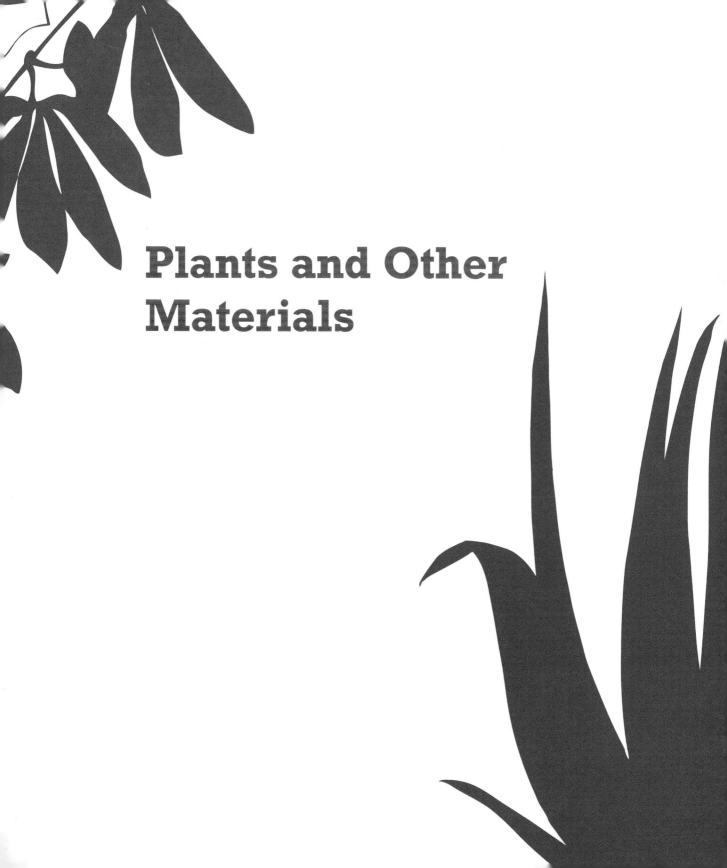

Plants and Other Materials

The use of unusual, innovative and frequently highly artificial-looking materials is one of the hallmarks of landscape conceptualism. It plays into the questioning of nature and our responses to it, which is one of the main preoccupations of conceptualist designers. However, it would be wrong to suggest that these designers as a generality do not exhibit enthusiasm for plants and their potential, or display a knowledge of them gained through long experience. Indeed, the juxtaposition of living plants with plastics and other materials is one of the most fruitful tensions in the work of a number of landscape designers in the conceptualist vein.

But there is a fairly sharp divide between those who regard plants as just one more material to use in landscape and garden spaces and those for whom plants mean much more, both theoretically and emotionally. It has to be said that a proportion of the designers featured here have no meaningful relationship with plants, and that some of them actively resent the elevated role of horticulture in the history of garden and landscape design. As with the attitude of designers to nature in general, the relative belligerence of such an attitude is no indication of the value or quality of their design work – it is just one of those elements which adds individuality to a signature look or tone. Conceptualist designers' relationships with plants do indeed tend to be highly personal, and it is impossible to make useful generalizations. Perhaps it would be best to look at a few individual cases in order to provide a sense of the range of opinion on this topic.

William Martin is unique among the designers in this book because his contribution has been confined to his own private garden, Wigandia, in Victoria.

His approach to horticulture is conceptual because it is a constituent part of his attempt to create a new (and partly satirical) garden vernacular for Australia, which also utilizes recycled industrial and agricultural detritus such as corrugated iron sheets and black plastic piping. In some ways, his horticultural observations appear quite conventional – the use of a 'layering' technique in plantings, or the 'obsession' with pairs of identical plants – but ultimately this is a case of a private gardener creating much more than a 'garden' as it is usually understood. The approach bears comparison with that of Derek Jarman at his seaside garden in Dungeness, a scheme which is not illustrated here simply because it is already so well known and has been widely published (Ian Hamilton Finlay's Little Sparta in Scotland is excluded for the same reason). These are gardens in which plants play an important conceptual role by creating allusion, providing orientation and combining to produce mood or atmosphere.

This engagement with plant material is most evident among conceptualist designers in Britain, where the horticultural tradition is more or less unavoidable and any talk of gardens that excludes serious consideration of plants is almost unthinkable. Brita von Schoenaich – a German designer domiciled in Britain – shows a deep understanding of plants and their capabilities in her conceptualist work, but projects such as the annual planting schemes for Tate Britain, where she has used a random dice-throwing generator for plant selection, also display an iconoclastic impulse towards horticultural method and the traditions of border design which remain so strong in Britain. The sculptor Julia Barton has made the technical and scientific properties of

living plants both her subject matter and primary material, as with her current experiments on the capillary function of plant stems and how that might be evoked through design. 'Horticultural installation artist' Tony Heywood is actually a head gardener as his 'day job', with a team of gardeners answering to him at several private housing blocks in central London. Heywood has repurposed his professional horticultural knowledge to artistic ends, using diverse and often fantastical living plant material to create a new and personal language that makes reference to culture and nature, and where the two might intersect in imagination and reality.

Away from Britain, it seems all the more remarkable that designers with a conceptualist attitude should exhibit a predilection for plants, which always demand a certain technical proficiency and often require maintenance in the future. Topher Delaney of San Francisco is perhaps the designer who holds conceptualist thinking and horticultural aptitude in the most fruitful balance. In a Delaney garden design, it is difficult to perceive any fundamental difference in attitude towards plants and other materials, in that they are used for spatial effects and to create meaning even while they may also be playing a relatively conventional decorative role. A Delaney garden gives the lie to the notion that conceptualism is only for people who don't like plants.

The Dutch designer Lodewijk Baljon is unusually strident among conceptualists in his insistence on the value of plant material: 'Contact with plant material is the basis of landscape architecture,' he says. 'You have to be confident using soft and tender green materials.' Key features of Baljon's work include plantings of roses with grasses intermixed, and fruit trees: 'If there is an

opportunity I try to create an orchard, whether it is a private garden, a public park or an office building. As well as the fruit there is an abundance of flowers, good autumn colour (if you choose well), and in a small garden you can introduce a sense of rhythm.' New York-based Paula Hayes calls her landscape design work 'large-scale ikebana', in that she reuses techniques learned in her career as a sculptor. Hayes's attitude to plants is original and engaging because it simultaneously displays both intimacy and distance: the intimacy with plantlife which led her to create 'Plant Packs' – urban backpacks containing plants designed to soothe and 'heal' city-dwellers as they went about their business; and distance, in the way she perceives massed plantings as essentially sculptural moves.

'Eco' is a vexed question among many conceptualists (see the essay on 'Nature'). Wolfgang Betz of WES & Partner, for example, states unequivocally: 'Let's forget green. We are working with spaces and we have to create strong concepts which have real clarity but at the same time allow for some ambiguity . . . We work in cities and we work with spaces, not landscapes.' Some conceptualist designers have developed a meaningful relationship with plant material, however, which cannot simply be bracketed with the ecological opportunism occurring now in mainstream landscape architecture.

Australia's Taylor Cullity Lethlean consistently use native or local plants in their design, especially cycads, lily-like dionellas, kangaroo paws and banksias, as well as trees such as eucalyptus (particularly the lemon-scented gum), paper-barks (malalucca) and the angophora, or apple gum. These plants are not arrayed in imitation of wild habitats, but rather used to bolster the

conceptualist scheme. Since so many of TCL's designs are 'about' Australia and
its natural landscape, this usage seems highly appropriate in context. Antonio
Perazzi is a conceptualist who has made native or wild plants the mainstay of
his work; he generally eschews hard landscaping in favour of plantscapes.
'I am interested in the relationship between plants and man,' he states.
'I consider myself more a plantsman than a designer – in Italy everyone is
a designer!' Perazzi's work is poised at that moment where plants and humans
meet, and several of his designs illustrate the way the man-made world can
easily be overrun by the fecundity of nature.

But it is this very man-made world which most often provides inspiration
for conceptualist designers, who habitually utilize a thrillingly exuberant and
vivid array of artificial materials in their landscape design. Artificial turf, mist
machines, painted logs, glass gravel, Styrofoam, stamped concrete forms,
moulded plastic objects, multicoloured Plexiglas, steel boxes, kitschy
ornaments, found objects, industrial materials, clothing . . . When it comes to
materials, anything goes in conceptualism. Plastics in particular have been used
widely. These materials may be perceived as unusual, funny or subversive, but
conceptualists argue that it does not make them any less 'authentic' than natural
materials, particularly in an urban setting. As Claude Cormier remarked of one
his most exuberant projects, 'It is all about this notion of something that is
artificial, but not false.' Indeed, it is possible to formulate a practical rationale
for experimentation with new materials. This is something Paul Cooper has
done. 'The challenge of the urban environment,' he says, 'with its lack of ground
space, has persuaded me to employ materials and methods of construction not

traditionally associated with the garden.' Cooper's gardens represent a response to contemporary lifestyle including, 'twenty-four hour gardens' with specialist lighting and theatrical effects. Among the epithets he uses to describe his work are 'instant', 'portable', 'reusable', 'multi-storey' and 'prefabricated'.

Familiar everyday objects can be given a surreal twist through enlargement, miniaturization or re-colouring. This appropriation of familiar objects can be traced back to Marcel Duchamp's use of found objects, and it therefore represents one specific intersection with conceptual art. An example of this in landscape design is the way designers use a familiar vocabulary, such as items of street furniture (bollards, zebra crossings, streetlights), and then enlarge and colour them to make them both part of the design and more practical. It is important to note that such artefacts are not 'sculptures' – conceptualist gardens are always weaker when built around a single sculptural artefact.

There is also a consistent use of pattern in conceptualist work. This is derived from a sense among many designers that on one level garden and landscape design is all about taming the chaos of nature, and large-scale pattern is one way of achieving that. An insistent, repetitive, rhythmic visual sequence is a thread that runs through much conceptualist work, though never in the pristinely geometric manner of architectural Modernism. It is notable how many conceptualist designs have some kind of linear grid sequence (perhaps formed by wooden strips) underpinning them, and the use of sinuous ribbon shapes is also prevalent. Such grids and patterns are generally disrupted in some way, as part of the narrative of the designed space. Optical illusion is

another useful tactic adopted by conceptualists, as well as partial views created by holes pierced in walls or screens, or coloured materials that alter vistas.

Water and fog is often a key component in conceptualist gardens and can be used in all kinds of ways, including as a method of constructing a linear narrative through space (as in Herbert Dreiseitl's work, where the watercourse often tells a story). Generally water is used in horizontal situations and the cliché of vertical fountains is avoided. However, it must be said that for technical and practical reasons conceptualist designers have been less innovative and exploratory in the use of water than in other areas; the mist machine is an overused feature, as is the sequentially programmed multiple fountain that spurts straight from the ground to the delight of children.

Scientific and cosmological theories have become a subject for conceptualist garden designers, and this often results in gardens that are less symbolic in tone, but more like demonstration gardens. Charles Jencks's 'Garden of Cosmic Speculation' is a case in point, being more literal than conceptual. It does thrillingly showcase the possibilities of land form, however, something which has been used in an exceptionally expressive way by conceptualist designers, and has also proved a particularly attractive 'entrance' into the landscape milieu for architects. But the use of shaped grass berms is now so commonplace as to be almost a cliché itself, and specifically redolent of the 1990s.

It is colour, above all, which materially distinguishes conceptualist landscape architecture from the mainstream, an emphasis that is to some extent a legacy of Pop Art. There is a feeling among many conceptualist designers that

contemporary society is colour-phobic. The use of bright artificial colours –
particularly greens, pinks, yellows, blues and reds – sets many conceptualists
apart from designers working in a Modernistic vein, for whom a palette of
tasteful greys and beiges is de rigueur. This is to some extent a legacy of Pop
Art. The attitude to colour can even be used as a kind of gauge – a way of
seeing how close to Conceptualism or Modernism a designer is. The best
conceptualist designers never use colour in a cavalier way, however. The
attitude of Maike van Stiphout of DS Landschapsarchitecten is revealing in
this context: 'We use a lot of colour,' she explains, 'but not a lot of colours, so
you never get this fantasy-land look. It remains abstract in that sense, although
it is all part of giving the piece meaning.'

Plants and other materials – their choice and disposition – are one way of
distinguishing conceptualist landscape design from the mainstream, but they
are not its defining feature. Materials are used as part of the designer's overall
effort to enrich and specify the start and end point of the space: the concept itself.

Helle Nebelong

Gentofte (Denmark)

Environmentally ordered children's playground design.

The Copenhagen-based designer is best known for her revolutionary approach to children's playground design, which – like all such design – is intended to set free the imaginations of young users. In this case, however, this is not to be achieved through the use of a plethora of brightly coloured, artificial-looking and often expensive play equipment. Nebelong believes this will always to some extent prescribe (and proscribe) the children's play themes, so she uses as much of the natural surroundings of the park or playground as possible. A Nebelong playground appears to merge with its surroundings, or even grow out of it, and there is no sense that the children have been fenced off from the rest of the park or public space (ostensibly for their safety). In fact, she claims that there is no fundamental difference between designing for children and for adults. Unusually – if not uniquely – Nebelong takes into account the importance of socializing among children of all ages in playgrounds. 'You have to design a space where they can meet each other,' she says.

'I don't use standardized equipment,' she continues. 'I make a design that fits the location. I try to find the spirit of the place, and what kind of children are living there. Children like to play in natural surroundings where they can create spaces themselves. They are not so interested in using equipment which has just one use or appearance. It is possible to design something where they are able to use their imagination and creativity. They need a sense of an opportunity to play "free", to be less controlled by adults.'

Nebelong recalls being exhorted to work in a more architectural manner during her training in landscape architecture, and resisting that approach. (Ironically, it was a Dane, Carl Theodor Sørenson, who pioneered a new attitude to children's playground design in the mid-20th

century.) Her earliest projects were sensory gardens for multi-handicapped children, which of course depended on means other than structure. 'These really influenced me,' she recalls. 'The children didn't demand much, in a way – the little things were the miracles.'

There is also a social mission underpinning Nebelong's attitude, a feeling that a feel for nature is intrinsically good. 'You have to make beautiful, aesthetic spaces for children

LEFT AND OPPOSITE Nebelong responded to the brief for an imaginative space by creating a children's playground of multi-levels, places for hiding and asphalt surfaces for games, along with sand, tiles, paths and uneven stones, forest floor, woodchips and gravel. The result, Nebelong says, is 'a little oasis with organically shaped planting', complementing the monumental presence of the surrounding buildings. Murergården, Copenhagen 1996.

because it will make them into better people,' she suggests, echoing the paternalistic ideals of city planners in Victorian Britain, now updated in the contemporary mantra of 'designing out crime' by means of public space. 'Public spaces are not about escape but about encouraging people to come back to themselves,' she says. 'I like the city and urban life, but you don't have to identify public spaces as only urban.'

Nebelong does not suggest that her unique approach is a model which might be rolled out across the majority of playgrounds – as ever in this sphere, variety is of paramount importance, particularly in urban areas where children and parents can often exercise a choice over which play areas they might visit.

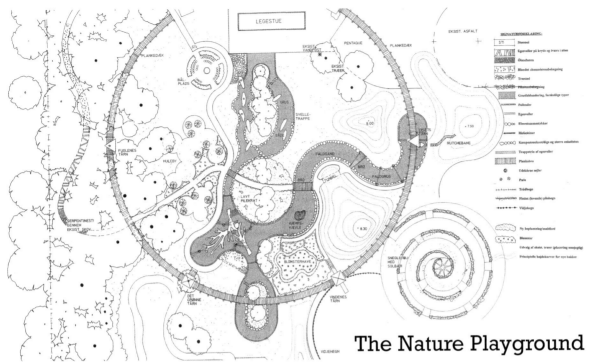

The Nature Playground

VALBYPARKEN (DENMARK) 2006

The primary materials used for this large park were the recycled tree trunks of dead elms from the city streets and grass seed. Otherwise, Nebelong depended on the existing landscape and woodland, which is enlivened by small hills. 'In Denmark there aren't many hills and no mountains at all. To the toddlers, these hills are like big mountains!'

The wood from the elms was used to create walkways, while whole tree trunks were reused to create natural climbing apparatus, the branches of each one presenting a unique challenge. Meanwhile, the grasses have now grown up to create mysterious pathways, hiding places and areas for camp-making.

Another part of the brief was to make 'unique play towers'. A series of these was designed by students from the Danish design school, on the theme of nature. Conceived as sculpture rather than as 'play equipment', these structures exist at the very fringes of health-and-safety requirements, and are all the more popular for it.

Helle Nebelong **213**

Ålhom School

COPENHAGEN 1998

This design for a school playground for seven- to sixteen-year-olds is all the more successful for not being stuffed with features. Indeed, at first glance it does not look like a children's playground at all, but a public space designed for adults along abstract minimalist lines, somewhat reminiscent of the work of the Californian Modernist Dan Kiley.

Nebelong took her creative cue from the children's love of a sculpture of a lion drinking from a trough, the only feature to be retained from the existing playground design. 'The head teacher wanted it taken out, but the children loved it,' Nebelong recalls. Referring to the grid of plane trees, she explains: 'I was thinking of the lion courtyard at the Alhambra.' Each class planted its own tree.

Simple, geometric blocks of stone set in gravel create an abstract setting, with swirling serpentine paths linking the different spaces of the play area. The circular asphalt mound represents a 'blue island in a big ocean'. Nebelong

adds, 'I didn't want to fill up the space with lots of colours.'
The stump of an old, multi-stemmed tree has proved
inexhaustible as a source of play opportunities, while
Nebelong has also been careful to provide a variety of
tone in the space. 'There are many places just to sit,'
she explains. 'Children don't just "play". They like to sit
and watch and talk.'

Nip Paysage   Montreal

Delicate and cheeky park and
garden design.

Nip Paysage are five young landscape architects who
met at the University of Montreal in 2001: Michel Langevin,
France Cormier, Josée Labelle, Mélanie Mignault and
Mathieu Casavant. All of them had gained experience in
Boston as interns in the offices of either Martha Schwartz
(p. 256) or George Hargreaves (and in Langevin and
Mignault's case, both). This makes the young team unusual
among conceptualist designers in the sense that they have
been schooled in a conceptual approach through the 1990s,
instead of coming by way of the Modernist inheritance.
Langevin talks of 'a new spirit of landscape' and
acknowledges Claude Cormier (p. 70) as the pioneer of
the movement in Quebec, a region which has emerged as
a hotbed of this kind of work. The annual garden festival
at the Jardins de Métis has played an important role as a
catalyst for conceptualist landscape work in the region,
encouraging local designers as well as attracting big
international names. Montreal is emerging as a place
that is beginning to be defined by conceptualist landscape
design by a variety of companies, in a way unmatched by
any other major city worldwide. The 'Montreal School' is
represented in this book by Cormier and Atelier Big City
(p. 10), as well as Nip Paysage, but there are other, newer
outfits developing in the creative atmosphere fostered by
the city's universities and institutions, including the Centre
Canadien d'Architecture (CCA).

BELOW For a comedy festival, large 'boxes' (wrapped scaffolding)
were sited along the two main thoroughfares: green boxes containing
natural materials, and red ones that used such objects as protruding
shop-dummy legs. Just For Laughs, Montreal 2006.

This lack of aesthetic 'baggage' has perhaps freed up these designers, creatively and emotionally. Nip Paysage's themed environments are often playful and amusing in tone, which makes their work genuinely popular with the public, as evinced by such several projects as Pause (see above) and Virage Vert (see p. 221) in public spaces in Montreal. Another possible reflection of their relative youth and educational generation is the way Nip Paysage displays a genuine engagement with ecological issues. Anyone who went to school in the 1990s could hardly emerge without some sense of impending ecological disaster, and Nip Paysage display none of the belligerence towards nature and natural forms which can be a driver to creativity among a (slightly) older generation of conceptualist designers.

ABOVE This installation consisted of four giant (3.5m) Adirondack chairs in a public park, near a Metro station. Langevin explains: 'It's very busy, with people going to work or shopping. We were trying to say it's OK to stop and sit down.' Pause, Montreal 2005.

Unity Garden

MONTREAL 2006

The Unity apartment development in downtown Montreal consists of two buildings: an old factory and a new aluminium construction. The brief was to create 'unity' by means of a courtyard linking the two. As is often the case with such schemes, the courtyard is built on top of an underground parking facility, so planting and weight had to be kept to a minimum. Langevin and his colleagues often turn to natural materials instead of concrete, plastic or asphalt, and in this case they opted for large expanses of

Canadian cedar decking to create an exterior 'dance floor' or terrace. 'We said, "Let's do something more homey, using wood",' Langevin recalls. The conceptual element is always there, however – in this case, in the way the angles of the wooden planks continue the lines of the building's footprint. 'We took the grid of the building and extended it so that the buildings could "meet" in the middle,' Langevin explains. The rock-filled gabions are described as the stone filling of a sandwich in which the wood is the bread.

In Vitro

MONTREAL 2001

This was Nip Paysage's first collaborative project, for the Jardins de Métis festival. 'It is about the forest, culturally – what it means now (a source of timber) and what it was,' Langevin says. 'It is about conservation and the genetic code of the pine cone.' This genetic code is buried in the colour sequence of the jars.

A statement from Nip Paysage reads: 'Fundamentally, the forest fulfils three roles: cultural reference, industrial resource and leisure space. Questioning the aesthetics and mythological aspects of forestry, the garden exhibits, in the foreground, a nomadic spruce façade growing out of blue barrels. A linear wood floor runs through the site and is crossed by blue plastic woodchip veins, on which are installed metal structures. Each steel frame is lined with enigmatic jars. The numerous transparent jars are filled with "spruce gum" and "pine cone jam", simultaneously provoking aesthetic pleasure and question: hasn't the contemporary forest transformed itself into a laboratory, a factory, a supermarket, a museum or a leisure centre? Finally, the ground plane recalls the drama of deforestation and burning of woody matter. Metaphorically, the carbonized zone is transformed into playground, scattered with giant transgenic blueberries used for sitting and bouncing around.'

The fact that this looks like a scorched garden, with the laboratory references defining the space, makes this an effective critique of contemporary ecological malaises achieved in conceptualist spirit.

Virage Vert

MONTREAL 2006

This popular installation consisted of predominantly green plants (among them sweet potatoes, irises, Nicotiana and ornamental grasses), crushed green recycled rubber underfoot and hundreds of small green balls, each inscribed with the name of one of the plants. Nip Paysage describe this as 'a green chiaroscuro of colours, plantings and textures'. In the centre of the garden is a quiet space, where park users can sit on large green balls.

Antonio Perazzi Milan

Sensuous planting design with conceptualist underpinnings.

After studying architecture and landscape in Milan, Antonio Perazzi travelled to Kew in 1991 to take part in a summer school taught by John Brookes. 'In Italy we tend to focus on history and analysis,' he says,' but we don't have much training in how to do the projects professionally. I learned so much.' On his return, Perazzi began a long-term collaboration with a leading architectural firm. His own practice grew, fulfilling a range of private and public commissions – mainly in central Italy – and he branched out into landscaping projects around five power stations for ANL, which was then Italy's public energy company.

Perazzi is highly unusual among conceptualist designers in that his focus is unequivocally on the plants: he uses relatively little hard landscaping or non-organic material to create the structure of his designs. Plants are used naturalistically, in large drifts which often incorporate grasses, ramblers or ground cover, and Perazzi particularly favours local species which might be growing wild nearby. 'I had one project where I used a lovely rose,' he recalls, 'and the client said, "Oh, it is so delicate – does it come from Japan?" I said, "No, it comes from that woodland at the back of your garden over there." The Italians do not appreciate the force of the wild Mediterranean plants.' Perazzi often uses a linear or grid-like pattern to underpin his designs, but he always allows it to be visibly disrupted and compromised by the plant-life.

'I am interested in the relationship between plants and man,' he says. His work is poised at that moment where plants and humans meet, and his designs often illustrate the way the man-made world can easily be overrun by the fecundity of nature. From this basic premise, Perazzi creates more nuanced meanings in each work, illustrating the way that nature can surprise, delight or even threaten us. This ecological–conceptual standpoint is unusual among Italian garden designers. 'I consider myself more a plantsman than a designer – in Italy everyone is a designer!' Perazzi claims. 'They want to be avant-garde in terms of the latest fashion, but no one cares very much about their own style.'

LEFT The underlying concept for this show garden at the Jardins de Métis festival was that the blue flowers it contained were a message of hope and reconciliation, an idea inspired by the French Surrealist Raymond Queneau's 1965 book, *Les Fleurs bleues*. The vivid blue meconopsis is also the signature flower of the gardens at Métis. The surrounding 'gravel' is in fact made of cherry stones. Bleu de Bois, Montreal 2003.

Riviera Golf Club

SAN GIOVANNI IN MARIGNANO (ITALY) 2004

The landscape design of a new luxury golf club resort near Rimini was a massive project which had to be completed extremely quickly: 'I was designing it while we were building it,' Perazzi recalls. The stock of entire nurseries was bought up as Perazzi sought to create a sense of place, using, for example, a million narcissus bulbs to line the entrance drive and some 100,000 small, fruitless and fast-growing olive trees to create hedges. The central building, ringed with distinctive blue terracotta tubes, was encircled by a 'border' of *Stipa tenuissima*, *Vitis vinifera* 'Purpurea' and yucca, followed by sections of lavender, rosemary, perovskia, santolina and teucrium. Another challenge was the creation of thirty-two gardens connected to apartment suites, each of which had to be different. Perazzi achieved his effects through plants alone – a 'red' garden, for example, or a scented space, or one defined by variegated leaves – with the fruitless olives forming a dense, uniform hedge to the front, to make each garden space a surprise.

Plant Toronto

Rehabilitation of difficult sites through 'experiential design'.

Lisa Rapoport, Mary Tremain and Chris Pommer first met as undergraduates studying architecture at the University of Waterloo. In 1995, they formed the multidisciplinary outfit Plant, its name a reference both to botanical forms and to the industrial idea of a 'plant' as a place where things are made. The office remains small (just seven-strong), but over the past decade they have realized a wide variety of commissions, from private gardens to interiors to graphic-design projects. 'We all do a bit of everything,' Tremain explains. All three partners teach design studios at the University of Toronto, and perhaps as a result they are not averse to making theoretical declarations. However, the statement 'The practice is best known for creating work that resolves difficult site conditions or highlights conditions that might otherwise be overlooked' is justifiable enough. Another useful description of their method is 'experiential'; that is, they respond to the garden space intuitively and spontaneously, and try to honour that feeling, which can mean leaving sections of the site alone.

Most garden- and landscape-design outfits with a conceptual leaning like to arrive at a site and then remake it completely – in so doing making reference to the history, ecology and function of the space. Plant is unusual in that the designers seek to enhance the existing characteristics of the space either by leaving them alone or by intervening in a gentler way, so that the original character of the place can be discerned beneath the layer of their involvement. This approach takes a certain confidence, and the designers make reference to the tradition of Land Art in this respect (particularly in its 1960s and 1970s American incarnation: Robert Smithson, et al) because they are happy to allow the artefacts and decorative elements in their gardens to stand alone as statements in their own right.

This can lend their designs a certain disparate quality – a sense they have been bolted together on some level – but Rapoport argues that this does not necessarily lead to a sense of confusion or disunity: 'The work itself is very discursive, like a conversation, both between the elements on the site visually, and between us in the office.' Tremain points up the functional rigour which underpins their work and helps secure a client base: 'It's really a sense of lifestyle. We want people to be able to live in these places.'

A contrast in materials, often founded in the less interventionist stance of the designers, is a recurring theme in Plant's work. Typically the lavish use of wood,

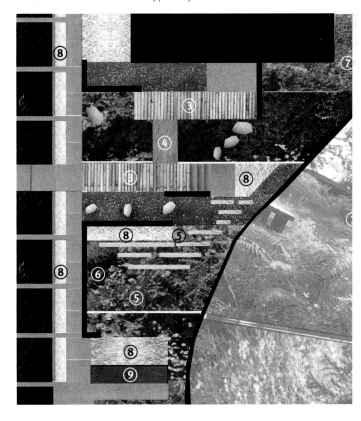

often laid in horizontal slats or boards, is set against metallic finishes or smooth stone. The designers' interest in what they term 'the cultural aspects of waste, domesticity, industry and agriculture' can result in a tension between smoother or more obviously designed areas and a roughly rustic or industrial feel adjacent. This sensibility follows through to the ground plan, where strident geometric motifs abut organic or natural forms. As Tremain says approvingly of one project: 'It's not slick.'

In their design, Plant rail against the classic Modernist garden move of a deck right outside the rear of the house, which floats a foot above an unadorned yard just beyond. 'Decks often make people feel exposed – or so our clients say,' Rapoport explains. 'So we take away that deck and reintegrate the back of the house with the garden. In fact, we often site our dining areas at the far end of the garden.'

LEFT AND OPPOSITE This landscape for a six-unit apartment building marries a linear design to a native woodland garden. Alternating stone and wood bridges, lit from below, float above the plants and are punctuated by concrete walls and large boulders. The planting is arranged in strips, woven like a quilt. Ravine Forecourt, Forest Hill, Toronto 2006.

Cabbagetown Garden

TORONTO 2005

At Cabbagetown, the client's main request was for a dining area that afforded some privacy in a seriously overlooked residential garden, 6m wide by 21m long. Accordingly, Plant made a terrace at the top of a gentle slope at the far end of the garden, reached via a shiny metal staircase which was intended to 'float' above a sea of waving perennial plants arrayed in height-graded horizontal bands, producing what Rapoport describes as 'this amazing experience of walking through plants'.

Tremain adds: 'The symmetry came from the [Modernist] house and the site. We did two schemes, one geometrical and one meandering, and we chose this one because of its simplicity.' Height and structure in the planting is provided by three varieties of oak-leaved hydrangeas and ribbons of alliums and staked clematis. Massed perennials – mainly pink- and white-flowered – include artemisia, Japanese anemones, astilbes, speedwell, perovskia and cimicifuga, while ground cover is provided by creeping ivy, phlox and campanula.

Plant's trademark use of contrasting materials can be seen here, particularly in details such as the use of old fencing and stained cedarwood boards for the walls of the garden. And the reuse of the old bricks within the gabions reflects the theme of the recycling of existing material. 'It's new but old,' Rapoport says.

Ravine Garden

MONTREAL 2005

This garden is sited to the rear of a typical city lot, but is unusual in that it borders a steep ravine slope on one side and a large municipal park on the other. The garden was already shady because of three existing ailanthus trees, and seven more native trees have been planted to ensure this will continue to be shady long into the future. The planting selections were guided by ecological precepts: that the plants should be native, and chosen to form a natural woodland community which could perform an aesthetic construct as much as a restoration.

Making trees the centrepiece of the planting scheme is the foundation of the slope stabilization strategy, provides year-round interest, shade for the garden and south-facing windows, and transforms the upper floors of the house into tree house-like rooms. By creating outdoor rooms, the ground-floor living area has increased by 30 per cent. The textured bark and tall perennials provide a foreground, and the aluminium stair and frame to the ravine invite the long view. Flowering dogwoods provide vibrant spring colour as a foamflower and fern carpet unfurls on the ground. Throughout the summer, clusters of vivid perennials shoot colour from the mottled ground cover. The rhythmic vertical fencing modulates transparencies, and will support a variety of climbers.

The project overlays industrial materials onto heavily planted areas to highlight material contrasts: the reflective aluminium stairs hover over a dark, green fern bed; galvanized re-bars support the scrambling of downy clematis; and the painted steel frame provides a sharp edge through which to see the ravine foliage.

Philippe Rahm   Paris and Lausanne (Switzerland)

Theoretical explorations of the conceptualist
landscape through thermal modelling.

'As an architect I work in the language of architecture and
landscape, but also with temperature, humidity and light.'
One of the most exciting and innovative architectural
theorists at work today, Philippe Rahm's ideas impact
on landscape quite as much as they do on the built
environment. The idea of manipulating climate, humidity,
light and other supposed constants of the natural world
is key to his work, which can be viewed as almost satirical
in its most extreme incarnations. The subject of this satire
is that familiar trope among conceptualist designers: the
fallacy of an inviolable nature which must be deferred to,
or even worshipped. By advancing the idea that architecture
can create new notions of time or manipulate the seasons,
Rahm emphasizes the essential artifice of landscape
architecture (another core conceptualist idea).

For Rahm, nature might instead be altered or utilized to
create inspiring new spatial and physical experiences which
will have sensual effects on the human body, ultimately
making us feel closer to nature rather than farther away
from it. Taking his lead from Maurice Merleau-Ponty and
other phenomenological thinkers, Rahm posits the body
in its most physical sense as the key to understanding our
relationship with the world, and to that end he endeavours
to create environments that respond to the status of the
human body – as the 'client' of the space – which can also
be altered and manipulated by that person to create the
desired environmental setting.

'The relationship between landscape and architecture
is not just something visual, but is related to the body,' he
explains, 'whether we are naked or whether we are moving
around, for example. The house might respond to that
movement and become like a set of clothes.' There is
no distinction for Rahm in this sense between the indoor
and outdoor environment of a dwelling. It is as if traditional
in-house controls, such as air conditioning or heating
systems, have been extrapolated and enlarged so that the
whole house and its setting become flexible and responsive.
he adds. Rahm is also unusual in that his focus is not on
creating a building and a surrounding garden or landscape
that might function of itself as a beautiful art 'object', a
'house beautiful' – they are simply the means to an end.
It is an apparently uncompromising position which is born
of the integrity of the design philosophy.

LEFT The aim of this project (holiday homes in the French
countryside), according to Rahm, was 'to construct an architecture
for which the climate is in profound relation with the earth and the
subsoil'. Canadian Houses, Vassivière (France) 2005.

House Dilation

CUMBRIA (UK) 2006

This installation at the celebrated Grizedale sculpture trail in England's Lake District aims to 'distort the limit between outdoor and indoor so that the relationship between them is unclear. It is a progression made up of different layers and there is variation between the different elements; the landscape – the forest – is the final "skin" of the house.'

The inspiration for this design came from the French writer George Perec, who considered having his living room in the Latin Quarter, his study near the Champs-Élysées, his bedroom in Montmartre and his bathroom on the Île de la Cité. 'The idea,' Rahm explains, 'is that that an apartment can be disseminated throughout the city of Paris, finding the rooms in various places, according to hours of the day, to the environment of the district, to the desires of the moment and the season. The thresholds between two rooms, normally a doorway of a few centimetres thick, dilates then over hundreds of metres.'

This notion has been translated to Grizedale's forest setting, where the landscape becomes the final skin of the dwelling, filtering the light, containing or repelling moisture, heating or cooling, according to the situation and time of day. Three sites have been selected: the meadow, the boundary of field and forest, and the forest itself. Each site is determined by its specific climatic qualities: the light, temperature and humidity created by the trees. According to the hour and season, the interior quality of the rooms will vary. Activity in each dilation will relate to the particular and required climate: the heat of the night forest, the warmth of the field in the winter during the day, the freshness of the forest edge in the spring.

Philippe Rahm **231**

Maxims Towards a Conceptualist Attitude to Landscape Design

A landscape that is devoid of meaning is merely an agglomeration of materials.

Materials exist in time; meaning is for all time.

Nature may abhor a physical vacuum – conceptualism abhors an imaginative vacuum.

Landscape designers must be the psychoanalysts of places.

Gardeners
are storytellers.
They should
cultivate their plots.

We already have
alpine gardening, bog
gardening and vegetable
gardening . . . What about
mind gardening?

When we perceive
a landscape or garden,
we do not just see it
'as it is' but as 'how we are'.
We are all co-creators of
the places we experience.

The fallacy of function and
the moral expediency of 'eco':
people need nourishment from
the spaces in which they live;
that nourishment can sometimes
honour emotional and imaginative
needs rather than of 'functional'
or ecological imperatives.

Conceptualism is not vague: it is an evocation and celebration of the piquant and the particular.

It is a commonplace that 'beauty' endows a space with value. This is in part because we experience an intimate reaction with the place during the very process of recognizing beauty. We form a relationship with it. A similar relationship can arise by means of other meaningful emotional or intellectual interactions with spaces, and this too can endow them with equal value.

All landscapes 'speak' to us. What do our towns and cities say as we pass through them? Public spaces are the way a city can interact with its inhabitants – to reassure, to placate, to warn, to embrace, to love.

Don't talk to the plants. Let the garden speak to you.

A garden can be a retreat. Or it can be a strategic withdrawal. It might equally be an attack.

Are we building spaces for birds, bugs and butterflies, or for people? By attempting to heal or atone for our ecological crimes through the (re)creation of 'natural' landscapes, perhaps we are using landscape to punish or satirize humanity for its treatment of the planet. What good are such gestures?

For 'naturalists' and romantics, topiary – the clipping of hedges into shape – is an act of perversion. Perhaps this makes conceptualism – the clipping of ideas into shape – an act of subversion.

Every garden is a political act. Every plant is a political prisoner.

Designers: ask not what you can do for a landscape, ask what the landscape can do for you.

Problems with Plastic #1. We already live in a plastic landscape. What is more, we can bend it, shape it, colour it and even imbue it with meaning and emotion.

Problems with Plastic #2. A hatred of plastic is a hatred of humanity. But plastic is neither better nor worse – morally speaking – than trees, plants, stone and water. It is our own mental processes which accord these elements their meaning and worth.

Problems with Plastic #3. Plastic toys can be more fun than wooden toys. Plastic trees can be more fun than wooden trees.

Vivid colour is not always 'funny'. Vivid colour is not always 'feminine'. In landscape – as in all nature – colour is a source of potent power and can be harnessed, borrowed or wilfully intensified.

What is artificial is true to itself.

If form has to follow function, why not think of function as the ability to delight?

When it comes to strident geometry, if it ain't broke . . . break it.

The world is filled with colour – why excise it from landscape design?

A landscape or garden has no beginning and no end: it flows like fluid into every other corner of the earth, irrigating and mingling with other space flavours. It also flows into the brain, body and personality of every person who experiences it, and is nurtured and enriched by the symbiosis of emotions and ideas between person and place.

It is right to be wary of the power of colour, but that is no reason to relinquish it.

The Victorians believed that well-ordered public spaces make for a well-ordered populace. Can it be that thinking public spaces will make for a populace that thinks?

All architecture and landscape architecture is an effort of will that is doomed to decay and destruction. Only in the realm of landscape is this inevitable fact not only acknowledged but celebrated and ritualized – not simply as 'defiance in the act of construction', but as a recognition of the endless mutability of form, the fallacy of the 'object' in art, and the endless flux and continuum of the universe.

The infinite nature of space, the elasticity
of time and the mystery of consciousness have
proved impossible to comprehend. Yet it has
been believed since Newton that place is
defined by the parameters of space and time,
as experienced through our consciousness.
Aristotle, however, included 'where' as one of the
defining or beginning characteristics of any
object. Perhaps place is not contained within
space and time, but space and time are
circumscribed by place, the cosmic 'where'.
If so, the potential value of landscape as a
commentary on humanity and the cosmos can
be understood. In this sense, a garden is
more than simply a nice place to be.

Eco-mania
=
Ego-mania.

A joke lasts
longer than
an oak.

Going organic:
a symptom
of panic.

RCH Studios   Los Angeles

Exploratory and interdisciplinary conceptual landscape design.

Mark Rios studied at the University of Southern California and then the Graduate School of Design at Harvard. In 1985 he set up in practice in Los Angeles with fellow GSD graduate Charles Pearson, with the intention from the outset of creating an interdisciplinary outfit offering everything from graphics to furniture design to city masterplanning. 'From the very beginning I've wanted to blur the boundaries between the disciplines – you get unexpected synergies,' Rios says. The practice now employs some forty-five people, including Rios's long-standing colleagues, co-partners Julie Smith-Clementi, Frank Clementi and Robert Hale. Julie and Frank have worked with Rios for the past fifteen years, and Robert for five. 'The work gets better as you develop a shorthand with each other,' Rios explains. 'That takes time.'

RCH Studios like to take on projects which allow for such an interdisciplinary approach, so there is often a holistic feel to the work, with interior segueing to exterior seamlessly. There is also a light touch to the design,

perhaps the result of a continual process of experimentation. 'I think our development is based on simple curiosity,' Rios explains. 'We're constantly digging, scratching and pushing, trying to be inspired – it's kind of like being curiously hungry.' As with many practices founded in Modernism, RCH Studios have been pushing the boundaries in recent years – using more colour, compromising linearity and expressing ideas in a conceptual way. 'What we do not want is what you see elsewhere: a perfection of forms which are then reiterated until they become a kind of brand,' Rios says. 'The biggest compliment for me is if someone looks at a project and says, "Hmm, I wonder who did that." Clients come to us because they know they're not going to get a typical

solution. They want something with a kind of velocity about it. Our work isn't simple, it isn't quiet – it's a little louder.'

Rios acknowledges that the company's design ethos is founded in the tradition of American, and specifically Californian, Modernism. 'The work of the office comes out of the ideas of Modernism, but we're not afraid of culture or of pattern or of trying to identify the particular. Pure Modernism is devoid of the concept of site – its expression comes out of the way things are pieced together. Our work is the opposite: we use the sense of place. It comes out of a connection with memory, the place and the culture. Our work tries to turn up the volume on experience.' Rios frequently mentions the idea of culture as key to the design attitude, as a way of unlocking what is important about the space. 'I talk about our role as storytellers,' he says. 'We need to solve people's problems, but the main thing is to find out what story there is to tell.'

The brief for one of the firm's more recent projects was to design a headquarters for the California Endowment (see opposite) that included a community centre, library and café, and a large courtyard garden that would be open to the public. The distinctive buildings are faced with metal slats, and the three colour palettes used – green and olive, rust and red, and gold – act as a reference to the look of the neighbouring urban buildings. 'The buildings and landscape are the result of that surrounding scale and texture and variety,' Rios explains. 'We did a study of the surroundings and tried to find a new way to fit with it.' The courtyard, with raised beds, trees and a still reflecting

pool, was a reference to the regeneration of the nearby river. 'There are lots of river-edge plants in there,' Rios says, 'things like sycamore and bamboos.' Rios's take on ecology is that it is one of the more straight forward aspects of landscape design: 'I use the word "fit",' he says. 'You need a design that fits with the ecology, something that will thrive in its location.'

OPPOSITE Here at the California Endowment, the design 'emphasizes the positive relationships possible between indoor and outdoor environments in California'. California Endowment, Los Angeles 2007.

ABOVE Housed in the fictional headquarters of the *Terminator* movies at Universal Studios, this design, centred around an interactive water feature and providing relaxation and dining areas, features biomorphic curves in silver-grey. T23D, Los Angeles 1999.

Baroda House

BEVERLY HILLS (USA) 2005

The Baroda residence near Beverly Hills, once the home of Gary Cooper and originally landscaped in the 1950s by cult Californian Modernist Garrett Eckbo, has recently been substantially enlarged through the purchase of adjacent land. As well as the creative restoration and remodelling of the house and its interior, RCH Studios undertook a 'pastoral' redesign of the large garden, which features a 8m-deep arroyo, or small, dry ravine. 'The house is very clean and modern and diagonal, so we wanted a landscape that was rough and exciting,' Rios recalls. 'The arroyo is very self-contained, whereas up top the views are expansive.' The garden contains a variety of sections, including a camellia garden, a succulent garden, a eucalyptus area and a fern dell.

Chess Park

Glendale is a busy commercial and residential area
in northern Los Angeles, heavily populated and boasting
an especially active community of chess players. The brief
here was to create a pocket park for the players in a slither
of land that acts as a passage between a car park and the
main shopping boulevard. There was another particularity,
as Rios explains: 'Chess players typically have jobs, so they
want to play chess from 10 p.m. to 2 a.m.' Lighting was
needed, so the main decorative move became the five
chess piece-shaped, fabric-covered light fixtures. Much
of the wall and floor cladding was created using Treks, a
recycled material made out of glass and wood. The facility
is run by the chess club, and the chess pieces are locked
away under the chessboard tables at night.

LAUSD Primary Centres

LOS ANGELES 2003

RCH Studios were engaged by the Los Angeles Unified School District to create a pair of prototype schools less than a mile apart – on a strict budget. A primary concern was providing the maximum number of seats for the fewest dollars, so modular classrooms and support buildings were designed to streamline both production and construction time. The exteriors of the buildings and the ground plane of the playgrounds were decorated with colourful, naive or graffiti-like graphics along two themes: transport for one school (using pink, indigo and chartreuse), and nature for

the other (green, red and yellow). 'We were trying to make a
learning landscape in an interesting Latino neighbourhood,'
Rios says. 'A lot of the local stores use pictographics for
selling milk and vegetables, so we borrowed that idea.'

Janet Rosenberg Toronto

Versatile conceptualism that works on all scales.

After university degrees in urban planning and environment and then landscape architecture, Janet Rosenberg worked for a planning and engineering consultancy for six years before setting up Janet Rosenberg Associates in 1983. Since then she has established herself as one of Canada's leading designers, winning numerous design competitions for prestigious public projects in Canada – including, most recently, beating Kathryn Gustafson (p. 122) in the Toronto waterfront redevelopment competition – while maintaining a thriving residential practice. Rosenberg now employs fourteen fellow landscape architects in her Toronto office,

and prizes above all the diversity of their commissions and the versatility of their working methods.

Rosenberg does not wish to have her work labelled, but the functionalist tradition of Modernism can be seen to be strong in the work. There is an emphasis on usability in all the practice's designs, coupled with a respect for the site itself and for the brief from the client. 'I do believe that in the end it is the clients – or the end users – who are the facilitators,' Rosenberg says. 'What's the point of designing something that no one is going to use?'

It is this adaptability – a fluidity in response to both site and client – which leads to remarkable diversity in Rosenberg's output. Critics might note a lack of coherence in individual projects, or the lack of a consistent tone through the output as a whole, but Rosenberg points up the practical virtues of the versatile approach and its potential for innovation: 'One of our strengths is that we can "do the other". For example, we know we can put a certain softness into a design if we want to.' Rosenberg is also keen to collaborate more with architects: 'The next step for our profession is to forge successful relationships with architects, and I think the ecological and environmental movement will enhance those possibilities.'

Since the work ranges from straightforward Modernism to traditional English gardening, from Italianate formalism to conceptual installation work (and is often a mixture of two or more of those styles), it is difficult to make generalizations about Rosenberg's designs. However, one constant is attention to detail. Rosenberg ascribes this

LEFT This installation was created as a feature garden for Canada Blooms, one of the largest garden shows in North America. The bronze angels, by sculptor John McEwen, sit in boxwood spirals punctuated with alliums. Dream Garden, Toronto 2000.

emphasis to her practice's beginnings in domestic garden design, the idea of a residential sensibility in the sphere of public landscape. 'The residential work takes us down to a micro-scale. We do the same amount of detail on our big public projects as on the small scale,' she explains

Unlike contemporaries such as Gustafson and Martha Schwartz (p. 256), who concentrate almost exclusively on big public projects, Rosenberg still relishes private commissions. 'When I hire people, I find that if they haven't worked on that residential scale, I can't work with them,' she says. 'They have big ideas but can't implement them. There are designers out there who spend years entering design competitions and never actually build anything. I'm a builder: I love to design, and then I love to build it.'

ABOVE AND ABOVE LEFT The design for this private garden, in which a 'unique symphony of materials was blended to complement and harmonize with the natural elements of wind, sunlight and water', was inspired by its lakeside setting. Waterfront Residence, Toronto 2006.

Barrel Warehouse Park

WATERLOO (CANADA) 2001

As with a number of other contemporary landscape architects and garden designers who come from a Modernist background, over the past five years or so Rosenberg's work has become more conceptual in tone – incorporating playful artefacts, brighter colours and a specific symbolic narrative that underpins the design. This can be seen in her plan for Barrel Warehouse Park, completed in 2001. The two giant buildings that loom over the space are old barrel warehouses for the nearby Seagram whisky distillery, which have now been turned into upscale apartment blocks.

Rosenberg and her team decided to make reference to this industrial past through the placement of big-scale industrial artefacts along one side of the space, which act like abstract sculptures. The massed planting of miscanthus grasses refers to the use of grain in the distilling of whisky. The modern aspects of life in Waterloo – now a base for high-tech industry – is honoured by the use of ultra-smooth cut-stone walls (which top traditional rubble walls), smooth pavers, lines of sculptural plane trees and stainless-steel boardwalks that cut through the grass. It is a fusion of old and new, made attractive and practical for users through the introduction of a formal pool and cascade, narcissus plantings among the grasses and benches bisecting grass mounds. 'We looked at it as a series of transitions through spaces, which is how we look at all our work,' Rosenberg explains. The final transition is into the adjacent street area, where the edge of the park has been blurred through the use of linear tree planting.

Mario Schjetnan
Mexico City

Socially motivated Conceptual–Modernist work informed by history.

Despite his non-Spanish name, Mario Schjetnan is a Mexican-born designer whose work is steeped in the culture and history of the country of his birth. His paternal grandfather was a Norwegian commercial attaché who arrived in Mexico at the turn of the 20th century to oversee railway construction, while his father was an architect with a predilection for designing golf courses. Schjetnan studied architecture in Mexico City and then at Berkeley, emerging – like many of his generation – with an enthusiasm for Modernism and a sense of social injustice.

Schjetnan's first job, from 1972, was as head of urban planning at the new Housing Institute for the Workers in Mexico City, after which he co-founded landscape firm Grupo de Diseño Urbano in 1977. Since then Schjetnan has worked on a wide variety of projects, from large-scale designs for public parks and nature reserves, to gardens for museums and government offices. Schjetnan is unusual among contemporary landscape architects and designers in that an explicitly politicized social mission – rather than a vague desire to create useful and pleasing spaces – is the core of his design philosophy. He looks back to the 1960s as key to the formation of his leftist political ideals, especially his time at Berkeley (1968–70), where he was first taught how to 'relate social aspects to environment'.

He is also deeply interested in the pre-Hispanic culture of Mexico: 'I have studied very closely how Mayan, Toltec and Aztec buildings are placed in the landscape, how they are set within views and in relation to the cosmos in general.' Schjetnan is keen to point out that he does not make specific reference to these ancient architectural forms in his work, but allows them to inform his design in deeper ways. This sensibility has contributed to a sureness of touch in large-scale situations – a confidence to allow empty spaces to speak volumes. Finally, Schjetnan's talk of the layers of culture in a given place is reminiscent of the preoccupations of contemporary conceptualist designers, and in this sense he can be seen as a precursor of that burgeoning movement.

Much of Schjetnan's work is distinguished by a sense of openness and width within an overall design that is nevertheless tightly controlled. Into this dramatic, sculpted landscape setting Schjetnan frequently inserts sculptural artefacts or architectural elements. 'I come from a tradition of architecture,' he explains. 'I am still a practising architect – I do buildings. Sometimes we address landscape as architecture.' A fondness for bright colour, reminiscent of the work of Luis Barragán, is also evident in his work, and this can give even his largest projects a jaunty quality. The work may be couched in the familiar vocabulary of Modernism, but sculptural inventiveness and the use of colour set it apart from the buttoned-up, often corporate tone of 'straight' Modernist work.

Small Tribute to Migrant Workers

SONOMA (USA) 2004

This politically motivated show garden was one of the first installations at the Cornerstone Festival, and its polemical aspect was refreshingly original. The garden is defined by three walls (one painted blood red, one made of corrugated iron, and one made from rocks encased in wire gabions) that enclose vegetables and a miniature vineyard, a reference to the winelands of Sonoma. Visitors can find gardening tools strewn around, broken pots underfoot, and printed notices in waterproof folders pinned to the walls.

These notices elucidate the garden's polemical message: the fact that an estimated 85 per cent of agricultural workers in California are illegal immigrants with no access to housing or health insurance. As visitors turn the final corner they are confronted by a 'wailing wall' adorned with photographs of the workers who built the gardens at Cornerstone, many illegal immigrants themselves. The direct emotional impact of this space makes it one of the most effective show gardens of recent years.

Martha Schwartz

Cambridge (USA) and London

The pioneer of conceptualism, always moving forward

Martha Schwartz is the designer who is justifiably credited as the driving force and best-known advocate of landscape conceptualism internationally. All conceptualist designers must express their individuality in different ways, and some will dissent from certain emphases in Schwartz's work (her use of humour, perhaps, or Pop Art-inspired artefacts), but during scores of interviews and site visits not a single one has sought to undermine Schwartz's position as the pioneer, leading protagonist, and, in many cases, the inspiration for this kind of work. Other designers can be credited as early developers of conceptualism, but none of them were on the scene as early as Schwartz or have garnered a comparable international profile subsequently.

Schwartz's contribution to landscape design has been fully documented elsewhere (see *The Vanguard Landscapes and Gardens of Martha Schwartz*, published in 2004), but perhaps it is appropriate here to recall how it all started. In 1979 Schwartz was living in Boston and married to Peter Walker, then as now one of the leading Modernist landscape architects in the US. Trained as an artist and printmaker, Schwartz was just starting out as a landscape architect herself, but was dissatisfied. 'I was frustrated at the discrepancy between my goals as an artist and what it appeared I would be doing as a landscape architect,' she recalls. 'The remaking of our front yard became an increasingly beguiling opportunity to create a project and to keep my hands and imagination busy.'

But Schwartz was worried, justifiably in hindsight, that she and her husband might clash over her idea for their garden. So she decided to redesign it in secret. She waited until Walker went away on a business trip, did her work in the garden and then invited friends round for a drinks party just in time for her husband's return. Walker was shocked – first to find a party going on, but even more at the new garden of their townhouse, which consisted of a double row of (real) bagels arrayed round the box hedges of the front yard, with a grid of bright-pink geraniums at the centre (see below). In the weeks before, Schwartz had individually varnished every bagel in the makeshift workshop she had created in the attic, entirely unbeknownst to her husband.

The garden was half Pop Art, half 17th-century parterre design, and in every way infuriating to the landscape profession, which exploded with anger when images of the garden appeared on the cover of *Landscape Architecture* magazine (the editor was sacked). 'A bagel is not an appropriate material for a garden,' Schwartz observed. But landscape design would never be the same again.

ABOVE The landscape design surrounding a new office headquarters for a German insurance company divides the site into four quadrants, each assigned a different colour: red, blue, yellow, green. Swiss Re Headquarters, Munich 2002.

OPPOSITE Schwartz's infamous garden of bagels caused shock waves throughout the garden world, but has become immortalized as the first contemporary conceptual landscape garden. Bagel Garden, Cambridge (USA) 1979.

Since those heady days, Schwartz has built up an international reputation – she split with Walker in the late 1980s – developing an immediately recognizable style that combines high concepts, witty commentaries and a plethora of unusual artificial materials. Her gardens are emphatically not about plants, which has led some to dismiss her out of hand – but Schwartz claims that in the public sphere, where she mainly works, an obsession with solutions that are 'quick, cheap and green' has paradoxically led to a coarsening of the man-made environment. She believes that contemporary society,

and particularly male society, is colour-phobic. Her thrilling use of brightly artificial colours sets her apart from other designers working in a Modernistic vein, for whom a palette of tasteful greys and beiges is de rigueur.

Since Schwartz believes that on one level garden and landscape design is all about taming the chaos of nature, and large-scale pattern is one way of achieving that. Insistent, rhythmic patterning is a thread through all her work, whether it is realized through the serpentine benches in a public square (as at Jacob Javits Plaza in New York) or through the simple placement of a large orange dot on each parking place in an irregular space ranged round a Japanese apartment block. Schwartz has been accused of shallowness and frivolity by some landscape architects, but she is unrepentant: 'God help the person who thinks that humour is frivolous. I think the fire-and-brimstone preachers get listened to a lot less than the comedians.' Many Schwartz designs raise a smile, or even a laugh. Her design for a shopping centre in Atlanta incorporates an army of 350 gilt-painted frogs, which appear to be worshipping a large red geodesic dome. Not many designers have the confidence to use humour in this way. For Schwartz, it is a trick learned from Pop Art, and also a useful way of expressing anger or dissatisfaction. In the case of the frogs, however, the intention was simply to cheer up shoppers in a depressed part of the city.

But it had all begun in 1979, with the Bagel Garden. 'It kick-started my career,' Schwartz says, 'established me as a presence in the profession and created a mark in the sand that eventually defined the beginning of the Postmodern era in landscape architecture. I thought, if it's this easy to make a flap in this profession, then maybe it is necessary that it happens.'

Grand Canal Square

DUBLIN 2007

This thrilling new urban plaza is at the heart of the redevelopment of Dublin's South Docks area. The Daniel Libeskind-designed Grand Canal Theatre (unfinished at time of publication) will take up one end of the square, while the other looks out over the canal itself, with an office block and new hotel flanking the space. The architecture (all of it distinguished) is realized in a panoply of styles, so the landscape design had to provide a sense of unity.

Because of what Schwartz accurately describes as the 'cultural celebrity setting' of the new square, a scheme was developed featuring a central 'red carpet' that leads from the theatre out onto the canal and vice versa. A green 'carpet' connects the new hotel to the office development. The red carpet is paved in a newly developed bright-red resin-glass material, and is completed by glowing, angled lightsticks that mimic the 'bustle' on the real red carpet. The green carpet has a calmer expression and offers ample seating at varied heights on the edges of the planters. The planters themselves are extruded polygons of the green carpet, planted with marsh vegetation as a reminder of the historic wetland for which this area was formerly well known (and hated by the people who had to live there). Some of the planters offer immaculate lawns for lingering.

Pushing out of the plaza is a water feature of randomly stacked green marble that overflows with bubbling water. The square is further criss-crossed by narrow granite-paved paths that allow for movement across the space, while providing space for activities such as markets or fairs. Several metallic structures serve as as entrances to the stairwells leading down to the underground car park.

Gifu Kitagata Apartments

KITAGATA (JAPAN) 2000

This apartment complex comprises four buildings, each designed by a different female architect, and landscape spaces designed by Schwartz. For the latter, Schwartz considered the needs of different kinds of families and the various and distinct age groups who would need to use the spaces. 'We created a variety of small but age-specific mini-landscapes, where everyone could be in his or her own space while still all being together,' Schwartz explains.

Since the site was formerly home to several rice paddies, a structural vocabulary of dykes and sunken spaces was used to differentiate the spaces, or episodes, of the landscape. The Willow Court is the most private space: a sunken, flooded area of willow trees and wetland vegetation bisected by a boardwalk. The Four Seasons Garden was intended for teenagers: four spaces enclosed by coloured Plexiglas that evoke the seasons. And younger children enjoy the Stone Garden, with its stepping stones and pink boulders that double up as randomly spitting water fountains. A wooden dance floor was requested by older residents, while the Bamboo Garden, Cherry Forecourt and Iris Canal provide more traditional horticultural delights.

Mesa Arts Centre

MESA (USA) 2004

The challenge here was to create a visually and socially appealing cultural centre for an Arizona city that had previously lived without a central core. The strong light of the region led Schwartz to the central concept of this large-scale and extremely rich design: shadows. The grand promenade into and through the complex became a 'shadow walk' – a place where the interplay of overlapping shadows, trees and architectural canopies creates a cool and inviting environment. In addition to shadows thrown by vegetation, a series of glass canopies and raised glass screens cast coloured shadows on the ground and spray mist down to the walkway from above. Translucent glass walls, back-lit by the afternoon sun, hold the shadows of cacti and other distinctly textured plants in silhouette.

In parallel with the shadow-walk theme is a water 'story' appropriate to the Southwest USA: a boulder-filled arroyo runs along the western side of the shadow walk for its entire length. From time to time, a strong pulse of water rushes through the riverbed from north to south, recalling the flash floods characteristic of the region. A welcome side effect of this exciting event is the cooling and humidifying effect of water evaporating from the wet boulders.

Another motif running through the Shadow Walk is that of the banquet table. The coloured glass forms used to catch light cast shade, and colour shadows also take the form of sculptural and symbolic tables and chairs. These forms are abstracted to create a poetic statement about people coming together in celebration, a family-orientated image for the arts centre and the community it serves.

The Conceptualist
Garden Show

The greatest international showcase for conceptualism as a landscape-design attitude has arguably been the summer-long garden shows established over the past twenty years and particularly during the past decade. These events – which tend to host between fifteen and twenty-five design teams each year and last for four or five months – have given landscape and garden designers (as well as several architects and artists) the opportunity to experiment with conceptual ideas and new ways of thinking about outdoor spaces. They have also proved to be useful diversifications at historic gardens, where it has been found that a contemporary festival of this sort encourages repeat visits by locals and can produce a revitalized international profile for the garden itself.

The downside is that such festivals require a huge investment of time, energy and faith on the part of the organizers and volunteers, who can then be subject to the vagaries of public-funding decisions once the show is up and running. Several excellent festivals, including the Westonbirt International Festival of the Garden in the UK, have been closed as a result of a lack of imagination and understanding from the original sponsors.

However, new conceptualist garden initiatives are opening every year: in 2007, for example, Ireland opened its first-rate International Garden Festival at Emo Court, while the city of Bilbao also hosted its own urban conceptualist garden festival (an idea pioneered in Glasgow and Lyon). London's Hampton Court Flower Show, organized by the august Royal Horticultural Society, inaugurated a conceptualist gardens section in 2006, which caused a big stir and has fostered extremely high-quality work. Meanwhile, Canada's International Flora show has only entered its second year. Several such

festivals have opened in places which could fairly be said to be rather off the beaten track, such as the excellent new festival at Ponte de Lima in northern Portugal (a delightful yet touristically underpopulated area), or the well-established Jardins de Métis festival in Quebec. On the other hand, such venues are often in up-and-coming tourist destinations, with the garden festival counting as another, refreshingly different attraction within the region.

The visitor profile of all these garden shows reflects the fact that 'normal' people visit gardens – with their families, at the weekends, or on holiday. Clearly visitors are not put off by the idea of conceptualist gardens because of the setting and context, whereas they might ordinarily be resistant to or apprehensive about the idea of gallery-based conceptual art. Historically, there has been a tendency among artists and designers to proclaim the democratic and populist credentials of their work, when in reality their audience consists of urban sophisticates who understand the jargon and gestures used. The paradox with conceptualist garden shows is that they are pitched extremely highly, in terms of their conceptual content and challenging subject matter, but the audience is overwhelmingly made up of people who have no declared interest in contemporary art. This is another example of the way that gardens and landscapes can slip under the radar of notice in the hierarchy of the arts. Anecdotally, at conceptualist garden shows all over the world it is possible to witness all kinds of people, engaging with the show gardens at precisely the sophisticated level envisaged by the designers. In this particular context, complex artistic statements do not necessarily appear threatening or exclusive to a popular audience.

It is a paradox that conceptualist garden shows have attracted very little
attention from the mainstream arts world, which tends to view the garden
sphere in its entirety as irredeemably bourgeois and congenitally trite.
The fact that any garden or landscape could potentially be treated as a vast
outdoor art installation, temporary or permanent, which changes with every
second of the day and with every nuance of the season, has occurred to very
of the few critics and curators who happily visit biennale art shows.

The first conceptualist garden show, and still the best known, is the annual
Chaumont Festival in the grounds of the château of the same name in the Loire
Valley. Founded in 1992 by Jean-Paul Pigeat, it has provided the model for
all subsequent conceptualist festivals: Gothenburg, Lausanne, Mälmo,
Ludwigsburg, and the Cornerstone Festival in California's Sonoma Valley,
as well as those already mentioned. Most of these festivals have a genuinely
international flavour, although one or two recent events have displayed a
regrettably parochial attitude in terms of designer selection. Such festivals
usually last for a period of months over the summer, so they are able to grow,
change, mature or decay as the artists and designers might envisage.

Given the 'problem' of a lack of engagement with a sense of place in
conceptualist work, it is interesting to note that each show has its own particular
atmosphere, which affects the gardens and how they seem to visitors. At a show
such as the biennial Jardins de Métis, for regular visitors even specific garden
spaces seem to retain the ghostly impressions of previous gardens on that spot.
Métis's own atmosphere is tied up with its position in woodland overlooking the
St Lawrence River, and the guidance of festival director Alexander Reford,

whose family formerly owned the house and garden. Of all the garden shows, this is the one which seems to grapple most closely with a sense of place, actively encouraging designers to work within the geographical context: there is no declared theme at Métis, but some kind of engagement with the site and its history is seen as mandatory.

Chaumont has a pleasantly jaunty atmosphere, almost like a carnival or fair with sideshows. The hedged ground plan of the site was devised at the outset by the Belgian designer Jacques Wirtz; in retrospect it may have made more sense to have introduced less rigid parameters and, in certain cases, larger garden spaces. Every year a theme is chosen, and to date these have been:

1992: Inaugural festival – no theme

1993: The Imagination in Crisis

1994: Acclimatization

1995: Gardens of Curiosity

1996: Is Technique Poetically Correct?

1997: Water! Water!

1998: Ricochet

1999: Vegetable Gardens Only

2000: Free theme (in honour of the Millennium)

2001: Carpet Bedding (or 'Mosaiculture')

2002: Garden Erotica

2003: Bad Flowers!

2004: Long Live Chaos!

2005: Gardens and Memory

2006: Garden Games

2007: Movement

There is an infectious sense of humour in many of Chaumont's gardens, which conversely makes it more difficult for serious or bleak gardens to work. The selection process here tends to favour more theoretical design ideas, with a number of student outfits winning through each year, and a notable bias towards French designers. There is also a perennial problem with build quality at Chaumont – many of these installations seem decidedly flimsy and the planting can seem less than adequate. But despite these shortcomings, the festival is always stimulating and surprising.

Westonbirt's strengths lay in quality of design and build, and in horticulture. Unlike Chaumont and Métis, Westonbirt was less purely 'conceptual' in its style, a reflection of not only different horticultural traditions, but also of different philosophical milieux. There was a pragmatic edge to some of the gardens, a sense that these were designed gardens which might find a place in the real wold, but this was balanced by numerous purely conceptualist experiments. Westonbirt was also perhaps the happiest conceptualist festival in its setting, in long grass next to the rich woodlands of the arboretum, with plenty of space between the exhibits. Of all the shows, Westonbirt displayed perhaps the most enlightened international attitude, with a good mix of designers and styles.

Cornerstone is just finding its voice. It is on a difficult site, next to a major road, with all kinds of visual pollution, but as shelter belts of trees are added, and telegraph poles rerouted or obscured, it should settle down. The tone of the design here is different again, a reflection of the United States' own design culture: there is a Modernist rigour to the work which reflects the commercialized milieu of American landscape architecture and the professional status of the

designers invited to collaborate. From the beginning, Chaumont has enjoyed substantial funding and support from local and national government, a reflection of France's civic attitude to the arts, whereas Cornerstone has been set up and is managed by an entrepreneurial individual and his team with no state aid whatsoever. The hope is that the show will pay for itself and make a profit from the substantial retail village on the site.

Cornerstone's founder, Chris Hougie, made his money as a toy manufacturer (luminous plastic stars for bedroom ceilings were his biggest success) and had been captivated by Chaumont while on honeymoon in France in 1996. With the help of landscape architect Peter Walker, Hougie put together a wish-list of top US designers, made speculative trips to Napa and Sonoma, and, after a long search, acquired a roadside plot well placed for the passing tourist trade heading into the wine country. Walker's name helped ensure that almost all of the big players on the original list – Martha Schwartz, Topher Delaney, Claude Cormier, Ken Smith – agreed to take part, despite the small combined fee and budget for each garden of $10,000. Cornerstone is now an established element in the conceptualist garden scene and is unique in that it remains open all year round. It also follows a relaxed policy with regard to novelty, keeping a number of gardens in situ for a few years while rotating other spaces – a process of slow evolution rather than an exciting revamp each season.

All the shows have something unique to offer; the differences between them add strength to the movement as a whole. Yet there have been several instances of show gardens moving from one venue to another, almost as if they are on tour (Claude Cormier's 'Blue Sticks' is probably the most travelled). The value of

'exchanging' gardens from site to site, and other close collaborations between festivals, is perhaps debatable, despite the clear financial and other practical benefits. There is a danger that this could potentially stymie creativity and lead to a certain homogeneity between the shows, although admittedly this may be a rather purist position to take. The quality of build and design across the established festivals has got better over the few years of their existence, and the depth and sophistication of the ideas behind the designs has also improved with time. Some design companies, such as Land-I, have poured a great deal of creative and intellectual effort into this unique genre, with impressive results.

The conceptualist garden show goes to the heart of some key questions – or problems, perhaps – for landscape conceptualism as a whole. Key issues include: the temporary nature of the work; its supposed lack of integration with place; the way budgetary constraints affect build quality; the way show gardens tend to fade from memory more quickly than 'real' gardens, perhaps because the visitor sees a number in a short space of time; what it is these shows are offering to visitors in practical terms – horticultural, political, moral, spiritual, intellectual – and whether that should be of serious concern to makers and organizers; the value of such festivals to designers, in encouraging newer practices and stimulating more established ones; the way they encourage dialogue and collaboration between architects, artists, landscape architects and garden designers; whether garden festivals should be themed, or be judged; and ultimately, what makes a good conceptualist show garden?

The answer to this last question is essentially the same as that to a query about the value of specific conceptualist designs in the 'real' world: some of

them work well in an almost didactic sense, with a clear message or concept espoused and consistently evident throughout, while others are more opaque, in which case words such as 'simplicity', 'balance' and 'poise' come to mind. Conceptualist garden shows offer the opportunity for new perspectives on old ideas, and act as laboratories for the development of landscape and garden design. The majority of show gardens deal to some extent with the idea of mankind's relationship with nature – the oldest topic of all in landscape design – or else are stimulated by a gleeful subversion of some of the clichés surrounding the tradition of gardening. It is noticeable that those makers who come from outside this tradition tend to hone in on the 'big' concepts surrounding our ideas of nature, whereas those who already work in landscape tend to be more specific (and more often successful).

One area which might be worthy of further design exploration is politics. Surprisingly little interest has been shown in this potentially explosive and challenging topic, but the example of the garden made by Mario Schjetnan at Cornerstone illustrates its power: 'Small Tribute to Migrant Workers' serves as a radical mausoleum to the Mexican workforce, often illegal and underpaid, who tend the gardens of California's wealthy cities and suburbs, as well as its vineyards. As one local journalist put it, this close-to-the-bone experience 'leaves the visitor with a tight throat and an uncomfortable knot in the stomach'.

Every subject is a fit subject for conceptualist design – not only those which are predicated on symbolism, ideas and materials drawn directly from nature – and it is to be hoped that designers will widen the parameters of their subject matter even further in future.

Vladimir Sitta · Surry Hills (Australia)

Surreal and uncompromising conceptual design.

Vladimir Sitta studied landscape architecture at Brno University in (what was then) Czechoslovakia, and practised for eight years through the 1970s as a landscape architect under the Communist regime. 'It was nearly all public landscapes,' he says. 'There were a lot of spas in Czechoslovakia, and most of our work was in the spa parks. But there were also a few gardens for party officials – a garden was a form of bribery, I guess.'

When Sitta won a design competition for a project in Essen, he began travelling to and from West Germany on work visas. 'One day I decided I wasn't going back,' he recalls. In 1981, after two years in Germany, Sitta emigrated to Australia. He admits that the decision was made almost on a whim: 'I always say, "I was young and stupid", but actually at the time the Australian government put ads in the newspapers and on television to encourage emigration. A friend showed my wife and I one of these. We went to Sydney because I was interested in rock climbing and I knew the Blue Mountains were nearby. That's it.'

For most of the 1980s Sitta worked in Sydney for a landscape company that specialized in educational theme parks, while also pursuing his interest in sculptural ceramics. When that company went under, Sitta started to concentrate on his own practice, called Terragram, and since then has designed and built a number of highly original private gardens. In 1985 Sitta formed interdisciplinary partnership Room 4.1.3 with Perth-based academic Richard Weller, and the pair have entered numerous competitions (with some success) while developing a rigorously theoretical attitude. Their biggest project to date is the controversial landscape surrounding the Museum of Australia at Canberra, which features a baking-hot 'pit' designed to echo the inhospitable terrain

of the country's interior. Sitta's instinctive approach to on-site design is in direct contrast to that of Weller, who has penned a number of theoretical articles about how, for example, their work 'extends the mytho-poetic terrain of the garden as a constructed idea'. For Sitta, the process of garden-making embraces spontaneity as well as critical theory. 'Richard likes to write a scenario and then graft the work onto it,' he explains. 'I'm more intuitive than that. I like the journey, what is unexpected.'

In some ways, Sitta's work appears rather stark and barren, and he is aware of the stereotype of the intellectual émigré artist: 'Somebody said to me, "It's this tormented mid-European soul", and I suppose that is true to an extent.' But as he talks about his work, Sitta reveals a

sense of humour which crosses over into his designs. Many of his conceptual ideas are in fact little jokes that have arisen from problems with the site, or characteristics of the owners or their families. The true spark of Sitta's creativity seems to be a fantastical and unbounded sense of humour akin to that of the Surrealists.

Sitta does not create naturalistic or romantic gardens, still less those which utilize a native plant palette. Instead, he designs landscapes in which a central conceptual idea dictates everything. Fissures, craters, cracked rocks, monumental boulders and reflective water are all recurring features, a geological language which is sometimes used to reflect our own deeply embedded psychological ideas. His work can also be seen as a reaction to the stridently ecological nature of much recent Australian garden work. 'When I arrived in Australia I didn't recognize anything, not a single tree,' he remembers. 'It was a totally alien world – although the food was just as bad as it had been in Czechoslovakia. There was a strong desire to depart from English paradigms, and it was expressed in an almost naive nationalism, where no trees except for Australian ones were acceptable. I'm not a "native Nazi" like some people; I'm much more eclectic. I will go for any plant I like.'

OPPOSITE AND BELOW The Garden of Walls, designed with Maren Parry, Sitta's partner at Terragram, is part of a series of unique gardens that includes the Garden of Reflections (see p. 276) and the Garden of Fire. Each garden makes use of a limited palette of plants and materials. Garden of Walls, Sydney 2005.

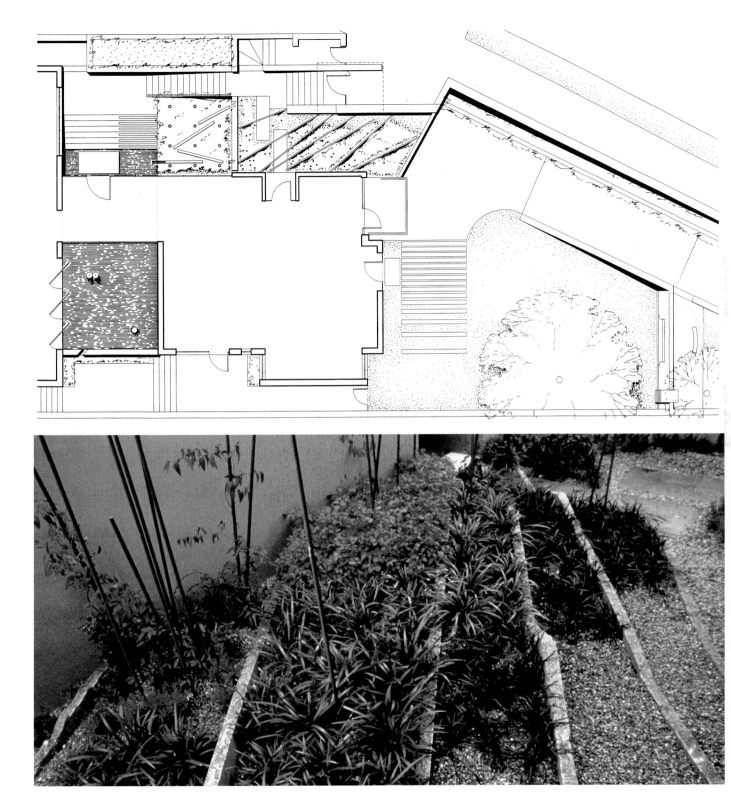

Garden of Reflections

SYDNEY 2005

At the Garden of Reflections in Sydney, Sitta worked in collaboration with an architect to create five separate courtyards around a new Modernist house. 'Those spaces are very simple, stark and restrained, like the architecture,' he says. 'We were able to build the earth up to the right depth rather than just use planters, which is usually the case in these projects.'

A limited palette of plants and materials was used – principally the verticals of bamboo, the bamboo-like wombat berry (*Eustrephus latifolius*) or copper rods, set against various coloured aggregates, straight rills and lines of uniform architectural plant species. 'Most of our gardens are for people who are not gardeners,' Sitta explains. 'The type of garden that is filled with plants can be superficial: you don't notice things like the dew on the leaves, or the way shadows cast patterns on the walls. This sort of garden creates a different kind of richness.' The principle of repetition is common to much Modernist and Postmodernist design, but Sitta's artistic sensibility here gives it a uniquely characterful twist.

SLA Copenhagen

Conceptual design which aims to capture a balance between nature and urban experience.

Founded in 1994 in Copenhagen by senior partner Stig L. Andersson as a specialist in 'new urban experiences', SLA aim to 'create genuine amenity values that in an unorthodox way add a new layer of meaning to the everyday environment'. Over the past fifteen years, SLA's work can be seen to have developed away from more conventional Modernist architectural expression – using geometric plans and grids, axes of trees and paths, or else a strident ground plan together with a certain spatial freedom – towards a more conceptualist approach, weaving new ideas and fruitful contradictions into public spaces. SLA's ground plans now resemble colourful collages which develop along emotional and aesthetic lines, as opposed to strictly rationalist criteria. In addition, the practice has developed from pure landscape architecture and into the realms of interdisciplinary urban planning, site analysis and conservation – there are now four principal partners and some twenty-nine employees in total, including seventeen landscape architects.

SLA's style and attitude can be summed up as a reconciliation between the natural environment and the reality of contemporary city life: their designs do not recreate simulacra of natural scenes, but instead build up urban environments that hold the urban and the natural more or less in balance, in terms of both the materials used and the prevailing atmosphere. It is easy to state this as an aim, but extremely difficult to achieve in practice; SLA are one of the few firms internationally who have been consistently successful in this respect.

The concept of change has been a preoccupation for Andersson from the beginning, and grew out of his extended trip to Japan in 1986, soon after graduating, where he was impressed by Japanese design precepts.

'Organizing physical matter within a spatial context and then waiting to see what happens, thus allowing for unforeseen coincidences should always be the starting point of landscape architecture,' Andersson states in a 2006 essay published in *Topos: Grow!*. 'Working this way means that an unlimited number of experiences are created, not a static image or object. Contemplating the urban space or landscape as a picture of beauty – in one final and ideal form – is a misunderstanding that ignores the overwhelming qualities of change.'

He concludes: 'The landscape architect cannot and should not control unforeseen developments. Future interruptions – which are always part of a dynamic society and force the project to change suddenly – should be

looked upon as an integral part of the project, even with a potential to maintain the dynamic of the system. We have to design urban spaces with interruptions in mind, to focus on context and make the city simulate an ecosystem, where parts interplay and react, but without the closed boundaries of the classic biotope.'

Andersson's urban spaces are redolent of this notion of landscape space as a continuum affected by all kinds of influences, not least human interaction.

ABOVE AND OPPOSITE This cemetery funded by the Danish Arts Association consists of two parts: 'A Plot' by SLA and 'Megaron', a 3.5m-high sculpture by Morten Stræde. A Plot consists of thirty patches of grass or red sandstone, laid into the ground in varying sizes and at different angles. A Plot, Nørrebro (Denmark) 2004.

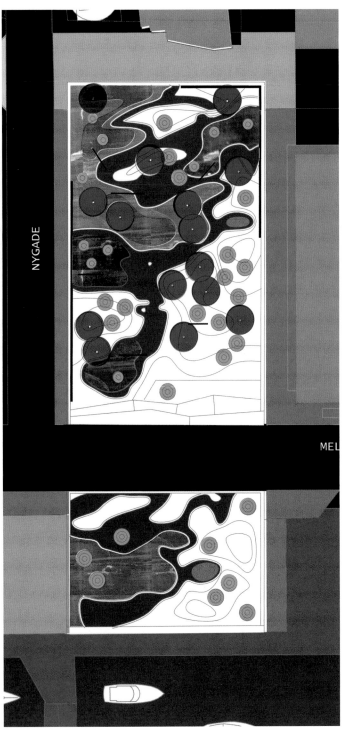

Urban Garden

NØRRESUNDBY (DENMARK) 2005

This public space was constructed between the town's quayside and apartment buildings. Paths of crushed mussel shells wind between amorphous areas of asphalt containing vertical jets and pools of water. The space is surrounded by beds of willow trees, bracken and moss, and defined by a semi-transparent steel fence. A blue rubber-coated stairway links the space with the quayside itself.

The play of water and light on surfaces is a constant theme in SLA's work, and the linking conceptual idea here is rainfall. 'Bringing a sense of nature into an urban context through the means of technology and a few components was the conceptual starting point of the Urban Garden,' Andersson states. 'By cultivating the processes of weather, we can make weatherscapes out of cities and turn technical measures into sensuous interplays.'

He continues: 'Much too often people complain that nature is lacking in most cities. What they mean is, of course, that nature is not present as a representation or image, at the same time forgetting that nature as a process is present almost anywhere. Just think of how the changes of weather affect us, no matter where we go. This illustrates how making a representation of nature in the city is not really interesting in itself, but that what we should focus on is what nature really does. In that case, we have many different options of expression: trees not only form clumps, but also cast shadows, sounds excite the imagination, and shifting levels of humidity draw patterns on the pavement.'

Charlotte Garden

COPENHAGEN 2004

This urban landscape was created to complement
a traditional courtyard block in the Oesterbro area of
Copenhagen. A geometric ground plan was rejected in
favour of this arrangement of natural curves and contours,
apparently in imitation of an agricultural landscape, though
also in reference to the nearby natural dunescape. The
planting consists mainly of grasses, including *Festuca
glauca*, seslevia and *Molinia caerulea*, creating an ever-
changing landscape of colours and forms that seem to
flow into each other. The simplicity and apparent
naturalness of the space have made it extremely popular,
and not just with residents of the overlooking blocks.
The materials used will naturally change and develop with
time and require a minimum of maintenance, which will
enhance the sense that here is a stylized piece of nature
in the city. As Andersson remarks: 'Urban spaces should
provide flexible frames, not by containing a planned
transformation, but by really making change possible.'

Ken Smith New York

The conceptualist who disavows concepts:
startling urban interruptions.

After graduating from Harvard's Graduate School of Design
in 1986, Ken Smith joined the office of Peter Walker and
Martha Schwartz (p. 256), who were in partnership both
professionally and domestically. Thus Smith was involved
with landscape conceptualism from the very start. (One
now has a sense that he feels his early contribution has
not perhaps been sufficiently acknowledged.) Smith was
certainly an integral creative element of Schwartz's team
until he left to form his own practice in New York in 1992.
Like Claude Cormier (p. 70), another Schwartz alumnus,
Smith can be viewed professionally as a scion of the
design 'family' fostered at Schwartz's Boston office.

After a slow start, Smith has built up a thriving practice
and a deservedly international reputation as an iconoclastic
landscape conceptualist who is unafraid to break taboos
concerning colour and materials, but who will also
undertake commissions which either have a conservation
element or are relatively 'straight' compared with the rest
of his output. An example of the former is his masterful
restoration of the forecourt of Lever House in Manhattan,
with sculptures by Isamu Noguchi, while the latter can
perhaps be exemplified by his horticulturally exuberant
new plaza at 55 Water Street, also in New York.

Smith is unusual among landscape conceptualists in
that he cites two major artistic influences on his creative
identity (most conceptualist designers prefer to describe
their development as some kind of personal reaction to
architectural Modernism, or as a personal artistic
expression). Marcel Duchamp is the first, particularly
in terms of his original emphasis on what Smith calls
'cultural production involving appropriation, found elements
and transformation of common objects'. Smith is the only
landscape conceptualist in this volume to have cited

Duchamp – or indeed any leading figure in conceptual art –
as an influence, which is perhaps testament to the distance
that lies between the genres.

The second major influence is Robert Smithson, the
pioneer and major theoretician of Land Art (indeed, its only
coherent theoretician). In Smithson's inspiring writing lies
the core of Smith's personal take on conceptualism. He
explains: 'Of particular importance is his concept of "non-
site", a constructed or theoretical site that makes direct
reference to actual sites through abstraction. Smithson
used the non-site as a conceptual container to bound,
signify and represent landscapes without imitating their
outward image or form.' In other words, it is possible to
create landscapes which in aesthetic terms exist primarily
as references to other places – possibly imaginary places.

Smith's attitude also differs from that of most other
conceptualists in his contention that his designs need not
(should not) be read in any particular way. Any central idea
or concept will be realized in a relatively loose way in his
work – it is often a matter of the repetition of unusual
materials or forms, rather than a literal narrative or a
connection with the history or ecology of the place. 'I am
committed to working on projects of public impact,' he has
stated. 'Public work is the most important work one can
engage in. It is also some of the most difficult work,
involving multiple constituencies and complex contextual
situations. For this reason, I try to create work that has
both specificity of content and abstraction of interpretation
and meaning.'

OPPOSITE The idea here was to create a 'vertical wall painting', says
Smith, 'with tropical epiphytes, orchids and bromeliads, very much in
contrast to the New York landscape.' The ground was covered with
rubber to create a 'forest floor'. Atrium Garden, New York 2005.

Triangle Park

NEW YORK 2006

The seventh building in Manhattan's former World Trade Center complex was connected to the plaza via an elevated walkway. While it did not suffer a direct hit in the attacks of September 11, 2001, the building's superstructure was compromised by falling debris from the collapse of the adjacent twin towers; the forty-seven-storey building then caught fire and collapsed at 5.20pm that day.
A replacement building was constructed on a smaller footprint, providing the space for this triangular public park between Greenwich Street and West Broadway, designed by Smith. The building was heralded as an example of 'green' architecture since it comprised such features as a rainwater collection system, which is used as the sole means of irrigation of this park.

The design of the space utilizes rigidly portioned groups of pink, green and purple flower and foliage plants in the diagonal beds surrounding the central 9m-wide vertical jet fountain (which originally boasted a 3m-tall Jeff Koons sculpture and is now used for other temporary art installations). The fountain area is surrounded by marble benches and a ring of light columns. Rows of sweetgum trees emphasize the diagonal orientation, while the box hedges and azaleas below bolster the structure during the winter months.

Twin Roof Gardens

NEW YORK 2005

Smith's idea for the twin roof spaces at the Museum of
Modern Art was based on the concept of camouflage –
as an intersection between urban style and natural
landscape, and also as a comment on the inescapably
artificial qualities of all man-made landscape design.

There is no access to the garden spaces: they must be
looked down on from above at a steep angle, and in that
sense they function as parterres in the Baroque sense
(the design satirizes the tradition of such 17th-century
gardens as Het Loo in the Netherlands). One disappointment
is that the new gardens are not viewable by museum
visitors, only by those working in overlooking buildings –
but distant views can be obtained from the rooftop bar
of the Peninsula Hotel on Fifth Avenue.

The amorphous ground plan – derived from the
camouflage fashion pattern – is made up of quantities of
ultramarine crushed glass, white crushed marble, black
recycled plastic, green plastic boxwood topiaries and white
and black hollow plastic cones. Flesh-coloured dividers,
made of Styrofoam, allow these artificial gardens to
clamber round numerous immovable vents and skylights.
With no weight capacity, irrigation or maintenance budget,
these had to be gardens made entirely of lightweight,
cheap, non-living materials; the result is amusing, original,
absorbing to look at and made on a surprisingly large
scale. The temporary – or 'slow-temporary' – nature of the
materials, which will probably last for less than ten years,
is one of the controversial aspects of much conceptualism.
Echoing Martha Schwartz, designers argue that if a space
has been a success, there is usually no reason, beside
budgetary ones, why it should not simply be renewed.

Taylor Cullity Lethlean

Functional, imaginative, distinctively
Australian work.

Princes Hill and Adelaide (Australia)

TCL was set up in 1990 by husband-and-wife team Kate
Cullity and Kevin Taylor, who were joined five years later
by Perry Lethlean (he now heads up the Melbourne office
while Cullity and Taylor work out of Adelaide). The company
now employs more than twenty-five people and undertakes
a wide range of work, from urban design involving modern
artworks, to signage and landscape architecture in national
parks, to playground design, to residential work. Lethlean
sums up the different skills of the three partners: 'I have an
urban design interest; Kevin has a deep sensitivity towards
the Australian landscape; and Kate has an artistic and
finely detailed sensibility. Kate, in particular, thinks about
projects in an artistic way.'

TCL's attitude is underpinned by four 'streams of
investigation': contemporary urban life and global culture;
the inherent elemental power of site and landscape; artistic
practice in a range of disciplines; and the creation of a
sustainable future. Contemporary culture informs all of the
company's work, explains Lethlean: 'Parks and gardens in
the past might have been considered as places of escape
or refuge from the city, but we try to create spaces that are
totally integrated with the life of the city. The way we do that
is through a certain robustness; we allow for a range of
activities in our public spaces – festivals, markets, sports
and simple day-to-day use. The other layer could be called
poetic: we try to tell a story in our work, in the context of
the site's history or the people who might use it.'

Unusually for a conceptualist outfit, TCL also finds
inspiration in the natural Australian landscape. 'It informs
all our work,' Lethlean says, 'the patterns, the forms, the
materials, the colours.' What results is something akin to
Outback Modernism, with a savour of the surrounding
natural world introduced in a non-naturalistic way.

The artistic element of the company's work is most often
realized in collaborations with sculptors and artists, while
Lethlean insists that the references to sustainability in their
statements are not just a way of pandering to contemporary
trends and increasing the chances of commissions from
public bodies. 'Yes, you can use the idea cynically,' he says,
'but in Australia it is increasingly important that we don't
just pay lip service to sustainability. We can be poetic or
conceptual in our work while also being sustainable.
Eco-design does not have to look like eco-design.'

At first sight, TCL's output appears to come from the
mould of corporate Modernism, with its emphasis on
a strong linear masterplan, repetition, and high-tech
detailing in the lighting, paving and water features.
However, a closer look reveals that there is something
peculiarly Australian about all their work. For one thing,

the same colour keeps cropping up: a kind of dull terracotta, the colour of the Outback. 'We love that colour,' Lethlean says. 'Even though our communities tend to congregate round the coasts, we all recognize that colour as uniquely Australian.' The use of native plants used en masse (i.e., not naturalistically) is another trademark – especially cycads, lily-like dionellas, kangaroo paws and banksias, and trees such as eucalyptus (particularly the lemon-scented gum), paper-barks (malalucca) and the angophora, or apple gum. 'In the '60s and '70s there was a "bush garden" movement, in which people replicated the Outback,' Lethlean explains. 'They didn't use it creatively, in new and unusual ways. That is what we try to do.'

ABOVE AND OPPOSITE Intended as the centrepiece of the new Melbourne Museum complex, this design consists of a 50m-by-25m rectangular space into which a forest fragment has been inserted. Forest Gallery, Melbourne 2000.

Garden for Australia

CRANBOURNE (AUSTRALIA) 2006

Intended to function as a stylized microcosm of the natural landscape of Australia, this 25-hectare landscape was commissioned by Melbourne's Royal Botanic Gardens to constitute a new botanic garden at Cranbourne. TCL's statement reads: 'The garden highlights the tension between the natural landscape and our human impulse to steadily change it. This tension is not eliminated; rather it is the driving creative impulse for exploration, expression and interpretation of the landscape and its flora.'

To that end, TCL has not shied away from including elements of human intervention in its design, as a way of illustrating 'the evolving relationship between the Australian people and [its] landscape and flora'. Indeed, the garden itself can be seen as another chapter in that relationship.

The ground plan is based on a series of ellipses, bisected by straight lines. The western side of the garden echoes the flowing contours of the natural landscape – dunes, hills, forests, marshes – while the eastern side introduces the human element, culminating in a series of designed gardens. Fingers of woodland which partially span the site hint at reconciliation between the two halves. Water becomes the mediating element, cascading into shallow rockpools at the entrance until finally growing in size and power until it encircles an island at the garden's north end.

Customs Plaza

GREATER GEELONG (AUSTRALIA) 2001

Sixty miles southwest of Melbourne, the historic port of Geelong was the centre of Australia's wool trade. Today the docks have closed, but the city now wants to attract new business and retail development. In the city centre, a shopping mall had lost its connection with the surrounding streets. To remedy this, TCL introduced roads into the mall to create 'a sense of busy-ness and a feeling of security and surveillance'. Low, bubbling fountains were set in a paved design of directional arrows and lines of columnar lights in stainless steel were lit from above and below, with plane trees continuing the linear narrative at a higher level.

Perhaps the most important aspect of the city's redesign, however, was the 2.5km-long waterfront. 'Lots of people had never even been to this part of Geelong,' Perry recalls. TCL got rid of most of the clutter and connected the area back to the city by introducing new view-lines and pedestrian walkways away from the main promenade deck. Small 'harbours' were created along the waterfront and concrete ribs connected to the ugly sea wall to create a sense of rhythm, with seating added around the major gateways to create 'areas of intensification' for visitors.

A new park was also created in front of the historic Customs House, adjacent to the waterfront. What had been the car park was transformed into a plaza made up of landformed grass berms in the shape of waves, and a timber deck with amorphous shapes in gravel planted with angophora trees. A long rill divides lawn from deck. 'We wanted to relate the history of the site through the landscape,' Perry explains. 'So we created these cargo boxes, each of which tells the story of a particular ship.'

Eucalyptus

MONTREAL 2005

The eucalyptus was chosen by TCL for their show garden at the Jardins de Métis as the plant perhaps most emblematic of the Australian landscape. 'The enormous height and robustness of the eucalyptus tree, combined with the decorative and delicate nature of the leaves and limbs, have inspired the design of this garden,' they state.

Staggered metal screens, which together form the shape of the eucalyptus leaf, are perforated with magnified microscopic designs that recall the plant's cell structure. The verticality of the screens refers to the way the leaves present themselves to the sun, an adaptation in a hot and dry climate to prevent water loss. The fine transparency of the screens projects patterns of light and shadow on the red ground, reminiscent of the filtered light that breaks through the leaves and makes them appear filigreed. The experience of walking through the installation is one of gradual progression from openness to partial closure, changing with each step and turn of the head. A sinuous ribbon of eucalyptus seedlings alludes to the way the plant grows opportunistically along ephemeral waterways.

Topotek 1 Berlin

Conceptual landscape design with a light and humorous touch.

Topotek 1, the Berlin landscape firm founded by Martin Rein-Cano, is a decade old. It has developed rapidly during the past five years or so, with a high success rate in competitions for public work – which is how landscape architects in Germany obtain most of their commissions. There are now seventeen employees at the company, and Rein-Cano has been joined by partner Lorenz Dexler, with whom he studied at the University of Hanover. Rein-Cano's training included a year with the Swiss 'poetic rationalist' (as Rein-Cano calls him) Dieter Kienast, and an internship in 1991 at Peter Walker's office in Boston. It was the latter which proved to be the more important influence, as it was Walker and his ex-wife Martha Schwartz (p. 256), in the office next door, who pioneered conceptualist design and the loosening of Modernist structures regarding colour, pattern and the idea of decoration. As Rein-Cano observes, 'In the end it was the Postmodern movement which brought forms and colours back to landscape design.' Rein-Cano's work has developed along conceptualist lines, and his personal charm and enthusiasm has meant that projects which have started out quite strait-laced have developed into something more innovative.

Rein-Cano sees his chosen direction as a radical departure from the mainstream of 20th-century landscape design, which has been predicated on functionalist Modernism with a soupçon of ecological polemic. 'In Germany, the social and ecological movement dominated landscape design for decades until the early 1980s,' he explains. 'Anything "designed" was seen as suspicious and bad; it was the era of the researchers, trying to find things out: how many children were playing in parks, how many birds were singing. They tried to prove things all the time, to make design seem scientific, somehow.' The conceptualist strand of Postmodern landscape design offered freedom from these constraints. In any case, Rein-Cano believes there is less reason for functionalism in landscape as opposed to architecture – while there is a need to make a building warm and weatherproof, gardens and landscapes historically have been places where people have created direct expressions of their identities and aspirations. Rein-Cano says he has the confidence to think in this way partly because he was born in Argentina and only moved to Germany when he was thirteen, which gives him the ability to feel both an insider and an outsider.

Like other conceptualist landscape and garden designers, Rein-Cano often uses clear linear patterning or mapping in his work. This is partly for practical reasons –

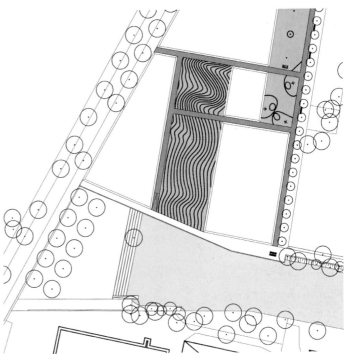

ABOVE AND OPPOSITE In the Spandau district of Berlin, Topotek 1 created a 'meeting place' to rejuvenate this former industrial area near the Maselake canal. Dynamic, contour-like markings 'create a playfully topographic effect that blurs the different dimensions' of the space. Open Spaces Maselakekanal, Berlin 2006.

to produce a sense of orientation for users in a large or confusing area – but it is also a play on the traditional Modernist obsession with spatial construction. By creating linear patterns which are illogical or curved, the designer can transcend rationalist Modernism while also imposing a sense of structure on nature. 'The Baroque tradition is most important to me,' Rein-Cano says, 'especially in the way they made paintings on the ground with parterres.' Rein-Cano says he is also painting on the ground, but in an abstract way.

One crucial area of difference between Rein-Cano and most other conceptualists is in his attitude to the idea of meaning in design. He often talks of a certain 'looseness' in this regard, a reluctance to produce specific symbolic meanings or to engage directly with history. 'In that sense my work is close to art,' he explains. 'Sometimes it's more about sensuality, a feeling, than a need to explain, or to refer to history. We often make that feeling quite easy-going and loose – in a park, we don't want to make people feel oppressed. I don't believe in the idea of having to explain a design.'

Castle Park

WOLFSBURG (GERMANY) 2004

The rejuvenation of Wolfsburg's public park was part of efforts made by the city authorities to improve amenities in order to prevent the possible relocation of Volkswagen, the company for which the city was essentially built during the Nazi era. It is still very much a company town.

The English landscape garden on 23 hectares below the castle was a pleasant but not particularly notable example of the genre, and after some conservation work including replanting and the opening up of vistas, the city authorities asked Topotek 1 to do more. Rein-Cano's essential plan was to emphasize the movement and episodic nature of this type of garden, so as part of the wider scheme he inserted three circular gardens on the themes of sculpture, the rose and the forest, which for him represented distillations of the existing atmosphere of the park. Each garden has a different character: the sculpture garden is closed and hermetic, like the castle adjacent; the rose garden is open and expansive, 'a show-off like the garden show'; and the forest garden is mysterious, labyrinthine and scented, like the woods all around. Mirrored stainless-steel sculptures are a constant in all three gardens.

Faced with legions of white-painted park benches, Rein-Cano decided to paint them all pink, and this colour theme was continued in the fences of an adjacent paddock and in a large, inflatable children's playground designed for summer use. 'That was the pink era,' Rein-Cano says. Now: 'No more pink!'

Unter den Linden

BERLIN 2006

This small courtyard of the offices constructed for the Bayer pension plan headquarters is characterized by a floral pattern similar to a Baroque embroidery ornament. 'When viewed from the upper floors, the yellow paint on the asphalt formally dissolves from the courtyard space as its visual structure leads boundlessly beyond its confines,' say Topotek 1. For the visitor in the courtyard, the idea is that the floor design creates the impression of an interior with a carpet, historic tapestry or brocade material. The austerity of the architecture, with its strongly contrasting, shining black granite surfaces and brass axes, is given a playful note by the similar tonality of the yellow colour on asphalt. 'In this way,' the designers say, 'the significant charm and massive materiality of the façade are accompanied by an almost decadent pleasure in exuberance and an extravagance of form and colour. Flanked by a shining black granite wall illuminated in a randomly generated rhythm, the courtyard space evokes an atmosphere which – with its finely carved production of cinematographic sequences – reminds one of a courtly ritual.'

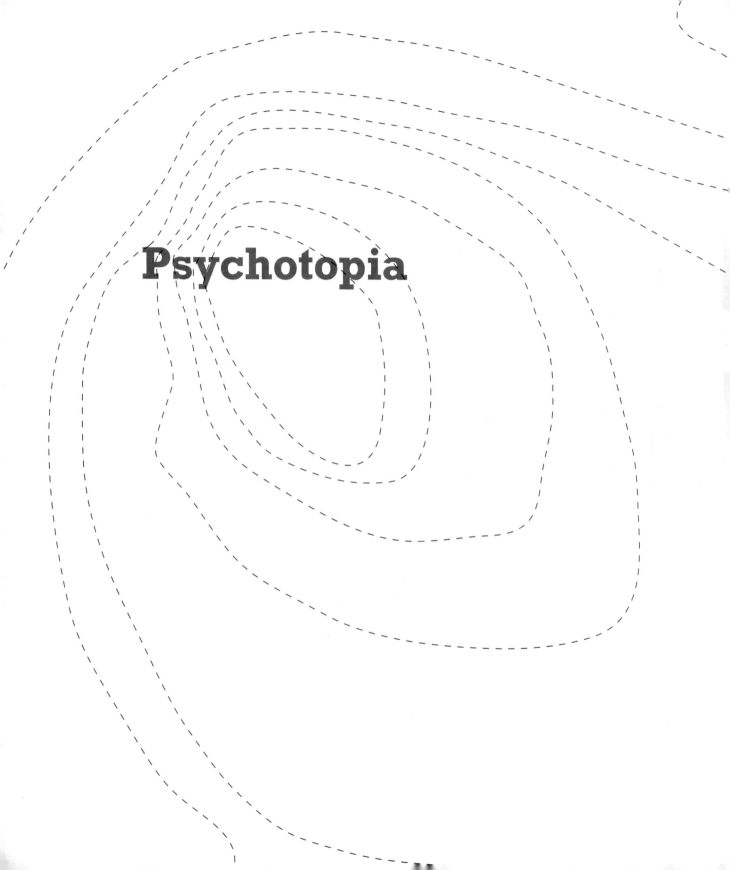

Psychotopia

Conceptualist landscape design is predicated on the idea of meaning, metaphor or narrative inserted into spaces. How, therefore, are these meanings communicated? This can occur in a literal manner, through visual symbolism, but there are other, more mysterious ways in which landscapes can 'speak' to us. Since ancient times the idea of the 'genius of the place' – to use Alexander Pope's formulation – has survived: the notion that spaces are possessed of some kind of presiding atmosphere or spirit. This notion does not necessarily have to take on a 'spiritual' or quasi-religious dimension to make sense or become useful. And the fact that it is unquantifiable and difficult to describe does not make it inherently 'irrational', as any contemporary physicist would aver.

It is clear that the object of the landscape architect and the garden designer is not simply to fill up spaces with 'features' which may or may not affect the minds and emotions of those who experience them. The cumulative effect of the designer's work on the space constitutes much more than the sum of its parts. Practitioners are usually quite at home with some kind of idea of the 'genius of the place'. At the very least, it is clear that a place's meaning tends to be wrapped up in its invisible, as well as its visible, qualities. In recent years, the word 'place' has been appropriated by geographers and others as a way of describing space that is freighted with meaning or character, but this appropriation effectively jargonizes the word, since it does not replace or transcend the word's other usages except in academic contexts. I offer up a new, more specific term – 'psychotopia' – as a shorthand for a way of describing places as they are actually experienced in life, not how they are 'objectively' assessed, described later, or assimilated into existing theories.

Psychotopia is 'place' understood not just in terms of location, but also in terms of meaning – its history, use, ecology, appearance, status, reputation, the people who interact with it, its potential future. It refers to the actual life of the place as it is experienced by those who visit it, and therefore also encapsulates the psychic impact and assimilation of human consciousness. It does not only describe 'the atmosphere of a place' as apprehended by the human mind; the landscape is not passive in that sense: psychotopia addresses the dynamic manner in which the atmosphere of places works on us, and – more controversially – how, in turn, our minds and experiences act on and influence places. Psychotopia is place seen anew, supercharged with meaning and life.

The word is an amalgam of 'psyche' and 'topos'. Topos refers to place, of course, but psyche, meaning 'mind' or 'animating spirit', has a dual application here. It refers to the spirit of the place itself – its 'mind', which exists independently of us and can, in a sense, speak to us. It also refers to our own psyches, in that I would argue that we become co-creators of places as soon as we experience them, and inevitably influence the prevailing sense of place through our own interaction. (The idea for psychotopia, in fact, emerged from the realization that garden and landscape designers are, in a way, the psychoanalysts of places, which itself stemmed from Gaston Bachelard's coinage of 'topo-analysis'.) Thus, the mental traffic travels both ways in a symbiotic process of mutual accretion: humans influence places, places influence humans. A psychotopia is a place where human psyche connects and combines with place-psyche. This is not to suggest that a place might have a 'brain', free will or a personality in a quasi-human sense; but on the

other hand, it is not to deny that a place can actively work on us, and that it can be possessed of a kind of memory, which can be expressed.

Do places have innate atmospheres, whether natural or engineered? It is generally accepted that landscapes and gardens are imbued with meanings that are derived from how and why we know them, and who we are. The perceived properties of all objects depend on the personality and culture of the viewer; therefore, as we perceive a place visually, we instantaneously interpret its meanings. Each person sees each place in a different way – in this sense, we see gardens not as they are, but as we are.

Some natural settings seem to possess a character largely derived from the topography and the way the plants and trees are grouped, and perhaps it is this alone which produces a sense of the spirit of a place, the consistent space flavour that emanates and is then absorbed and transmuted by all the different people who experience it. Man seems instinctively to ascribe spiritual values to natural places. In Ancient Greece, places with pronounced natural qualities were associated with particular deities: for example, those with a fertile atmosphere were dedicated to Demeter and Hera, and mountains with a 360° view were dedicated to Zeus. But perhaps it is more useful to examine the question from the standpoint of aesthetics rather than spirituality, which is precisely what the contemporary phenomenological aesthetician Arnold Berleant has done in studies such as *Aesthetics of Environment*. 'The human environment', he writes, 'has sensory richness, directness and immediacy, together with cultural patterns and meanings that perception carries, and these give environment its thick texture. Environment, then, is a complex idea,

the more so when we consider it aesthetically.' Gardens and landscapes
are complex places, whether we like it or not. It is impossible to conceive
of them simply as agglomerations of surface detail.

As visitors at gardens or landscapes, I would argue we are not just passive
observers. We are co-creators, and every time we experience a garden we
remake it for ourselves and others. In this most mutable of artforms, the
physical appearance of the place and its ecological diversity might actually
be less important to the sense of place than the cumulative meanings accorded
it by previous visitors. Gardens and landscapes are not unique in that visitors
participate in the creation work of art – in painting, Ernst Gombrich first pointed
out our role as co-creators in terms of optical effects – but our interactions are
perhaps more profound and dynamic. By some unquantifiable but describable
process, the meanings accorded to a place by successive visitors, and the
nature of their interaction with it, become absorbed: every time we visit a
landscape we contribute something to its richness. The ghostly impressions
of our interaction may be faint or imperceptible, but they remain nevertheless.

People can have different kinds of relationships with gardens: as part of
a community, on an individual level and in terms of a legacy after death. The
aesthetic geographer Yi-Fu Tuan believes space becomes place as it becomes
endowed with value and meaning: the garden is made into a cultural landscape
by its users. The essential difference between untouched wilderness and other
types of landscape is that the latter is always culturally transformed to some
degree. The potentialities for landscape designers – particularly those in the
conceptualist milieu – can be seen coming to the fore here.

In terms of a local community, a place can take on the character of 'a community of memory', in Josiah Royce's phrase. The landscape becomes a physical realization of that community. Just as it is a commonplace to note that a garden is often an expression of the owner's personality, it can also be true that a landscape is a reflection of the community which interacts with it. Albert Camus put it like this: 'Sense of place is not just something people know and feel, it is something people do'. These are not uncontroversial statements when one considers the architectural development of cities and their neighbourhoods. A city can seem to speak to us quite distinctly, as Louis Kahn suggests: 'A city is a place where a small boy, as he walks through it, may see something that will tell him what he wants to do with his whole life.'

Berleant has summarized the importance of place in our lives: 'For most people, the lived, living landscape is the commonplace setting of everyday life, and how we engage with the prosaic landscapes of home, work, local travel and recreation is an important measure of the quality of our lives. How we engage aesthetically with our landscape is a measure of the intrinsic value of our experience.' In aesthetic terms, simply being outdoors creates a completely different spatial, emotional, cultural and artistic context. There are so many variables and distractions. In one sense, nature is chaos. Landscapes and gardens are places where we might have what feels like a visceral, emotional, almost unmediated interaction with the world of raw experience. Compare our experience of physical engagement with a garden with the quotidian realities of a life lived mainly indoors, where we travel around in cars and segue from one indoor space to the next. Outside, we are physically and emotionally

vulnerable, and therefore more sensitive to our surroundings. Our effortless engagement with the landscape that surrounds us is in its way as intense an engagement as the one we effortfully invent when considering a painting or sculpture in the art gallery, though it is by its nature often more diffuse.

Martin Heidegger's influential 1951 lecture, 'Building Dwelling Thinking', introduced his concept of the four-fold of Earth, sky, mortals and divinities. The four-fold defines what it really means to dwell (in this context, simply 'to be') on Earth. 'When places are actively sensed,' he said, 'the physical landscape becomes wedded to the landscape of the mind, to the roving imagination, and where the mind may lead is anybody's guess.' It is a visionary explication of a dynamic process, although Heidegger also sees building, dwelling and thinking as a desirable human prerogative, in that dwelling is understanding our place in the cosmos, building is expressing those ideals, and thinking is our awareness of it. The psychic connection between people and place may not simply be emotional, but hold greater significance for us. Some of our worries about what a landscape or garden is – is it a space, or an object, or an experience? – mirror our concerns about our relationship with the cosmos.

The importance of place was appreciated by Aristotle, who included 'where' as one of the ten defining characteristics of any object. But in Newtonian physics, place became just another way of describing the physical compartmentalization of space: space is by definition empty and has no specific properties of its own. In recent years, a few philosophers and scientists have tried to reclaim 'place' as a defining aspect of humanity – more important than time, for example. A radical idea has been floated (by Heidegger): that space

and time are contained in places, rather than places in space and time. This idea of place as the beginning of all experience has been gaining currency. The philosopher Edward S. Casey has even suggested that the phenomenological 'lifeworld' be replaced by 'placeworld'.

Cosmologists have now given up on the idea of the linear progression of history through time, in favour of a view of the cosmos defined by the types of raw energies it contains. Time has been discredited: it varies from the top of a tall building to the bottom, time runs differently in space, and, in any case, the human conception of time is fatally biased towards the future. Perhaps we do not live 'in time' after all, because we do not understand infinity, rather we live in places, in the where, which we can more readily comprehend. Everything we do and perceive has to happen in some place. We cannot imagine time without place, and when we do, we call it hell. In 1967 Michel Foucault gave a lecture in which he introduced some potentially useful imagery: 'The present epoch will perhaps be above all the epoch of space. We are in the epoch of simultaneity; we are in the epoch of juxtaposition, the epoch of the near and far, of the side-by-side, of the dispersed. We are at a moment, I believe, when our experience of the world is less that of a long life developing through time than that of a network that connects points and intersects with its own skein.'

In this world throbbing with meaning, each place is a matrix of energy which is connected with thousands of others in our memories. Places are the interconnecting nodes of our experience. It is akin to a London taxi driver's 'knowledge': they do not carry a whole map of the city about in their head, but a series of little vignettes which they connect as they go. We could think of our

consciousness as thousands of such 'knowledges': A–Zs of friends, food preferences, the weather, foreign countries, and so on.

If places are the interconnecting nodes of our experience, a spatial plane which is perhaps more important than the temporal in terms of our relationship with the universe, then this must have a bearing on our attitude to death. We tend to think of death as the end of a life lived through time, and imagine that what we fear about death is the sudden extinction of that life. But perhaps this fundamental fear of death is founded not in anticipation of the absence of life, but in a fear of suddenly being nowhere. (In our society, the lowest castes of all are the placeless peoples: the gypsies, the travellers, the refugees, the asylum seekers.) To be in no place, psychologically speaking, is the worst fate of all, since it means either madness or death, whereas to be in a place that is right is paradise – which brings us back to gardens and landscapes.

Garden and landscape design is the aesthetic correlative of this meaningful relationship with the universe. Places, both urban and natural, are matrices of energy where thousands of strands of meaning enfold the visitor, who becomes a participant and co-creator of that place. Gardens are, for many of us, the most special places of all, filled with myriad threads of experience, emotion and memory which combine to make them meaningful. The ideas behind psychotopia do not require 'belief'. Psychotopia represents a descriptive attitude to be used for examining what it is in experience that makes places seem special or unique to us, taking into account both observable facts and more abstract intuitions. Its application to conceptualist landscape design is in the first instance theoretical, but may also, conceivably, become practical.

Trinidad Vienna

Theoretical outfit with groundbreaking conceptualist landscape ideas.

Artist and academic Mario Terzic has produced a notable body of theoretical and on-the-ground conceptual landscape work since the early 1990s, when he took up a post at Vienna University of Applied Arts. His most sustained and intense phase of work to date has been the Trinidad project, founded in 1997 in partnership with colleagues including Norbert Bacher and finally disbanded in 2005. Trinidad was one of the most irreverent and imaginatively unbounded conceptualist groups – probably one reason why so few of its speculative projects ever came to fruition. Since its value was as much theoretical as anything, this does not seem to matter overmuch in hindsight; Trinidad asked questions and made suggestions which other landscape outfits did not think to pursue.

Taken as whole, the output of Terzic and Trinidad can be seen as the most worked-out theoretical structure or manifesto of landscape conceptualism. Terzic's startlingly original and confrontational ideas – particularly those related to historic landscapes – constitute an antagonistic challenge to established notions of how best to create, conserve or curate sites (usually thought to be by 'treading lightly' on the ground, or honouring a romance of nature), since he invariably suggests some radical new artistic interpretation. Younger, angrier designers may posture as rebels, but this middle-aged academic of conventional appearance has the capacity to enrage quite as much as enthrall. He notes with grim satisfaction that he was recently cited as 'Public Enemy No 5 of Historic Landscape' in a recent state-sponsored handbook in Austria.

Terzic began his career in industrial design and was then assistant to Austrian sculptor Walter Pichler for five years. He began thinking more about landscape from 1978, when he curated an exhibition in Frankfurt for which he took artefacts from 'various museums and their storerooms' and put them together. 'For me the process of curating and exhibiting the artefacts was a way of placing more emphasis on the environment.' His next exhibition took place in the garden of the Vienna Belvedere. 'I tried to use sculpture to lead visitors through different spaces,' he recalls. 'The most important thing was a sense of movement.' In the 1980s, Terzic conducted guided tours to France and Italy; for one such trip, he persuaded the Juventus football coach to allow his party of thirty to watch the team train while they listened to the music of Erik Satie. In 1991 he began teaching graphic art at Vienna University of Applied Arts, and it was at this point that he took his students on a formative tour of seven British gardens, including Stowe, Claremont, Great Dixter, Derek Jarman's garden in Dungeness, and Stourhead.

Terzic's abiding conceptual concern has been the use and 'abuse' of history, in particular with regard to man-made landscape sites. 'We asked some questions,' he

LEFT AND OPPOSITE Trinidad's witty conceptual landscape schemes were often calculated to outrage the heritage and conservation lobbies. One early idea (opposite) envisaged a topiary garden featuring box shapes clipped in the form of designer scent bottles. 'Aerostat' (left) was 'a completely new kind of garden tour, using a one-person helium balloon' – in this case, over the gardens of Herrenhausen, in Germany. Exhibition, 1999.

recalls. 'Why should historic gardens remain in decay? Why should they only be restored in a historical way? We felt that some historic gardens could be developed by artists.' This is precisely what Terzic and his colleagues set out to do. The first Trinidad publication was a 1998 book about Baroque designer André Le Nôtre, a remarkable sketchbook filled with Terzic's pencil drawings, asking the question 'Who was André Le Nôtre?' on the first page. Trinidad's first major exhibition (and catalogue) – 'Immobilien und Realitäten' – was staged in Vienna in the same year, a magnificent outpouring of polemically inspired conceptual themes and ideas based round images and memories of historic gardens. The show was packed with original and provocative projects, such as open-air garden hotels, hot-air balloon guided tours of landscapes, athletics-track ornamentation, erotic retreats, lighting plans, and outlandishly themed topiary schemes. Many of these early ideas were revisited in later exhibitions and publications under the Trinidad imprimatur.

Terzic's contention with regard to the treatment of historical landscapes can be summed up as a conviction that they must constantly be reinterpreted conceptually in order for their meanings to remain live. In 2001 the National Trust admirably invited Trinidad to stage an exhibition at Osterley Park, an 18th-century house and estate in the western outskirts of London. The exhibition showcased such ideas as a bird's-eye-view garden tour of the Baroque garden of Herrenhausen, using a one-person helium balloon and harness hovering 60m above ground, and a 'Risk Pavilion', a large tent containing a screen showing video footage of 'natural catastrophes sparked off by faulty planning and over-exploitation'. Terzic states: 'Interpreted statically as a monument, a garden becomes a fossil. Art gardens are singular, megalomaniac or fantastical creations and must be understood as individual works more closely related to film, theatre, poetry or living music than to architecture. Their best protection is integration into the rhythms of the present.'

Among Terzic's realized projects is the 1999 installation entitled 'Noise Gate', at Gesmold Castle Garden in Lower Saxony. The boundary of the ruined castle's garden is in places just 30m from the Berlin–Amsterdam motorway, with the noise adding a frisson of 'panic' to any experience of the garden, hence the piece's subtitle, 'Panic Arcadia'. Visitors were given headphones on arrival and were thus able to enjoy an alternative soundscape to that offered in reality. Terzic calls Trinidad 'a polemical-theoretical movement', and continues his explorations today, as Studio Terzic, with a similar level of energy.

GDANSK, MŁODE MIASTO/YOUNG CITY · SITE OF THE FORMER "LENIN SHIPYARD" [SOLIDARNOSC GARDEN] — STRUCTURE CARRIED BY CRANES — OPEN TO LICENSED CRANE OPERATORS ONLY

Sportscapes Reviewed

INNSBRUCK 2004

The potential of sporting sites and sporting imagery was first realized as a missed creative opportunity, and then became something of an obsession for Terzic, resulting in the major 1999 project Harrach GT and the newspaper-format *Sportscapes*, with its variety of theoretical ideas.

Harrach GT proposed that Austria's historic Harrach Park and ruined Prugg Castle might be reinvented as a rally-driving course, an outrageous suggestion that seemed formulated to prick the sensibilities of the garden-heritage lobby. This was a fully worked-out and costed project envisioned on a large scale; like all of Trinidad's projects, it operated on the fringes of possibility but was actually achievable. Terzic's foray into the world of sport developed into a philosophy: 'Sports [have become] the most important point of contact between man and nature . . . It is all the more astonishing that landscape plays no (or a comparatively underdeveloped) role as a culture bearer of the sports world. Even the economic potential that lies in designing these cult sites is left out of account. One could say sportscapes are "neglected landscapes".'

Trinidad's other sporting projects include the 'Heroes' Paradise' at Mösle Stadium in the Rhine Valley; the Innsbruck Landscape Balcony (see opposite), which turns the great ski jump into a covered video installation walkway; and Silverstowe Pier, a 7km-long aerial walkway in Northamptonshire that links the Silverstone motor-racing circuit with Stowe Landscape Gardens. Similarly, this robust and imaginative theoretical method has also led to an exploration of the past, present and future of the old Lenin Shipyard at Gdansk, in Poland (see above).

Michael Van Valkenburgh

Sensual, experiential landscapes, mediated by raw nature.

New York and Cambridge (USA)

Treading the line between academia and professional practice, Michael Van Valkenburgh has built up a respected corpus of work, which is broadly Modernist in stance yet incorporates ideas about the episodic and psychological aspects of gardens gleaned from 18th-century English landscapes. Van Valkenburgh has been involved with Harvard University's Graduate School of Design since 1982, but in 1990 he made the decision to concentrate on his landscape practice. 'After I had become a full-time design professor,' Van Valkenburgh explains, 'and was wondering whether I could take on a really big project, a friend said to me: "You want to be a boutique practice all your life?"' He has since been able to take on more large-scale corporate and public work, as well as private garden designs, and has

opened a New York office. In recent years, Van Valkenburgh has turned away from Modernism and minimalism and has gravitated instead towards the irregular qualities of natural forms and environments.

At first glance, much of Van Valkenburgh's work appears to stem from the great mid-century tradition of Modernism in American landscape architecture, which has translated so successfully to the corporate and public sphere. But look closer, and a kind of shaggy Modernism can be discerned, honouring what he calls the 'playful, irregular, rowdy, undisciplined, unpredictable' qualities of natural landscape. Van Valkenburgh lets more of nature and natural form into his work than do most of his contemporaries.

'I do come out of a Modernist tradition,' he explains,

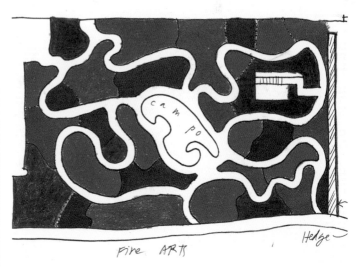

LEFT AND ABOVE Located on a roof at the Carnegie Mellon Institute, this 3,000m² garden is described by Van Valkenburgh as an 'inventive reconsideration of horticulture' and a 'bold artistic consideration of form and colour'. Kraus Campo, Pittsburgh 2003.

'but as a creative person I have to ask, "How can we stretch that medium?" Minimalism is over: it's the end of a Modernist era. What is the power of those landscapes? Where do we go from here? My critique is that there is no place to go, aesthetically. Eco-landscape brings in a more tolerant aesthetic – letting some of the messiness of nature inoculate the aesthetic experience.'

Van Valkenburgh is in fact scathing about the new conceptual strand in garden and landscape design: 'Cornerstone just disgusts me. I mean, why are these people trying to be artists? I say: respect your medium. Great art grows out of the capacities of the medium you are working with. The art of landscape is not about appropriating or being derivative of other artforms: the reason for studying art history is not to mine it for ideas.'

The unifying tone of all Van Valkenburgh's work lies in the way that the architectural austerity of Modernism is offset by natural effects. This is done in a variety of ways. The crisp, geometric lines of the design are blurred at the edges by massed plantings of grasses, lines of native trees and other naturalistic elements, so that the balance between the two creates tension and interest. 'We draw some of the power of the natural landscape into the design arena, but we don't let nature draw the aesthetic boundaries,' he explains. Sometimes this is realized simply as a quotation from the English Picturesque tradition (Mill Race Park at Columbus, Indiana, is an example). Then there are the juxtapositions of materiality: smooth stainless steel or concrete next to exuberant plantings which complement rather than obscure the artifice of the design. Van Valkenburgh says he has become more instinctive about this over time: 'It's what happens when you are confident with your medium. It's the difference between

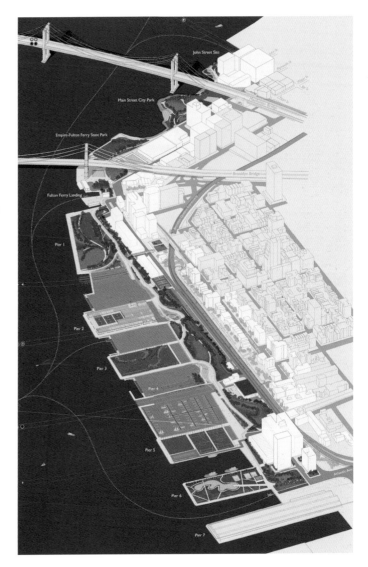

being thirty-five and fifty.' Finally, the physical, sensual, experiential elements of landscape are always to the fore: 'When you are standing in a landscape and the land in front of you is moving up and down, it is an incredibly physical experience,' he says.

ABOVE The masterplan of this project combines the site's industrial history with cultivated lawns and juxtaposes it against new pieces of wildscape, especially at the water's edge. Brooklyn Bridge Park, New York 2003.

Garden on Turtle Creek

DALLAS 1999

Because the client for this garden design is a keen birdwatcher and the site is on a perilously sloping parcel of woodland on heavy clay, Van Valkenburgh conceived of a stroll garden with a circular route hemmed in by thick, bird-friendly native foliage. This was planned in the spirit of an English landscape garden, as a sequence of brief but intense episodes. 'I spent a lot of time looking at those 18th-century landscapes,' Van Valkenburgh says. 'I realized that what is interesting in landscape is how people interact with it, how you are surprised spatially. What you get in the 1700s is an aesthetic where the human being becomes the engine of the experience of landscape.'

The garden has three distinct stages. The first is a green plinth of lawn next to the modern house, which begins to instil a sense of transition into nature for the visitor. Here, rectangular steel pavers are a stark architectural intervention, which nevertheless have an organic quality in their arrangement. The mid-slope is densely planted, with selected views open to the creek below. Encroaching vegetation contrasts with shiny steel steps and geometric concrete blocks. The lowest level has been left wild-looking, with the thick creekside vegetation supplemented by native birch, iris and palmetto. The concrete 'logs' on the bank form naturalistic stepping-stones.

Herman Miller Factory Landscape

CHEROKEE COUNTY (USA) 2001

Van Valkenburgh and colleague Matthew Urbanski's solution to the problem of landscaping – on a low budget – a rather anonymous furniture factory in rural Georgia (where 550 parking spaces were also needed) was to eschew muscle-bound corporate Modernism and opt instead for an ecologically aware design. The firm's statement on this reads: 'The current treatment of industrial landscapes usually condones chemically sustained lawns, massive expanses of impervious surfaces, and a static aesthetic of manicured tranquillity that often denies the site's individual character, seasonal dynamics and long-term health as a living ecology.' The vast factory roofspace and the area's high seasonal rainfall meant that run-off from the roofs might lead to serious soil erosion. As Van Valkenburgh puts it: 'The water basins we made were an ecological necessity, but they normally look like something a couple of beavers made at the weekend after a six-pack of beer. We thought we'd make these triangular forms integral to the car park.' The water from the basins runs off into the surrounding wetland meadows, planted with reeds, grasses and sedges, which have in turn become habitats for birds and insects.

Teardrop Park

NEW YORK 2006

Van Valkenburgh's ecological perspective found early expression in this popular park at Battery Park City, the southernmost point of Manhattan. The design responds to the challenge of making a park that is lodged within a courtyard surrounded by four apartment buildings, each taller than the site is wide. Although the park is not small – approximately two acres – the built context gives it an intensely urban feeling. The brief was to offer a variety of experiences for the full range of future users, to create places for children to play and explore a natural environment, as well as spaces conducive to relaxation and respite for adults and seniors.

The park's physical design takes clues from the landscape of the Hudson River Valley, freely bringing pieces of Upstate New York to Lower Manhattan. The design has a robust naturalism that continues some of the spirit of the upland area of South Cove Park, where the craggy stones and multi-stemmed trees create a space of both prospect and refuge. A material language and emphasis on stone and vegetation is extended into the park to form the essence of its material structure. In addition, Teardrop Park has an environmental agenda, giving nature a jump-start in establishing itself on a site composed of fill from the original excavation of the World Trade Center.

Tahari Courtyards

MILLBURN (USA) 2003

The twin 7m x 11m open courtyards near the entrance to this fashion-company office building and warehouse in New Jersey can be seen as a means of blurring the distinction between inside and outside in the conventional manner, but they also encapsulate some of the perennial concerns of Van Valkenburgh's practice. These gardens, with their robust textures and contrasting materials, insert a natural integrity into an otherwise austere modern interior. The ground plane is perhaps most striking: a moss carpet of *Plagiomnium cuspidatum*, together with areas of smooth grey river stones, bisected by a walkway of rough-hewn planks of black-locust wood (*Robinia pseudoacacia*), sawn so that the silhouette of the trunk's edges is not smoothed off. These rough, wooden planks are a typical Van Valkenburgh intervention: Modernist in conception, yet at the same time earthy and natural. An understorey of ferns, hellebores and narcissus gives way to a miniature forest of 9m birch and evergreen groves of bamboos, which act as screens for the office workers beyond. 'What's cool about the Tahari project is that it's not somewhere where the most glamorous people in the company get to go,' Van Valkenburgh says. 'It's a warehouse – it's where the bookkeeping gets done.'

Brita von Schoenaich

Petersham (UK)

Individualistic designer creating her own tradition.

Born in Hamburg, Brita von Schoenaich trained in landscape architecture in Germany and worked in a nursery there before going to Kew to study for the world-renowned three-year diploma in Botanical Horticulture. In 1991 she set up a design business with Tim Rees, and since then they have garnered an impressive client list that includes a number of stars from the wider art and design world, such as sculptor Anish Kapoor and textile designer Cath Kidston. Most of von Schoenaich's work is in Britain, though she has commissions in France and Germany and is designing the new garden for the British Embassy in Warsaw. Of her four colleagues, one is Italian, one French, one Polish and one English. She jokes: 'We are always being asked to do English gardens!'

Von Schoenaich is associated with the New Perennials look in horticulture – sculpted drifts of grasses and perennial flowers which look best in late summer and autumn – because she played a key role in its early development in Britain as the organizer of two seminal conferences at Kew on the subject, in 1994 and 1997. But now, she says, she has moved on. 'So many people were so passionate about this New Perennials thing, but for me it was never really a "school" or a manifesto,' she explains. 'I always want to try out new things – not to follow fashions, but to experiment on my own.'

At the moment, von Schoenaich is preoccupied with what she calls plant compatibility – the idea of using a pared-down palette of plants which will thrive together ecologically and aesthetically in almost any given situation. It is a kind of conceptualist horticulture, in that such designs are usually kept extremely simple or else given structure by an overarching metaphor. 'If you have eight or ten compatible perennials that can live together – in terms

of their colour, too – you can put them almost anywhere,' von Schoenaich says.

She expresses this horticultural approach as a linear style of planting – something which can be seen in her treatment of the wide borders in front and to one side of Tate Britain (see below and opposite), and to some extent in her recent design for the walled garden at Marks Hall (see p. 328), a public arboretum in Essex. For this look,

six to ten types of plant are arranged in straight lines, with no intermingling, to make a striking formal pattern. 'I'm trying to find a modern way of using annuals,' von Schoenaich says. 'It is planting design which has not developed since Victorian times.'

At Tate Britain, where she has been commissioned to redesign the bedding schemes twice each year, she throws a dice to determine which of the six plants to use for the next stretch, and then throws it again to ascertain the number of metres (one to six). On other occasions she has introduced highly unusual planting combinations,

ABOVE AND OPPOSITE Von Schoenaich has designed twice-yearly rectangular borders in the lawns in front of Tate Britain since 2001. These planted strips have provided the opportunity for much experimentation, though usually only two or three kinds of plant are used in each scheme. Tate Britain, London (ongoing).

such as a scheme in 2004 which comprised a strict grid of willow-tree whips of about a metre high, coming into leaf above a planting of white and pale green tulips. With the right plant combinations, von Schoenaich hopes this philosophy will increase longevity and reduce maintenance, while staying interesting all year round.

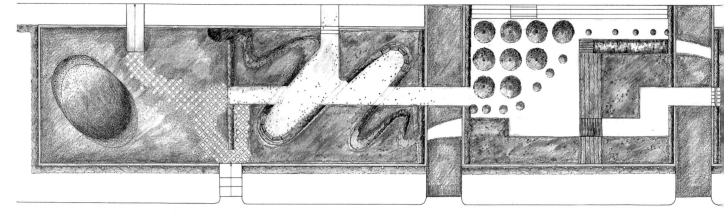

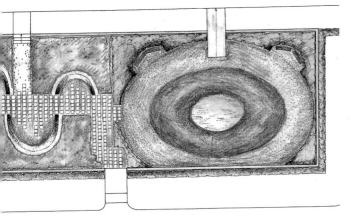

Marks Hall

ESSEX (UK) 2007

The 18th-century walled kitchen garden at this public arboretum in Coggeshall, Essex was redeveloped by von Schoenaich and Rees as a series of garden spaces flanked by a wide lawn on one side and a long border against the brick wall on the other. Von Schoenaich was responsible for the garden spaces, while Rees designed the border.

The walled garden itself is highly unusual because one long side of its rectangle is not walled, but bounded instead by a long, formal rectangular canal. This gives immediately on to a large apron of green lawn, bounded by a long yew hedge with the orange brick wall as a backdrop beyond. Von Schoenaich did not wish to compromise the simplicity of this, so she created the garden sequence behind the hedge where it cannot be seen from outside.

'I wanted to make a series of five garden rooms that are linked conceptually,' she explains. 'The first one contains an earth sculpture in the form of a scrape of earth. Some sort of movement is triggered off by this, which is then expressed through the curves that travel the length of the garden. In the second garden space pittosporum hedges continue the curve, and then stone walls take over. The central garden is open-sided – it is the only place where you can see out to the canal.' The meandering curves of the garden are finally resolved in the last space, conceived as a classical grove. 'It calms down at the end after all this movement,' von Schoenaich explains.

Linear planting is again the theme here, with combinations such as lines of lavender with blue bearded irises interplanted – 'lined up like soldiers', as von Schoenaich puts it. 'Usually with perennial plants it has to be a naturalistic scheme. I wanted to break with that completely.'

WES & Partner Hamburg

Flexible, functional spatial design based on conceptual artistic principles.

WES & Partner was founded in 1969 by Hinnerk Wehberg and Gustav Lange, who both came from art backgrounds. They started out creating sculptural pieces and installations in and around public and commercial buildings, but gradually moved into the sphere of landscape design. In the mid-1970s they were joined by Gundolf Eppinger, who had a background in practical horticulture, and by the 1990s the firm employed some sixty people. This period marked a watershed in the firm's fortunes, as it had expanded rapidly without an adequate infrastructure. Wolfgang Betz and Peter Schatz – both trained landscape architects – joined in 1996 when the firm's staff was cut to a third of its previous size and four of the six partners left.

Today the partners at WES are Wehberg, Betz, Schatz and Michael Kaschke. 'We have completely different characters and completely different attitudes and approaches,' Betz states with disarming cheerfulness, maintaining that the tensions this creates can have a positive effect on the work. At an early stage one partner will take responsibility for a project, but the dialogue continues as the other partners each form a critique of the developing work. 'It sometimes feels as if our office is a jury room,' Betz says. 'We discuss everything and we do not always agree.' Betz claims that all four are dominant partners, which is a highly unusual, if not unique, set-up in professional landscape practice. It does not seem to inhibit their creativity: WES has scored major successes recently in international design competitions, notably the 'Lansisatamanpuisto Jewel', a waterfront project in Helsinki.

WES & Partner is a conceptual landscape outfit in the strict sense of the word, in that each and every design is underpinned by a single strong idea that informs every detail: functional, decorative and ecological. The four

different sensibilities at large in the company make for a considerable range in the resultant work, but everything in a project goes back to a foundational idea. 'Even if we do a romantic and absolutely green garden, we first make a concept,' Betz asserts. The aim is to come to each project fresh, without preconceptions, so that the emotional and intellectual response is authentic.

Like many conceptualists, Betz has reservations about the current fashion for a chiefly ecological approach to design, although he points out that he has formed this opinion as a result of specializing in the subject during his training. 'My personal attitude is: let's forget green. We are working with spaces and we have to create strong concepts which have real clarity, but at the same time allow for

some ambiguity,' he says. Betz is also unhappy with the term 'landscape architecture' as too narrow a description for their work. 'We work in cities and we work with spaces, not landscapes,' he explains.

The sheer variety of WES's output is probably its most salient feature – the four-partner creative alliance makes it impossible to generalize about the 'voice' or tone of the work. There are a few constants, however. One is an affinity with artistic practice: Wehberg, Betz, Schatz and Kaschke are comfortable with the notion of their work reflecting a personal aesthetic response to the space and its needs, as opposed to the more objective and emotionally distanced functionalism of traditional Modernism. Unlike many conceptualist designers, WES do not appear to expend much time exorcising the demons of High Modernism absorbed during their professional training. Land Art is another clear influence, with WES designers frequently using grassy landforms and monumental sculptural interventions to break up naturalistic designs. There is also an abiding interest in the self-sustaining, self-repeating and constantly varying forms of nature used as a basis for design motifs. On paper, some of the large-scale works look like illustrations of the workings of chaos theory, with organically derived forms repeated and varied over large areas of space.

LEFT, ABOVE AND OPPOSITE Bringing light down into the relatively narrow inner courtyard was one of the challenges facing the designers at this apartment block. Mark-Brandenburg pine branches and slender stalks of bamboo emphasize the narrow proportions. Dorotheenblöcke, Berlin 1996.

Penthouse Garden

HANOVER 2005

Of his design for this penthouse garden in Hanover, Betz recalls, 'The client is an interesting person – he collects art and is a detail fetishist . . . The existing garden was a dense, jungly mass of plants with a pond, but I thought the client would want something more interesting than that. So I suggested an outdoor living room with the sky as its ceiling. That was the concept.'

The carpet of this 'living room' was created from turf enclosed by an inner frame of stainless steel, while the billowing purple-grey curtains were made from a type of hard-wearing, waterproof plastic that is used in swimming pools. An existing wall was covered with a bright-red plastic material, and WES designers also created the distinctive furniture. The white marble used for the floor of the interior of the penthouse was continued outside, to further enhance the indoor–outdoor sensation. The client wanted trees, so Betz sourced amelanchiers which now protrude from pure-white bases. He says they introduce a graphic element, like pictures on the wall of a real living room. This sparky and original space is a relatively rare example of a conceptual landscape design realized in a private domestic setting.

Autostadt

WOLFSBURG 2000

Wolfsburg is a company town, where the headquarters and factory site of Volkswagen and its sister marques, including Skoda and Bentley, are known collectively as 'Car City'. There is a patriotic tradition in Germany of customers travelling to Wolfsburg en famille to buy a new car. The company wanted to make this into a day out that was enjoyable for everyone (not just dad), and in doing so they have turned the car-showroom concept into a theme-park experience. Five exhibition pavilions, each one devoted to a Volkswagen marque, surround the central circular showroom, in which the cars for sale are on display. Each pavilion was designed by a different architect, with car-history displays leavened by such child-friendly gimmicks as a car vertically suspended on a wall (which explodes into smoke and noise every five minutes or so), the car appearing and disappearing as the wall rotates. WES & Partner were commissioned to design the landscape spaces which link these pavilions, and they decided to aim for a sense of relaxed transition between the frenetic, information-rich display areas. 'Our intention was to work with the hills and to mould the landscape,' Betz says. 'We tried to keep a little bit of calmness, so we just kept that one main idea in mind. If we had tried to "brand" the landscape around each pavilion with a different concept, it would have become unbearably chaotic.'

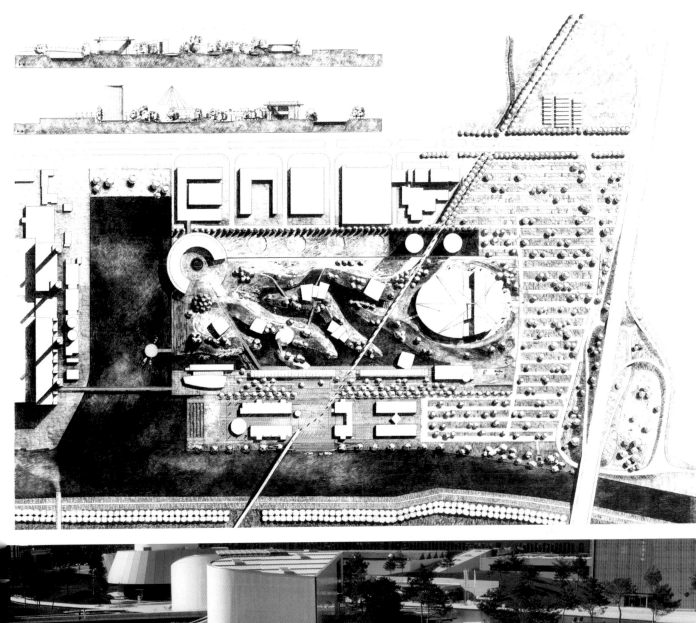

West 8 Rotterdam

Well-established conceptualist outfit working on a large scale.

The partners and senior designers of Rotterdam's West 8, founded in 1987, are Adriaan Geuze, Edzo Bindels, Martin Biewenga and Jerry van Eyck, though it is Geuze whose name is most associated with the company and who acts as its lead spokesperson. The emphasis in the work is firmly on large-scale city planning, to a degree unmatched by any other company profiled in this volume. Indeed, internationally West 8 can be considered the most successful conceptualist player in this large-scale realm.

West 8's mission statement is worth quoting: 'The knowledge that contemporary landscape is for the major part artificial, made up of different components – designed and undesigned – allows West 8 the freedom to respond by positioning its own narrative spaces. The basic ingredients

are ecology, infrastructure, weather conditions, building programmes and people. The goal is to incorporate awareness of these various aspects in a playful, optimistic manner, stimulating the desire to conquer and take possession of a space. On the other hand, the realization of an urban masterplan is a long-term process. It is not a ready-made object, but accumulates richness and beauty through time. Large-scale interventions in a city require a strong and understandable concept in order to carry a unique identity.'

The realization here is that a strict conceptualist or metaphorical scheme would be aesthetically inappropriate and practically unworkable at the city or town masterplan scale of design. But that does not mean that disparate areas and fine details should not have some kind of coherence – West 8's work is characterized by an exuberant artistic flair and originality which never undermines the functionalism of spaces. If they make a gesture, it tends to be grand and totemic – as with most conceptualists, theirs is not design which blends in with the background. The emphasis on playfulness and optimism is another abiding conceptualist concern that is missing from the austere pieties of architectural Modernism.

The company's methodology springs from an interpretation of the psychology and emotional needs of urban dwellers, with an emphasis on transport and movement through space: the speed which we travel at and the way that affects how we experience landscape. Geuze cites the morphing identity of the city dweller, as he or she

LEFT At this university garden, say the designers, 'the strict architecture of the building and the right-angled corners of the ground plane shape the ideal context for an introverted garden'. University Library Garden, Utrecht (The Netherlands) 2005.

LEFT The proximity of an ecological park dictated the careful design of the bank headquarters. The steel bridge and red sandstone blocks complement the labyrinth of box hedges and red gravel that wind through Bloeiendael Park into a birch copse. Fortis Bank Headquarters, Utrecht (The Netherlands) 1995.

shifts into different roles throughout the day. 'The hunting instinct of the Homo sapiens,' he writes, 'still exists in the contemporary city dweller, and his capacity to identify with the landscape is continuously evolving . . . The daily trips from work, to home, to school, to sports facilities or to friends and family are ritual journeys through challenging surroundings. On these trips, signs and symbols guide the route. In the classic city, life is captured in a static hierarchy. The Modernist city produces an efficient layout of urban programme and circulation. Contemporary urban planning should create non-identifiable objects, secret gardens and voids.'

West 8 reacts against the sheer banality of much modern landscape space, including the 'unofficial', in-between spaces – the liminal, the heterotopic. These can themselves be celebrated through the notion of 'unprogrammed space', urban breathing spaces possessed of an open design interpretation. Such 'blank spaces' are an important element in many of West 8's plans. Elsewhere, their work

positively celebrates the urban 'mess' and detritus which encroaches on designed space, because of its authenticity in a city setting. Variety is a key concern here. Geuze attacks what he calls the 'monoculture' of city life, where 'to accommodate mass-culture, the contemporary city is organized into a one-dimensional space and experience. Every single part is designed for one function only.' West 8's aim is to free up the individual – mentally and physically – in an urban context. And once again, here is a conceptualist landscape design outfit suggesting that city dwellers need to be challenged and delighted by urban landscape design, not placated and soothed by a green vision.

Geuze acknowledges both the vulnerability and euphoria of modern culture in his analysis: 'The city dweller is mobile and exchanging cultures: consuming like a supermarket shopper. The euphoria of mass-culture creates a numb individual. Efficiency, regulations and even law prevent the urban dweller from interpreting the environment in his own way. In modern functionalist urban planning, every site, every spot has a given specific meaning. To exist, a human being must be able to experience the environment in his own way.'

This is a critique not just of the supposedly static aesthetic of Modernism ('the hysteric celebration of the window view'), but of contemporary urban planning in general. Uniquely and most ambitiously, West 8 extends the conceptualist programme to cover whole city planning, not just parts of cities.

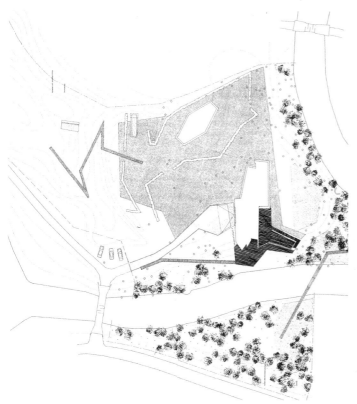

Möbius Garden

HET GOOI (THE NETHERLANDS) 1999

The site originally contained large rhododendrons and other species combined with the native oaks. The concept was to remove these large 'exotic' (but still very beautiful) plants and replace them with 'native' trees (*Pinus sylvestris*, *Fagus sylvatica*, *Quercus robur*, *Amelanchier lamarckii*), creating an overall woodland effect.

Around the swimming pool and leading up to the house, a distinction was made between 'wild' and 'tame.' A regularly mown 'English' lawn was established, while the grass beneath the trees was allowed to grow long as would naturally occur in a forest situation. Several species of fern (*Matteuccia struthiopteris*, *Dryopteris filix-mas*, *Polypodium vulgare*) of different sizes and growth rates were planted beneath the trees. Hedges (*Taxus baccata*) were planted at distinct changes in ground level. Once they have grown larger, the hedges will all be trimmed to the same level. A swimming pool is set in the middle of the lawn with shower and greenhouse nearby, while at the top of a small hill on the western side of the property lies a belvedere for chopping wood.

Apart from the existing bridge, which provides vehicular and pedestrian access for the inhabitants of the island, a small platform was constructed that provides the owners with private leisurely access by boat to the Möbius house and garden. The slate paving around the house is split on two levels. Grass is grown between the cracks to soften the greyness of the stone and to bring the green of the garden right up to the edge of the house. Leading from the driveway are zigzagging paths connecting the house and garden to the surrounding areas.

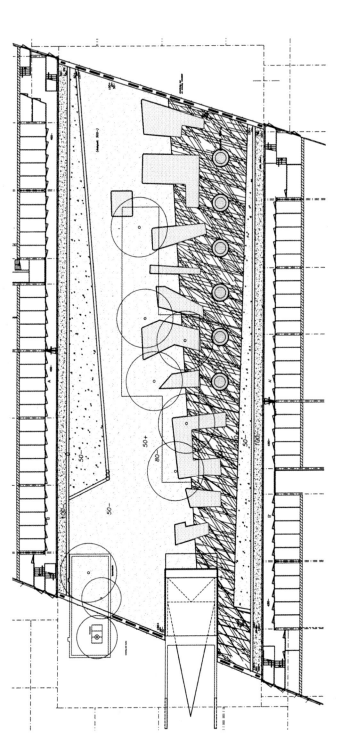

Sphinx Garden

AMSTERDAM 2001

The narrow courtyard of the Sphinx block in the large-scale Borneo Sporenburg development has characteristics of both interior and exterior. West 8's intention here was to make a 'poetic' garden as 'a natural still-life'. The zinc façades of the building inspired the design of four 5m-high free-standing vases, also made from zinc.

The vases were positioned in a surface of Norwegian slate, which reflected the silver-grey fishskin zinc façades. The other garden area consists of grass, blue flowers (hydrangeas) and shaped hedges. Eight large ginkgo trees create a surreal and contrasting botanical counterpoint to the architecture of the façades. The courtyard is bounded by a steel-plate fence featuring a graphic pattern based on the concept of ginkgo leaves.

Interpolis Headquarters

TILBURG (THE NETHERLANDS) 1998

The Interpolis headquarters lies on the axis of the station area of the city of Tilburg. The building is positioned on the north edge of a large triangular lot, so the garden covers one continuous stretch of approximately two hectares. This space forms a calm and introverted world, separated from its surroundings by hedges and a dark-green steel fence with a holly-leaf motif. In the daytime, it is freely accessible for employees and the Tilburg public.

It was felt that the large scale of the Interpolis headquarters called for large-scale garden design. Therefore Douglas firs were used, their long, lean shape offering a counterbalance to the tower of the building. The grass surface has a loose pattern based on the idea of tectonic shifts, with the edges defined by dark-grey concrete retaining walls. Canals or 'water tables' of varying lengths (20m to 85m), with an ecology of water lilies and frogs, form the central theme of the garden. Their shifting orientation and non-parallel shapes create a strong, constantly changing sense of perspective in the garden. Walking the soft paths paved with red-brown woodchips, one can find a seat on the broad edges of the water tables or the wood-surfaced retaining walls. The garden is

designed as a space for relaxation and enjoyment, where employees can work amid green surroundings. Several computer connections provide electricity and access to the headquarters' mainframe.

An elongated plateau of large slate slabs has been laid out directly against the building. This consists of various planes placed at different angles, a reference to the tectonic shifts in the grass surface nearby. Each spring the blossoms from the surrounding magnolia grove scatter themselves across the massive slates, the tender white blossoms contrasting with the rough, sharp-edged slate surface. A folded, wooden bridge crossing the plateau connects the entrance square with the garden. In addition to the two entrances in the fence, it provides a third, monumental entrance to the garden.

Geuze has suggested, 'The straightjacket of culture for the masses makes the city dweller crave for platforms inviting exhibitionism, apocalyptic sensations and the beauty of silence' – and something of that can be understood in this design.

Directory

Atelier Big City [10]
55 Mont-Royal Ouest, Suite 601
Montreal, Quebec H2T 2S6
Canada
T +1 514 849 6256
F +1 514 849 7013
E bigcity@atelierbigcity.com
W www.atelierbigcity.com

Lodewijk Baljon [14]
Cruquiusweg 10
Postbus 1068
1000 BB Amsterdam
The Netherlands
T +31 20 625 8835
F +31 20 420 6534
E postmaster@baljon.nl
W www.baljon.nl

Thomas Balsley [18]
31 West 27th Street, 9th Floor
New York, NY 10001
USA
T +1 212 684 9230
F +1 212 684 9232
E info@tbany.com
W www.tbany.com

Julia Barton [22]
Northumberland
UK
T/F +44 (0)1434 240990
E julia_barton@btinternet.com
W www.julia-barton.co.uk

BCA Landscape [26]
19 Old Hall Street
Liverpool L3 9JQ
UK
T +44 (0)151 242 6161
F +44 (0)151 236 4467
W www.bcalandscape.co.uk

Petra Blaisse [42]
Eerste Nassaustraat 5
1052 BD Amsterdam
The Netherlands
T +31 20 681 0801
F +31 20 681 0466
E office@insideoutside.nl
W www.insideoutside.nl

Jean-Pierre Brazs [48]
18, rue Georges Thill
75019 Paris
France
T +33 (0)614 194 554
E brazs@easyconnect.fr
W www.jpbrazs.com

Susanne Burger [54]
Rosenheimer Straße 139
D-81671 Munich
Germany
T +49 89 49 000 925
F +49 89 49 000 926
E buero@burgerlandschaftsarchitekten.de
W www.burgerlandschaftsarchitekten.de

Cao Perrot Studio [60]
3511 West 6th Street, Studio 5

Los Angeles, CA 90020
USA
T +1 213 458 2900
E stephen@caoperrotstudio.com

New York, NY
USA
T +1 213 458 2901
E andy@caoperrotstudio.com

28 bis rue Chauvelot
75015 Paris
France
T +33 (0)1 45 32 40 80
E xavier@caoperrotstudio.com
W www.caoperrotstudio.com

Paul Cooper [66]
Ty Bryn
Old Radnor, Presteigne
Powys LD8 2RN
UK
T +44 (0)7966 376 429
E paulcooper58@hotmail.com
W www.paulcooperdesign.co.uk

Claude Cormier [70]
5600 De Normanville
Montreal, Quebec H2S 2B2
Canada
T +1 514 849 8262
F +1 514 279 8076
E info@claudecormier.com
W www.claudecormier.com

E info@karresenbrands.nl
W www.karresenbrands.nl

Klahn + Singer [160]
Rastatter Straße 25
76199 Karlsruhe
Germany
T +49 721 884 101
F +49 721 882 906
E info@klahnsingerpartner.de
W www.ksp-landschaftsarchitekten.de

Land-I [166]
Rome, Italy
E land-i@archicolture.com
W www.archicolture.com

Die LandschaftsArchitekten [170]
Taunusstraße 47
65183 Wiesbaden
Germany
T +49 611 531 730
F +49 611 531 7388
E info@dielandschaftsarchitekten.de
W www.dielandschaftsarchitekten.de

Ron Lutsko [174]
2815 Eighteenth Street
San Francisco, CA 94110
USA
T +1 415 920 2800
F +1 415 920 2809
E mail@lutskoassociates.com
W www.lutskoassociates.com

Lützow 7 [180]
Lützowplatz 7
10785 Berlin
Germany
T +49 30 230 941 0
F +49 30 230 941 90
E info@luetzow7.de
W www.luetzow7.de

William Martin [184]
P.O. Box 46
Noorat, Victoria 3265
Australia
T +61 3 5592 5349
E williammartin@wigandia.com
W www.wigandia.com

Shunmyo Masuno [186]
Kenkoh-ji 1-2-1 Baba
Tsurumi-ku, Yokohama 230-0076
Japan
F +81 45 571 5201
E kenkohji@courante.plala.or.jp
W www.kenkohji.jp

Metagardens [194]
69 Shalimar Gardens
Acton, London W3 9JG
UK
T +44 (0)20 8993 6191
E info@metagardens.co.uk
W www.metagardens.co.uk

Meyer + Silberberg [198]
1443 Cornell Avenue
Berkeley, CA 94702
USA
T +1 510 559 2973
F +1 510 898 0488
E info@meyersilberberg.com
W www.meyersilberberg.com

Helle Nebelong [210]
Jaegersborg Allee 227 st. tv.
2820 Gentofte
Denmark
T/F +45 39 76 20 01
E helle@sansehaver.dk
W www.sansehaver.dk

Nip Paysage [216]
7468 rue Drolet
Montreal, Quebec H2R 2C4
Canada
T +1 514 272 6626
F +1 514 272 6622
E nip@nippaysage.ca
W www.nippaysage.ca

Antonio Perazzi [222]
Via Cesara Correnti 7
20123 Milan
Italy
T +39 (0)2 8940 4251
F +39 (0)2 8942 8652
E info@antonioperazzi.com
W www.antonioperazzi.com

Plant [224]
101 Spadina Avenue, Suite 208
Toronto, Ontario M5V 2K2
Canada
T +1 416 979 2012
F +1 416 979 1283
E studio@branchplant.com
W www.branchplant.com

Philippe Rahm [230]
12 rue Chabanais
75002 Paris
France
T +33 (0)1 49 26 91 55

Chemin de Noirmont 5
CH-1004 Lausanne
Switzerland
E info@philipperahm.com
W www.philipperahm.com

RCH Studios [242]
6824 Melrose Avenue
Los Angeles, CA 90038
USA
T +1 323 634 9220
F +1 323 634 9221
E mark@rchstudios.com
W www.rchstudios.com

Janet Rosenberg [250]
148 Kenwood Avenue
Toronto, Ontario M6C 2S3
Canada
T +1 416 656 6665

F +1 416 656 5756
E office@jrala.ca
W www.jrala.ca

Mario Schjetnan [254]
Fernando Montes de Oca No. 4
Colonia Condesa
Mexico City 06140
Mexico
T +52 5553 1248
F +52 5286 1013
W www.gdu.com.mx

Martha Schwartz [256]
147 Sherman Street, Suite 200
Cambridge, MA 02140
USA
T +1 617 661 8141
F +1 617 661 8707
E msi@marthaschwartz.com

65-69 East Road
London N1 6AH
UK
T +44 (0)20 7549 7497
F +44 (0)20 7250 0988
E llandels@marthaschwartz.com
W www.marthaschwartz.com

Vladimir Sitta [274]
L3 15 Randle Street
Surry Hills, New South Wales 2010
Australia

T +61 2 9211 6060
F +61 2 9211 6057
E room413@tig.com.au

SLA [278]
Refshalevej 153A
DK-1432 Copenhagen
Denmark
T +45 33 91 13 16
E landskab@sla.dk
W www.sla.dk

Ken Smith [284]
79 Chambers Street, #2
New York, NY 10007
USA
T +1 212 791 3595
E ksla@earthlink.net

Taylor Cullity Lethlean [290]
14-18 Holtom Street East
Princes Hill, Victoria 3054
Australia
T 3 9380 4344
F 3 9380 2983
E perry.l@tcl.net.au

7 Hutt Street
Adelaide, South Australia 5000
Australia
T 8 8223 7533
F 8 8223 3533
E kevin.t@tcl.net.au
W www.tcl.net.au

Topotek 1 [298]
Sophienstraße 18
10178 Berlin
Germany
T +49 30 246 25800
F +49 30 246 25899
E topotek1@topotek1.de
W www.topotek1.de

Trinidad [314]
Bäckerstraße 14
A-1010 Vienna
Austria
T +43 650 25 07 455
E mario.terzic@inode.at
W www.marioterzic.com

Michael Van Valkenburgh [318]
18 East 17th Street, 6th Floor
New York, NY 10003
USA
T +1 212 243 2506
F +1 212 243 2016
E mvva_ny@mvvainc.com

231 Concord Avenue
Cambridge, MA 02138
USA
T +1 617 864 2076
F +1 617 492 3128
E mvva_ma@mvvainc.com
W www.mvvainc.com

Brita von Schoenaich [326]
Greystone House
Sudbrook Lane
Petersham, Richmond TW10 7AT
UK
T +44 (0)20 8948 4445
F +44 (0)20 8332 6766
E info@schoenaich.co.uk
W www.schoenaichrees.com

WES & Partner [330]
Jarrestraße 80
22303 Hamburg
Germany
T +49 40 278 410
F +49 40 270 6668
E info@wesup.de
W www.wesup.de

West 8 [336]
Schiehaven 13M (Maaskantgebouw)
P.O. Box 6230
3002 AE Rotterdam
The Netherlands
T +31 10 485 5801
F +31 10 485 6323
E west8@west8.nl
W www.west8.nl

Picture Credits

Hanns Joosten 1, 298–303; Patricia Johanson 2, 154, 155; Atelier Big City 10–13; Rik Klein Gotink 14, 15; Maaike de Ridder 16, 17 (above right); Lodewijk Baljon 17 (above left and below); Thomas Balsley Associates 18–21; Carole Drake 22, 23 (left); Julia Barton 23 (above right), 24, 25; Roy Jackson 23 (lower right); Uniform 26; BCA Landscape/Smiling Wolf 27, 28; BCA Landscape 29, 31; Lee Brown 30; Inside Outside 42–46; J. Musch 47; Jean-Pierre Brazs 48–53; Susanne Burger 54–59; Cao Perrot Studio 60–65; Paul Cooper 66–69; Jacques Perron 71; Jean-François Vézina 72 (left and above right), 73–77; Denis Farley 72 (below right); CCAPI 74 (left); Topher Delaney 78–85; Atelier Dreiseitl 86–89; DS Landschapsarchitecten 90–95; Jimmy Söderling 106; Monika Gora 107; Monika Gora and Jan Lindstrand 108, 109; Urszula Striner 110, 111; Åke E:son Lindman 112, 113; Michael Betts 114, 115; Gross.Max. 116–121; Gustafson Porter, 122–124, 125 (above left and lower right), 126–129; Helene Binet 125 (above right and lower left); Fritz Haeg 130; Taidgh O'Neill 131; Eva Heyd 132; Richard Felber 2005 (courtesy of R20th Century, New York and Salon 94, New York) 133–135; Frank Oudeman 2006 (courtesy of R20th Century, New York and Salon 94, New York) 136, 137; John Sleeman 138–143; Karres en Brands 156–159; Ulrich Singer 160–165; Land-I 166, 167, 169; Mario Guerra 168; Michael Fehlauer 170–173; Ron Lutsko, Jr 174, 175; Marion Brenner 176, 177; 2006 Steve Whittaker 178, 179; Lützow 7 180–183; William Martin 184, 185; Shunmyo Masuno 186–193; Metagardens 194–197; David Meyer 198, 199; Helle Nebelong 210–215; Nip Paysage 216, 217, 220 (above), 221; Jim Verburg 218, 219; Michèle Laverdière 220 (below); Antonio Perazzi 222, 223; Plant 224–229; Phlippe Rahm 230, 231; Tom Bonner 242–249; Sharon Kish 250; Nelson French 251; Neil Fox 252, 253; Mario Schjetnan 254, Richard Barnes 255; Alan Ward 256,

262, 263; Jörg Hempel 257; Martha Schwartz 258, 260, 261; Tim Richardson 259; Vladimir Sitta/Terragram 274–277; SLA (photo: Torben Petersen) 278, 279, 283; SLA 280, 281, 282; Ken Smith 285–288; Peter Mauss 289; Taylor Cullity Lethlean 290, 291, 294, 295; Dianna Snape 292–293; Louise Tanguay 296, 297; Mario Terzic/Trinidad 314–317; Tim Kaulen 318 (left); MVVA 318 (right), 319, 323 (left); Paul Warchol 323 (right), 324 (left); Caroline Brown 320, 321; Anton Rocz 322; Jerry Speier 324 (right); Voorsanger Architects PC 325 (top); Elizabeth Felicella (325 (bottom); Brita von Schoenaich 326–329; WES & Partner 330, 331, 334, 335; Jörn Hustedt 332, 333; West 8 336, 337, 338 (left), 339 (below left and right), 340–343; Christian Richters 338–339.

Further Reading

J. Amidon, *Radical Landscapes: Reinventing Outdoor Space* (London, 2004).

G. Bachelard, *The Poetics of Space* (1969; reprinted Boston, 1994).

A. Berleant, *Aesthetics of Environment* (Philadelphia, 1992).

——, *Living in the Landscape: Towards an Aesthetics of Environment* (Lawrence, KS 1997).

E. Casey, *The Fate of Place: A Philosophical History* (Berkeley, 1998).

D.E. Cooper, *A Philosophy of Gardens* (Oxford, 2006).

G. Cooper and G. Taylor, *Gardens for the Future: Gestures Against the Wild* (New York, 2000).

——, *Paradise Transformed* (New York, 1997).

M. Foucault, 'Of Other Spaces', 1967 lecture printed in *Diacritics* 16:1 (1986):22–27.

M. Heidegger, 'Building Dwelling Thinking', 1951 lecture printed in *Basic Writings* (Oxford, 1993).

R. Hill, *Contemporary History of Garden Design: European Gardens Between Art and Architecture* (Basel, 2004).

G. Keeney, J. Dixon Hunt and A.S. Weiss, *On the Nature of Things* (Basel, 2000).

M. Merleau-Ponty, *Phenomenology of Perception*, trans. Colin Smith, Routledge (Oxford, 1962).

Modern Landscape Architecture: A Critical Review, ed. M. Treib (Cambridge, MA 1994).

C. Norberg-Schultz, *Existence, Space and Architecture* (New York, 1971).

——, *Genius Loci* (London, 1980).

M. Potteiger and J. Purinton, *Landscape Narratives: Design Practices for Telling Stories* (Hoboken, NJ 1998).

T. Richardson, *The Vanguard Gardens and Landscapes of Martha Schwartz* (London, 2004).

T. Schroder, *Changes in Scenery: Contemporary Landscape Architecture in Europe* (Basel, 2002).

R. Smithson, *The Collected Writings*, ed. Jack Flam (Berkeley, 1996)

Y-F. Tuan, *Space and Place: The Perspective of Experience* (Minneapolis, 2001).

——, *Topophilia: A Study of Environmental Perceptions, Attitudes and Values* (Upper Saddle River, NJ 1974).

Vista: The Culture and Politics of Gardens, ed. N. Kingsbury and T. Richardson (London, 2006).

U. Weilacher, *In Gardens: Profiles of Contemporary European Landscape Architecture* (Basel, 2005).

This book could not have been written without the
active cooperation of the landscape architects involved,
and I would like to thank all of them – and their offices –
for their help and professionalism. The team at
Thames & Hudson have been a pleasure to work with:
Lucas Dietrich commissioned the book and has guided
it through every stage with care and understanding;
Elain McAlpine has been an exemplary editor; and
Myfanwy Vernon-Hunt's designs are informed by an
instinctive understanding of the subject matter. I would
also like to thank my literary agent, Tif Loehnis, and the
team at Janklow & Nesbit. Finally, I would like to thank
Claire, my wife, for her support during a period when I was
researching and writing two major books simultaneously.